Advance Acclaim for *Reluctant Dissenter*...

"This book throws new light on a significant piece of post–Vatican II history. It portrays a moving struggle to preserve integrity which changed the life of a dedicated bishop. Carefully, honestly written."

—ANITA CASPARY, former president, Immaculate Heart Community, Los Angeles; adjunct faculty, Immaculate Heart College Center

"A most significant autobiography which should be read not only by every priest and Catholics of all ages, but by anyone interested in a moving account of an authentic spiritual seeker. This is the story of a man whose conscience compelled him to disagree with his superiors and church authorities. As a result, he was badly treated by them. This is a superbly written story of a brilliant resigned priest and bishop as he continues his journey through life."

—MSGR. JOHN J. EGAN, Assistant to the President for Community Affairs, DePaul University

"Jim Shannon is and has been a good friend of mine for almost half a century. This is an honest account of his life, difficult to write for any of us, but inspiring when he addresses faith, love, the ministry of service to others, honesty, and forgiveness. Thank God we are all judged by Him, the Fountain of love, understanding, and mercy. We will all need plenty of all three."

—(REV.) THEODORE M. HESBURGH, C.S.C., President Emeritus, University of Notre Dame

"Recounting candidly and irenically his life as a priest, bishop, and married man profoundly affected by Vatican Council II, James P. Shannon describes the interplay in his own conscience of the faith and friction within the Catholic Church, which, he affirms, is his only spiritual home. This is an easily read biography which will have a significant place in the history of the Catholic hierarchy of the United States."

—FRANCIS T. HURLEY, Archbishop of Anchorage

"James Shannon's life of dedication to the Catholic Church and to the deeper and greater truths and experiences of life is open to us in this remarkable book. One can enter it, as believers do the torrent, and emerge not only cleansed but healed and renewed to face life's challenges. The truth about James Shannon's life frees us, as it did him, not so much to put the past behind but to purify it and devote it to new but always life-giving and life-enlarging uses.

"This book is also a chronicle of a Minnesota boyhood, a career in Catholic life that destined him for a cardinal's red hat and great power in the church that he gave up for Thomas More–like reasons. This never-before-told story of the conflict between his pastor's heart and the demands made by the official church on the good people he served and his decision to leave and to be married will inform and move all readers. For this is not only a tale of a man of conscience facing a great institution but is also a story of love and its ever fresh power. What a treat for people who have never known Jim Shannon to meet him in these pages and to experience his remarkable, not to say mythic, life with him."

—EUGENE KENNEDY, coauthor of *Authority*

"Jim Shannon has been a great source of wisdom and inspiration to me and countless others. For the many of us who are looking for meaning and value in our lives, the story of Jim's extraordinary life is a guide to that search. For those exploring new options and experiencing change in their lives, this book demonstrates the triumph of one person's search for a fulfilled life."

—DOROTHY S. RIDINGS, President and CEP, Council on Foundations, Washington, D.C.

# RELUCTANT DISSENTER

# RELUCTANT DISSENTER

## A CATHOLIC BISHOP'S JOURNEY OF FAITH

James Patrick Shannon

*A Crossroad Book*
The Crossroad Publishing Company
New York

The Crossroad Publishing Company
370 Lexington Avenue, New York, NY 10017

Printed in the United States of America

**Library of Congress Cataloging-in-Publication Data**
Shannon, James Patrick.
    Reluctant Dissenter : a Catholic bishop's journey of faith / by James Patrick
Shannon.
      p.  cm.
    ISBN 0-8245-1758-X (hardcover) ; ISBN 0-8245-1847-0 (paperback)
    1. Shannon, James Patrick. 2. Catholic bishops – United States –
Biography. 3. Contraception – Religious aspects – Catholic Church –
Controversial literature. 4. Catholic Church – Doctrines –
Controversial literature. I. Title.
BX4668.3.S48A3 1998
282′.092 – dc21   [b]
                                                    98-13935

1  2  3  4  5  6  7  8  9  10      04   03   02   01   00

*This book is for*

RUTH SHANNON

*without whose original encouragement*
*and continuous support*
*it would never have been attempted*


*And for*

WARDE AND DODE WHEATON

*without whose friendship*
*and gracious hospitality*
*it might never have been completed*

# CONTENTS

# PREFACE

Almost three decades ago during the late summer and early autumn of 1968 I was unwilling to admit, even to myself, that my ministry as a priest and bishop was drawing to a close. But the progression of events narrated in this book eventually forced me to conclude that the pain of staying in the active ministry had reached a point which was, for me, intolerable. Only then did I begin to seek an alternative career and some kind of institutional support system which would give my life meaning and value.

Why should this narrative be of interest to the public? Friends whose judgment I trust have urged me to put my "odyssey" in print, partly to have a record of its steps and sequence as I see them, and partly to give a wider audience a specific illustration of how one person sought to reconcile his duty to self and his duty to an institution he loves and admires.

For personal encouragement long before this book was even a possibility I owe a particular debt to my friend Bower Hawthorne (now deceased). For their counsel, tact, and candor in reading parts or all of the completed manuscript I owe a similar debt to my friends Father Harvey Egan, Dawn Gibeau, Patrick Henry, Ronald M. Hubbs, and Charles I. Mundale. Readers of the finished product are indebted to these thoughtful critics for suggestions which clarified and refined many passages in copy once prematurely labeled "final draft."

At every stage of the composition of this book my dear wife, Ruth, has been my counselor, my critic, my best friend. Her abiding conviction that the story here is important and worth telling gave me the assurance I needed to undertake it and to complete it. But vastly more important than her central role in this book is her central role in my life. At a time when my world collapsed she offered to help me rebuild it. I thank her, above all others, for her courage and her faith in me then and since then.

JAMES P. SHANNON
*Wayzata, Minnesota*

# INTRODUCTION

In the first sentence of the Declaration of Independence Thomas Jefferson says that that document was issued out of a decent respect for the opinions of humankind and to declare the causes which impelled him and his associates to dissolve the bonds which had previously connected the American colonies to the British Empire.

In one sense this book is also a declaration of independence. It is also a serious effort to trace the values and the steps dictated by those values whereby a priest, later a bishop, at the age of forty-seven deliberately chose to resign from the active ministry of the Catholic priesthood and from the honor and the onus of the episcopacy. Out of a decent respect for the opinions of all those who could not then, or now, understand, much less endorse, that decision, this modest volume, more than twenty years in the writing, tries to connect the causes which led to that deliberate decision.

In a deeper sense this narrative is a declaration of dependence, a statement of devotion and respect for the Catholic Church, its doctrine, and its saving grace. The Catholic Church is the only spiritual home I have ever known. The values on which my life is built are those I learned in a Catholic family and in Catholic schools. I am not able, nor do I desire, to separate myself from that distinctive mode of Christian life and worship embodied in Catholic culture.

It is difficult for me to conceive a more satisfying or challenging life than the one I knew for twenty-three years as a priest and for four years as a bishop. The fellowship of the Catholic priesthood is one of the greatest human support systems known to humankind. Once to have been a member of it and then to have lost its support is as close to the dark night of the soul as I ever care to be.

Among mainline Protestants in the United States, freedom is a code word with favorable connotations. Historically, it conjures up the image of town meetings in New England, of democracy, and of self-determination. But in Catholic pedagogy (and among some Christian Fundamentalists) there is a tendency to suspect freedom, to equate it with license or dangerous forms of self-indulgence. In retrospect I realize that I was both a product and a practitioner of that pedagogy which felt obligated to qualify any discussion of freedom, to distinguish it quickly from irresponsibility and hedonism. The truth is that qualified freedom is not freedom. It is some form of regulated permission.

John Donne was right. No man is an island. Each of us identifies ourself in part by our affiliations and by the institutional system from which we draw support and to which we pledge to give support. For me the central institution of my life has been the Catholic Church. My lifeline has been that marvelous flow of sacramental graces which the church pledged to me through baptism in 1921 and holy orders in 1946, as I lay prostrate in the sanctuary of the Cathedral of St. Paul when I pledged my life to the service of the church.

The bonds other persons accept with other institutions may be less formal and not so precisely focused in time. But the process of pledging to give and to take support from an institution we admire is standard procedure for mature adults in any civilized society. No one goes it alone. We harness our energies to advance causes we consider important and we mature personally as we and these causes prosper. As we grow older these bonds are either maintained or replaced. They wax or wane. They cannot be denied.

There are push and pull factors at work in every life. If these are in reasonable equilibrium we tend to continue as we are where we are. But when pressures mount to the point where change is less painful than staying in place we begin to explore new options. Ordinarily the push factors begin to operate first. We usually conclude that our present position is intolerable before we begin the search for alternatives. This sequence, so often illustrated in historical studies of human migration, describes precisely the pattern of my experience.

My life in the decades since my resignation from the priestly ministry has not had the consistent quality of deep personal satisfaction which I knew continuously as a priest. I do not expect ever again in this life to experience that sense of rightness and fitness which I knew in my ministry as a priest. To say this is not to belittle in any way the cordial friendships, the professional achievements, and the generous love of a good wife which have taken the place in my life of my priestly ministry. My life today has new qualities of tolerance, compassion, freedom, joy, love, and affection which I seldom sensed with such intensity prior to my marriage. The principal source of these welcome new satisfactions is my beloved wife, Ruth, and the good life she has helped me build. This book is not intended as a tract to promote the concept of a married clergy in the Catholic Church. Nonetheless I do believe that if some priests had a loving relationship with a good wife, as I do now, they would be better priests and better Christians.

The discipline of writing this book has been salutary for me. Retracing my steps through a painful past period has renewed some old heartaches, but it has also convinced me that, given the same circumstances, I would make substantially the same decisions today as I did almost three decades ago.

As children, when my sister Mary or I scraped our knees or cut our fingers our mother would assure us that scar tissue is always stronger than ordinary skin. My dermatologist friends tell me that Mama was mistaken on this matter. I tell them that I still prefer her myths about injuries and healing. This book is a story about some deep wounds, some of them self-inflicted, and about the marvelous and mysterious process of healing. It is offered to the reader as one illustration of the universal dilemma faced by responsible adults who must make difficult judgments about their institutional loyalties. There is a psychic need in every human person to pledge one's talents, training, and time to the service of worthy ideals. Usually, fidelity to such pledges brings satisfaction and security to the pledgor. On occasion, however, we find the reciprocal promises of support between ourselves and our chosen institutions working badly or not working at all. In this dilemma one school of thought holds that loyalty to the institution, be it church, state, political party, or corporation, must necessarily prevail for the common good. I held firmly to that position as long as I could. In abandoning it I felt, initially, that my world had collapsed. I feared that my future would be bleak and empty. With grave misgivings I accepted a position as a tutor, later vice president, at St. John's College in Santa Fe, New Mexico. I shall always be grateful for that most welcome invitation at a time in my life when I was on the verge of despair.

There are threads of continuity linking the different periods of every life, the strands of sameness which do not snap as we change careers or places. These bonds help us maintain a sense of personal continuity as change happens around us. They also help us keep our hopes for survival and for future growth. For me the central bond between my past and my future was a kind of categorical imperative. Somehow I knew that I could only be happy in a career in which my talent and training were committed to the service and well-being of other persons. Being a priest for more than two decades means, at the very least, that one is by then unfitted for a host of other worthwhile and honorable careers which might have been viable options for him in his youth but which are so no longer.

The odyssey narrated in this book is only a story of one life, and that one not yet complete. It is a narrative of wrenching loss, of great subsequent loneliness, and, eventually, of an overpowering sense of personal freedom and a greatly increased sense of personal responsibility.

# CHAPTER ONE

# SOUTH ST. PAUL

From upstairs in our home in winter when the trees were bare and from any room on the east side of St. Augustine's School in South St. Paul one could see the Mississippi River valley. When I rode my pony after school from his pen in the stockyards we usually followed the west bank of the river, upstream or down, depending on the direction of the odoriferous wind from the packing plants. Later, as a student at the St. Paul Seminary, I often walked the eastern bank of the Mississippi where it marks the edge of that campus. Still later when I was named a bishop, I directed that two diagonal serrated lines, the banks of the Great River, be incorporated in the shield of my episcopal coat of arms.

I am no longer an unquestioning devotee of Frederick Jackson Turner's hypothesis that the Upper Mississippi Valley has produced this country's most creative citizens, but I admit to a lingering bias toward his admiration for the people of this region. As a graduate student at Yale, studying American history under such Connecticut Yankees as Samuel Flagg Bemis, Leonard Labaree, and George W. Pierson, I kept a discreet silence about my respect for Turner. But at this distance I can afford to say that I think Turner's hypothesis has a defensible kernel of truth, even if he did spend a lifetime overstating it.

I was the youngest of six in a family which was really two families. My mother, born Mary Alice McAuliff, had been a widow with four small children for almost a decade before she married my father. Her first husband, Fred Foxley, a cattleman, had died at a time that all of his assets, including his life insurance and their home, were pledged as security on a bank loan for the purchase of livestock. After his death Mother was unable to repay the loan and lost her home.

She took a job as a waitress in a restaurant and moved her four small children into a single room in the hotel above the restaurant. Although she had been a teacher before her marriage, she chose work as a waitress to be close to the children. One year later she became the manager of the restaurant. Two years later she bought it. By the time she married my father, nine years later, she owned two restaurants, a hotel, and a summer resort.

Everyone called her Mame, even her children. My earliest recollection of her is a curious one. She was in the basement doing the laundry. I was upstairs in the kitchen, painting the metal undercarriage of her Singer sewing machine a lovely iridescent red. When she saw my artwork she laughed out loud. I knew then that my mother was a woman of light and joy.

After surgery, before I was born, she had lost almost all her hearing. To compensate for the loss she later enrolled in a course in lip-reading. I remember helping her with her "homework." She would position my sister Mary or me across the room and ask us to read the headlines in the daily paper to her, but without sound. In later years I could always "talk" to her from as far away as she could see my lips.

During the Depression the basement in our home was the parish depot for used clothing for needy families. Hardly a day passed that a family did not ring our bell, with a note from Father Jeremiah O'Callaghan asking mother to outfit them. As a child I remember thinking that our house was some kind of public place, so many people walked through it so regularly.

In those days the mortgage on St. Augustine's Church and School was heavy. Parish-wide chicken dinners in the spring and harvest festivals in the fall raised the money to pay the interest on the debt. Mother was always in charge of the dinners. It was also her personal task to bake fifty pies for each dinner, twenty-five apple and twenty-five cherry. My special task was to carry them a block and a half from our home to the church hall. My bond with the church, even then, was more a bond of service than of liturgy or dogma. To me the church was the place where people helped other people.

In retrospect I often think that mother's single greatest contribution to our formation was her sense of humor. She had a marvelous laugh and a disposition like Beverly Sills. She considered a sense of humor part of a sense of values. She knew by instinct that a hangnail is not a mortal wound and wasted neither energy nor time over hangnails.

My father, Patrick Joseph Shannon, the oldest of eight children, was born in Hacketstown, County Carlow, Ireland. As a schoolboy he had learned sign language to help a deaf mute cattle dealer on "fair day" in their village. Once a week he was released from school to translate the hand signs of the cattle dealer, called a "cow jobber" in Ireland, and the words of the farmers as they bargained for livestock. In the process he acquired an unusual skill for estimating the weight of live cattle and for doing mathematical computations in his head. As a child I was often immensely proud of his display of these twin skills.

After finishing national (i.e., elementary) school he attended Knockbeg College in the city of Carlow. His academic records there indicate that among subjects he studied were Latin and Greek. In spite of its name, Knockbeg College is a secondary school, analogous to what we would call a minor seminary. My father never told us that he studied for the priesthood, but we infer that he did — for just one year. His grades in Latin and Greek were the lowest on his transcript, both fives on a scale of seven (highest) to one (lowest).

Our records lose track of him after his one year at Knockbeg. We assume, as the eldest of eight children, he returned home to help manage the family farm, which under primogeniture he stood to inherit.

But the call to America was too strong. When a cousin returned to Ireland from the USA (Minnesota) and decided to stay in Ireland, he sold the unused portion of his railroad and steamship tickets to my father. On May 10, 1907, exactly two weeks after his twenty-first birthday, my father boarded the White Star Steamship liner the *Cymric* at Queenstown (now called Cobh) in County Cork, and on May 20 he landed in Boston.

On arrival he learned that immigrants had to possess at least twenty-five dollars before they were allowed to enter the country. He had only his railroad ticket to Minnesota and ten dollars. He borrowed fifteen dollars from a shipmate, cleared customs, and returned the loan to his friend outside the immigrants' enclosure.

Two cousins and two friends had preceded him to South St. Paul, Minnesota. They helped him get his first job — as a bartender. In letters home he never admitted to his parents that he worked in a saloon.

From his days with the "cow jobber" in Ireland he wanted to be a cattleman. Rebuffed repeatedly in his efforts to get a job in the stockyards with James T. Crosby, the cattleman he considered the local leader in the business, he quit his job in the saloon and showed up the next day as an unpaid volunteer in Crosby's alley in the yards. Crosby told him he was crazy to work without pay. But at the end of the week when Crosby paid his men, he also had a check for the "foolish Irishman" who wanted work so bad he would do it free. After two years with Crosby, Father left to form his own firm, the Shannon Cattle Company.

He was a pious man. Religious exercises and prayer were important parts of his daily life. One of my earliest recollections of him is of his teaching me the Lord's Prayer. Like many immigrants he placed a high premium on education. He was also a bit of a showboat. He taught me, early on, to sing a homely classic of that era called "Red Hot Henry Brown," a feat I gladly and frequently performed at family gatherings.

He was a big man, well over six feet, and well proportioned. In the stockyards he wore a beige, snap-brim Stetson and rode a handsome blood-bay gelding named "Pig." On holidays when I would visit the yards, before I owned a pony, I would ride double with him, my hands around his waist. He could make Pig buck a little by snapping the popper of his cattle whip in the air. I thought this was great fun.

The night before he left Ireland for America his father pleaded with him not to go. Together they walked to the top of a hill on the family farm. As the eldest son, under primogeniture, Father stood to inherit the land. It is a good farm. But even when grandfather played his final card, "It will break your mother's heart to see you leave," my father confessed that the attractiveness of life in America forced him to leave.

Ever since the disastrous potato famines of the nineteenth century a dark memory of that dismal time has lingered in Irish folklore. It was strong in my father. To him the land was a symbol of possible betrayal, not necessarily a pledge of future security. He loved the land and its perennial promise of new fruit, but he knew, early on, that he did not want to make his livelihood tending a farm which could betray him in time of drought, plague, famine, or flood.

He also had the entrepreneurial virus. He loved to match wits in business with ranchers, farmers, cowboys, or "jobbers." I have seen him bet the horse and saddle he was riding that his guess on the weight of live range cattle in a Montana pasture was more accurate than the guess of the rancher who owned the cattle (and the horse). He won the bet, bought the cattle, and got the horse and saddle as a bonus.

He once told me that he flipped a coin to decide whether he would migrate to Australia or the United States. The push factor to leave Ireland was obviously stronger than the pull factor to any other specific place. He only knew that he wanted to be in some place of greater opportunity where he could exploit his entrepreneurial instinct.

He never regretted the move. Quite the contrary, he had an extravagant kind of gratitude to the United States. It gave him all he ever hoped for — and more. In his later years, when business was good and profits were high, he refused to complain about taxes. Maybe he would today, but many's the time I heard him say, "You only pay taxes when you make money. We make good money. I'm glad to pay the taxes."

It was taken for granted that my sister Mary and I would attend a Catholic school, as soon as there was one in our parish. When one opened we were among its first pupils, Mary in fourth grade and I in second. My transfer from Central Public School to St. Augustine's new parochial school, at the age of seven, began a love affair for me with Catholic schools in general and Dominican nuns in particular. In their white, floor-length, fine woolen habits the nuns seemed to me to be unreal visitors from some distant, good, and special place. I had been prepared for their style of firm discipline by my father's opinion: if a student had trouble with a nun, the nun was always right. Even when a nun was, in my view, dead wrong, I never questioned her. She may have been in error, but there was never any doubt that she was in charge. I horsed around a lot in grade school, and usually paid for it, but it never occurred to me that I could challenge any decision of any Dominican sister.

We are all the product of our own history. My formative years were spent in Catholic schools where I was expected to toe the line, do my work as well as possible, tell the truth, respect other persons and their property, worship God from whom all good things come, share the Eucharist every Sunday, confess my sins twice a month, and never talk back to a Dominican nun.

All this may not be a likely profile for an educational feature in *Psychology Today,* but it worked for me. And I sincerely believe that American society would be vastly more wholesome and healthy in the years ahead if more of its citizens had the benefit of Dominican nuns to shape their virtues in their youth. The mass closing of Catholic schools in this country in recent decades is a serious loss to the nation.

All through grade school I was in mildly hot water with each of my teachers, except in the fifth grade. The trouble usually involved my conduct, not my studies. In the fifth grade, Sister Jamesita Byrne once told me that with a little encouragement I would be hard to handle. I was not sure what she meant, but I knew she was giving me a friendly warning. The day I was eliminated from the *St. Paul Dispatch* Spelling Bee for misspelling "their" she asked me to stay after school. She wasted no time on sympathy but wrote three words in a column on the blackboard: "The," "There," and "Their." Then she drew a perpendicular line through the three words after the first three letters. I saw at once that all three words share the same first three letters. She said simply, "I'm sorry you lost the contest, Jimmy. But at least you won't make that mistake again." She was right.

Dominican nuns are by definition teachers. They all know how to spell. They also know how to handle kids who are a little hard to handle.

Our report cards in grade school marked us on "effort" and "conduct." I never got higher than a "C" in either category. Once, in the eighth grade, I got a "D" in conduct. It was something about my deliberately singing discord in the school choir. In the words of our teacher, that musical ensemble was not a barbershop quartet.

"C" was bad. But "D" was intolerable. When my father asked my teacher about it, she told him that I was simply a marginal student. By then I had been accepted for high school the next year at Cretin High School, named after Bishop Joseph Cretin and taught by the De La Salle Christian Brothers. From his days in Ireland my father considered the Christian Brothers the best teachers in the business. When he came back from his conference with the teacher concerning my "D" in conduct, he sat down at our dining-room table with me and said, "Your teacher tells me that you will not be able to meet the standards of study or discipline at Cretin." He had tears in his eyes. I asked, "Do you believe that?" He said, "No." I shook his hand and said, "You wait and see."

Cretin High School and the Christian Brothers were a whole new world to me. We wore uniforms, reported for R.O.T.C. drill each morning, and stood for inspection every Friday. We got report cards every six weeks, with marks in each of five subjects: Algebra, English, Latin, History, and Religion. There was a written examination in each subject every six weeks. It counted for 20 percent of the total grade. Marks were given daily for written homework and daily for recitation in each class. Each of these counted for 40 percent of the total. A perfect score of 100 percent depended on the three component marks (40–40–20).

Spurred by the prediction of my eighth-grade teacher that Cretin would be too tough for me, I resolved to prove her wrong. In the second semester of my freshman year I scored a perfect hundred (40–40–20) in every subject on every report card. My father was delighted. I was vindicated. But Mother, the teacher, was skeptical of a pedagogical system that told a thirteen-year-old boy that he had "perfect" marks. She considered the marking process of the Christian Brothers entirely too mechanical, and psychologically risky.

In our freshman year Brother Felix was our instructor in religion. He often talked about vocations to the religious life and shared with us the story of his own decision to become a Christian Brother. Under his influence, I began to ask myself whether that was the life for me.

Sooner or later he put the question personally to each of us: "Do you have any desire to serve God in the religious life?" My answer was a qualified "Yes, but." I admired Felix and the other Brothers enormously.

Their lifestyle and their dedication to the cause of Christian education made them attractive role models in my life just when I was beginning to comprehend that there is a considerable difference between the life of the intellect and simply doing homework.

The Brothers of the Christian Schools, their official title, have a quality of intellectual and personal discipline which I find extremely attractive. They are energetic and decisive. They make their students stretch. I recall being surprised that they all seemed to be happy in their work. Till then I had considered the religious life essentially a career of self-denial. It was a revelation to me to realize that the religious life is a positive affirmation of service, not a life sentence of penitence or mortification.

I was reluctant to tell Brother Felix, whom we called "Ajax" behind his back, that I felt more inclined to be a parish priest, like Father O'Callaghan, than a Christian Brother. When I did tell him my preference, he quickly put me at ease and urged me to pray every day that this "calling" would not wither.

At his suggestion I then began making daily visits for private prayer to the chapel in the residence of the Brothers. Alone in that chapel each day between classes or after school I began to understand that a religious vocation is basically a decision to commit one's life to serve the needs of others, as exemplified in the life of Jesus Christ. I sensed a bond of continuity, over centuries, between the earliest disciples of Christ and the Christian Brothers who were my teachers. The desire began to grow in me to plan my studies and to direct my life so that I might join that company of Christians who find the fulfillment of their personal potential in the service of others. Whole segments of those early meditations on the gospel and on my career come flooding back to mind, even today, whenever I visit that lovely little chapel in the residence of the Christian Brothers at Cretin.

As a freshman at Cretin High, I entered the Golden Gloves, learned the elements of boxing, and got my clock cleaned by a fighter named Pat Vaughan. The next year I won the Golden Glove for my division and decided to retire from the ring.

In my first year of high school my interest in public speaking grew as I began to realize that grammar, in Latin or English, is dull but that rhetoric is a whole new world of beauty. Till I saw the Christian Brothers in action I had never witnessed the eloquence of a low-keyed, polysyllabic, nonstop, two-paragraph, gentlemanly verbal dressing down of another human being the way they could give it to a student who needed it. It still delights me to recall the finesse of those marvelously artful performances. Somehow those flashing encounters built friendships and respect between the addressee and the addressor. The sons of De La Salle have reason to be proud of their pedagogical skills. And I am grateful that, briefly, it was once my good fortune to be under their instruction.

My growing fascination with language was encouraged by my father's admiration for eloquent speakers. There is a peculiar fondness among the Irish for the skillful use of language. True son of Ireland, he reserved his highest praise for persons who could speak persuasively, with beauty, and without notes.

Under his tutelage, my first public addresses all sounded like William Jennings Bryan's Cross of Gold speech, one of his favorites. Whatever the style, I did develop in those years a strong desire to build a vocabulary and the rhetorical fluency necessary to speak persuasively.

Like the Christian Brothers, my father always expected maximum effort and first-rate performance. It never occurred to me that his expectations were too high. I considered him a friendly critic who was always available for counsel or support when I needed it. One humorous image of him lingers in my memory. Whenever I was out late at night, no matter how late it was when I came home, I knew he would be sitting in the dark in our living room, in his long white nightshirt, smoking a cigar. As I closed the front door I could smell the cigar and see its red tip in the dark. Each time we had the same exchange. "Hi, Dad." "Hi, Jim, how was your evening?" "Just fine." "Did the car work all right?" "Yes sir." "Did you have a good time?" "Great." "Good, I'm glad you're home safe." Again it never occurred to me to think that I was being monitored. I now know that he wanted to be assured that I was home, that I was safe, and that I was sober. It also never occurred to me to come home in any other condition. Father had some of the same rhetorical skills which he and I admired in the Christian Brothers.

# CHAPTER TWO

# PRIOR LAKE

Summertime for our family meant Prior Lake. The day that school was out in June we packed the car and headed for the country. Then for three solid months my father made the daily round trip of fifty miles to work. He did the grocery shopping from a list on his way home each afternoon. Mother and Mary and I stayed at the lake until Labor Day. (By then the four Foxley children were gainfully employed.)

Our rented cottage was pretty modest. It had one bedroom, a small kitchen, and a full screen porch with no windows. Sudden rainstorms at night called for quick action to untie the canvas curtains furled at the top of the screens. Usually, by the time we could get them unfurled and hooked at the bottom our beds and pajamas were sprinkled if not soaked. There was no running water, and, for our first ten years there, no electricity. It never dawned on me that our lifestyle was extremely modest.

Small wonder. My mother could make or bake from scratch any dish for which anyone in the family could give her a reasonably accurate verbal description. She must have used some home-made "stretchers" to make the hamburger go further on occasion. But the dishes she served us were consistently delicious, varied, and abundant. At the lake, in season, we picked wild grapes, plums, blackberries, and choke-cherries and spent whole days late each summer helping mother can tomatoes, dill pickles, peaches, apple sauce, beets, and a half dozen varieties of jam and jelly, spiked with a jolt or two of pure choke-cherry juice.

The tiny kitchen at the lake had one small two-burner kerosene stove and one big wood-burning cook stove. To lessen the heat in the cottage, mother fired up the wood stove only once a week, on baking day. It was my job to gather firewood from fallen trees in a nearby woods. We carried drinking water every day in two three-gallon pails from the well at "Pop" Conroy's farm, a half mile away. We cleaned the chimneys of the kerosene lamps twice a week with old newspapers. And we got fresh milk and cream late every afternoon from "Mom" Conroy's farm kitchen, after we helped her turn the cream separator.

The cottage was not much. But the sandy beach and the clear water were paradise for kids. I could swim and dive and float by the time I was six. As one of the red-haired, fair-skinned Irish, I also got some of the most brutally painful sunburns known to medical history. Mother bought Unguentine in the large economy size every summer, and used every bit of it.

On one of his trips to Montana to buy cattle, father also bought a handsome chestnut Indian pony, with a bald face and four white "stockings," for Mary and me. At the lake we rode the pony every day, on land and even in the water. "Baldy" was practically a member of the family.

The days at the lake were easy and relaxed, with four parts leisure and one part light chores. In retrospect it seems to me that the gentle regimen of those summers, especially during the Depression, introduced me to the habit of simplicity. We had modest expectations but we thoroughly enjoyed a considerable variety of simple pleasures.

Writers my age often cite the Great Depression as a cloud on the memory of their youth. I cannot make that claim. I do recall one earnest family conference just prior to the opening of school in September 1930, in which mother explained to me that the family budget could not afford new "school shoes" for me. I was entering the fifth grade. I continued to wear my summer sneakers to school each day until the snow came. Somehow new shoes then appeared when it was too cold and wet for sneakers.

I also recall a telephone conversation at Christmas that year between mother and Frank Drkula, our family grocer. We were behind in our payments to him. She was calling to thank him for his patience and to assure him we would pay as soon as we could. Years later, long after supermarkets were in style, she would trade only with "Mr. Drkula" because he had been our friend and patient creditor in the days when we needed a friendly neighborhood grocer.

Our family was a close-knit group. The four Foxley children, Bill, Helen, Frank, and Pete, and the two Shannons, Mary and I, grew up together with a kind of warmth and mutual affection which I considered the norm for all families until I was old enough to realize that our family style was not necessarily typical of all families. We never spoke of one another as half-brothers or half-sisters.

As soon as each of the Foxley boys finished high school, he joined my father in the cattle business. Mother always regretted that family finances denied the sons of her first marriage the chance to go to college. Helen, the only daughter of that marriage, graduated from college and, like Mother, became a teacher.

Because I was the baby of the family and because the Foxley children were all older than I by at least a decade, each of them was a role model for me in different ways. In retrospect I often think that my Foxley siblings saw me as a "project" which they were to shape and mold.

Frank taught me to drive a car. Over a period of a year, when I was only thirteen, he spent hours with me, patiently showing me how to drive in sand, on ice, in snow, and in traffic. He considered an automobile a lethal weapon in the hands of an unskilled driver. On the winter ice at Prior Lake he taught me how to turn into a skid to correct it. In traffic he taught me to take advantage of every opportunity that is legitimately mine and to practice defensive driving as a regular habit.

Pete, the brother closest to me in age, taught me how to troll for crappies, how to saddle a horse, how to change a tire, how to throw a left jab and duck a left jab as a single operation, and how to fabricate, cheaply, new shear pins for the propellor of an outboard motor by snipping one-inch pieces off the end of medium-gauge copper wire.

In the summer Helen was usually away at school. She "liked nice things" and did not relish the simple life at the lake. During the school year she was my best friend whenever I wanted to see a movie. Most new motion pictures in those days were "uptown," a half-hour's ride by streetcar. On the weekends, before I was old enough to make the trip alone, Helen would take me to see Tom Mix, Buck Jones, Tim McCoy, Ken Maynard, or Rin Tin Tin any time they came to town. En route home in the streetcar she would analyze the movie for me, as though it were a book. Early on I came to consider motion pictures a form of literature, thanks to her commentaries in the streetcar. I never held it against her that she was a teacher, in spite of the fact that she never missed a chance to tell Mother that drinking coffee would stunt my growth.

In the diction of the cattle business my father was a trader, or a speculator. He was the middleman who bought grass-fed range cattle, usually in Montana, for shipment and sale to farmers in the Midwest who would fatten them on corn in farmyard feedlots and then sell them to meat-packers or local butchers. His Montana connection developed because that state produces an abundance of beef cattle and is on the main rail lines to the Midwest. Another reason, however, for the growth of his business in that state was that his Irish origins, and his evident brogue, gave him good contacts with several F.B.I. (Foreign Born Irish) ranchers who had settled there.

In the summer months he would contract to buy yearling and two-year-old-range cattle for an agreed price, with delivery to occur in

October. He was, in effect, buying futures in livestock, a dicey business, then and now. A drop in the market could wipe out a small investor. Yet his contracts were seldom in writing. A handshake and an oral agreement were sufficient guarantees for him and for the ranchers he dealt with year after year. When I was old enough to realize the riskiness of the business and the unpredictability of the market in livestock, my appreciation for the perennial durability of his "F.B.I." contacts grew.

Whenever father was away from home on business, the father-figure in my life was my oldest brother. To this day William Joseph Foxley stands out in my life as the most complete and well-balanced human person I have ever known. He had all the right virtues. He was extremely bright, tough, gentle, well disciplined, with a sense of values and a sense of humor that made him, in my eyes, truly a man for all seasons.

He had a genius for business and the nerve to stake his fortune on his judgment. In a life cut short by accidental death he made money and friends with equal ease but always knew that the latter are more valuable by far than the former. He gave the impression of always having more energy in reserve than he was using. He had kind words for everyone, even for those he no longer trusted. "I don't believe I'd like to have that fellow pack my parachute," was his description of a man he and I knew to be a scoundrel.

By the time I was ten years old I knew that I wanted to cultivate in my life the virtues I admired in my oldest brother. He was fond of saying that in any business or profession fewer than 5 percent of the practitioners either desire or strive to be the best in their field. Without ever lecturing me he made me aware that he expected me to be among that 5 percent. And yet his pursuit of excellence never seemed strained or tense. His power in reserve always made him seem relaxed. He had, in Hemingway's phrase, "grace under pressure."

After he married Eileen Conroy, the daughter of our landlord at the lake, they rented a cottage from her parents and became our neighbors in the summer months. They and their children became integral parts of my lifelong support system. Long before I heard of extended families I was a member of one, drawing strength from its strength.

The highlight of the summer at the lake was always July Fourth. In our family there was very little money to spend for fireworks or festive displays. But Francis McCormick, a cousin of my mother, and his family were also our neighbors. They made a marvelous production out of July Fourth. It all began just after sundown on that day. We could see it clearly from our porch. Skyrockets, pinwheels, Roman candles, and aerial bombs of several colors lit the sky for hours that night for all of us to see. It was the social event of the season. It was also the occasion of my introduction to that marvelous product of prohibition — home brew. There was never any alcoholic beverage served at our house. "Mac" McCormick, however, did not observe this rubric, at least on the anniversary of our national independence.

The saddest day of the year in my childhood was Labor Day. It marked the end of summer. To this day a cloud passes over my soul on Labor Day, as though freedom and light are somehow being subtly diminished when the folks at the lake store the family boat under the porch, close up the cottage, and head back to school.

# CHAPTER THREE

# ST. THOMAS ACADEMY AND COLLEGE

One day in the summer of 1936 our Irish pastor from South St. Paul, Father Jeremiah O'Callaghan, paid us an unexpected visit at the lake. He came to tell us that he had arranged a full tuition scholarship for me at St. Thomas Military Academy in St. Paul. Full tuition then meant $150 a year. It seems like a small amount today. It seemed large then.

I had no advance knowledge of the negotiations to obtain this scholarship. I still do not know whose idea it was to seek it. The logic of it, as explained to me that day by Father O'Callaghan, was that some of my teachers at St. Thomas would be diocesan priests and that if I had a vocation to the priesthood I would be more likely to pursue it if I attended St. Thomas, where I would have some priests as teachers, than if I stayed with the Christian Brothers at Cretin. The Brothers had already invited me to visit their novitiate in Missouri.

My parents assured me that the decision was mine to accept or decline the scholarship. I knew that accepting it would ease their financial burdens at a time when money was in short supply. I thought about my close friends at Cretin and about the keen rivalry between the two schools. With some apprehension that Cretin would regard me as a traitor and that St. Thomas might perceive me as a Trojan horse, I decided to accept the scholarship.

Some of my fears about the new school were well founded. A few cadets went out of their way to tell me that transfers from Cretin were unwelcome at St. Thomas. Once more I had a challenge to work against. I set my sights to be a cadet captain in two years, the highest position then open to seniors in the corps, and to be the commander of the Crack Drill Squad in my senior year, the position I considered the most attractive in the corps. Two years later I graduated *summa cum laude,* valedictorian of my class, with the rank of cadet captain and commander of the Crack Drill Squad.

A new friend came into my life shortly after I enrolled at St. Thomas. Reading lists for classes in English and Latin forced me and my classmates to rely on our neighborhood libraries for titles we all wanted at the same time. The public library in South St. Paul was three blocks from our house. Grace Dorival, the librarian in charge, was a huge, jovial lady whose first reaction to my long lists was one of amusement.

At first she merely responded to my queries about reference works and periodicals. But as we became better acquainted she told me that the "classical" curriculum at St. Thomas was, in her opinion, skewed in favor of ancient and European authors. What my education needed was a healthy dose of American titles.

She proceeded to develop a second reading list for me to parallel my class assignments. Thanks to Grace I first met Mark Twain, Willa Cather, Sinclair Lewis, Jack London, Lewis and Clark, and Nathaniel Hawthorne. At first I resisted her pressure to widen my taste in literature. But once I had sampled the fare she recommended I developed a taste of my own for the titles she favored.

Grace often went beyond the call of duty to help me with term papers and special reports. On the day I graduated from St. Thomas I went to the library to thank her. She looked at my diploma and remarked that she deserved at least a footnote on it for "saving" me from the ancient classics.

For each of us there are a few people who come into our lives at the right time and with a message suited to our needs and perceptions. One such person in my life was Grace Dorival. It wasn't that she disliked the ancient classics. She just considered American boys illiterate if they did not know about competitive frogs that jumped in Calaveras County and what homesteading was like on the Great Plains near Red Cloud, Nebraska. Keeping two sets of books in my youth, with the help of my friendly neighborhood librarian, made a difference in my life then and since. She helped me acquire taste and standards for judging and loving literature and history in the American grain.

St. Thomas Academy has since dropped the word military from its name and has deliberately deemphasized its former image as a military school, two decisions in which I played a part and in which I concurred. But in my day on its campus, military affairs were an essential part of its college preparatory curriculum. By military affairs I do not mean studying Von Clausewitz or Napoleon on the art of warfare.

As a cadet officer at St. Thomas I learned that every time I stepped in front of my command it was expected that I would know, with precision and with confidence, the elements of the drill or maneuver we were about to perform and the specific role each member of my command would play in it. A cadet officer who does not know the elements of close order drill and the manual of arms, or who lacks the timing to bring the platoons of his command evenly on line to pass in review, will be laughed at by his peers. There is no scorn like that of a classmate. And there is no reward so welcome as recognition from a peer who understands and appreciates the elements which constitute a solid performance. A successful officer, in an army or a corporation, is a catalytic agent who somehow manages to create the atmosphere in which he and his associates produce consistently and predictably at their highest level. I learned that lesson by trial and error as a cadet officer at St. Thomas Military Academy. It has made a considerable difference in my life.

The plan, shared by me and Father O'Callaghan, when I entered St. Thomas was that I would study to be a priest. In my two years at the academy only two of my instructors were priests. They and I were on cordial terms. But little was said to me or by me in those days about my future plans.

My two years at St. Thomas Academy introduced me to a social life I had never known. In the eighth grade I had fallen madly in love with a dark-eyed Irish beauty, but I never told her. At St. Thomas the Crack Drill Squad was expected to perform during intermission at all school dances. Till then I had never learned to dance and had never had a real "date." Determined to catch up with my more sophisticated classmates I enrolled in a crash course in ballroom dancing. I loved it. Students at all-male academies are sometimes caricatured as socially immature and ill at ease with girls. Nonsense.

With ten dance lessons under my belt I summoned my courage, called a girl I had known and liked in grade school (the Irish beauty had moved away), and got my first date. I bought her a gardenia corsage and had a great evening at my first dance.

When the drill squad traveled out of town to perform at other schools, we would be "fixed up" with dates by our hosts in other cities. I recall three lovely evenings, one in Hibbing, Minnesota, one in New Ulm, Minnesota, and one in Wisconsin Rapids, Wisconsin. I quickly acquired a fondness for gardenias. Even after they turn brown they still smell good.

In September 1938 I enrolled at the College of St. Thomas, using a scholarship awarded to me the previous June. With four years of Latin to my credit by then, I signed up for courses in Latin, Greek, history, theology, and speech, which I would need for admission to the St. Paul Seminary two years later.

As a classics major in college my introduction to philosophy was indirect. By threading my way slowly through the syntax of Aristotle, Plato, Homer, St. Augustine, Cicero, and Seneca I perceived, through the eyes of different thinkers, the outlines of humanity's perennial desire to understand oneself and the surrounding universe.

I have always been slightly suspicious of the adage that once you learn to read, all you need is some quiet time and a good library. G. K. Chesterton once said that self-made individuals always reveal the defects of their creator. Similarly, solitary students who memorize whole chunks of Shakespeare or plow through encyclopedias without benefit of third-party discussion invariably put the stamp of their own ignorance or mispronunciation on the classics they would master. The dialogs with Father Frederic Bieter at St. Thomas about what Plato and Aristotle and Homer said and what they meant are still solid bridges of understanding for me. Bieter was a classicist, not a philosopher. But I learned more philosophy under his tutelage, explicating the Greek and Latin classics, than I ever learned in any course in philosophy.

The liberal arts are called liberal because they are the skills which characterize the lives of free persons. My concept of human freedom and its correlative, responsibility, began to take shape in my first two years at the College of St. Thomas. Homer's *Odyssey,* Plato's *Dialogs,* Aristotle's *Metaphysics,* Seneca's *Moral Epistles,* Cicero's *Essays,* and Dante's *Divine Comedy* first raised for me an integrated series of cosmic questions about what truly constitutes the good life for a human person. These classical texts, taken together, describe the good life as one in which people actualize their potential by putting their talents at the service of the common good in society. They grow by being part of a value system larger than their private world.

Although these texts regularly praise the virtue of generosity in educated persons, they use the term to signify a sharing of talent, concern, or energy rather than a sharing of money or wealth. Generosity of spirit is that paradoxical quality whereby a person benefits as much from giving as do the recipients of that largesse.

In reading the Socratic dialogs of Plato as a college freshman, I realized that Socrates, who died four centuries before Christ, was, in separate dialogs, sounding variations on the themes Jesus Christ explicated later in the Sermon on the Mount. The Beatitudes of Christian doctrine could, at least in part, be culled from the Socratic canon.

The good life means, above all else, to be something, not to get or to have something. Achievements or possessions (money, power, academic degrees) are meaningless unless they somehow enable their possessor to actualize some potential to be more truly human. No one does this alone. One does it as a weight-bearing member of the human community. The Socratic paradox mirrors the Christian paradox: human beings develop their potential most fully when they spend time and talent to make the good life more available to others.

The best people actualize their human potential by serving the needs of others. The great discovery of my first two years in college came in Father Bieter's Greek and Latin courses, where I gradually perceived that the good life delineated in so many "pagan" texts is the same as that described in the New Testament: you get by giving. The big givers are the richest people.

That insight turned my world around. In one sense it made a vocation to the priesthood less awesome for me. If all educated persons are "called" to put their talents at the service of others, the priestly calling is not uniquely different from the calling of other educated persons. In another sense the priesthood became for me a much more attractive vocation because it provided institutional structure and systemic support for anyone able to make and keep the promises called for at ordination.

Given this new insight, it became vastly easier for me to make the intellectual and moral commitment required by a vocation to the priesthood. If my classical and humane premises were valid, and I was confident of them, it followed that every educated person has a vocation to serve the common good. Different folks respond to this call in different ways, but all those who hear it have a human obligation to respond in some way that is both possible and compatible for them. In this light the priesthood did not seem to me so much a life of sacrifice as a life of opportunity, with a regimen tested over centuries to help its members live, love, and grow under that mysterious paradox that the big givers are the world's happiest and richest people.

Early in my college career, Father O'Callaghan, our friendly pastor, had counseled me that a pattern of dating the same girl regularly might send me to the altar for a sacrament other than holy orders. He suggested that I keep up the social life required on campus, but avoid a "steady" date. This plan was acceptable to me, even though two of my gardenia-wearing partners were charming beyond description. I did want to be a priest, and I was ready to accept the plan Father O'Callaghan suggested.

At the College of St. Thomas it was also my good fortune to come under the influence of an attorney-turned-historian. Robert P. Fogerty's explication of American constitutional and economic history may well have planted the seeds in my mind which, years later, led me into an unexpected career in the practice of law. Good lawyer that he was, Fogerty insisted on the evidence. In his lectures he produced it, with style, ease, and authority.

He was the first bona fide scholar I had ever met. He handled evidence and ideas with deliberate respect. He was more than a teacher. He was a professional practitioner who could make vast amounts of discrete historical information intelligible by placing it in a conceptual context and by contrasting it subtly with similar but different contexts. In his history classes, I first became aware that some day I wanted to be a professor of history with at least some of the craftsmanship he brought to that discipline. In graduate school at Yale I later met and worked closely with many historians of international rank. But none ever influenced me as deeply as Bob Fogerty.

The College of St. Thomas was known for its strong tradition in forensics. Its debate teams, coached by a retired attorney, Owen P. McElmeel, had been national champions twice. McElmeel's theory was simple: you learn public speaking by speaking in public. He offered his students freely (and free) as speakers to any service club, church benefit, or veterans' affair that would invite them. Putting William Jennings Bryan behind me, I decided to copy the informal style of FDR's "fireside chats" and willingly made "Prof." McElmeel my booking agent. I often wonder what I had to say as a college freshman that all those service clubs would listen to.

McElmeel also had a theory about how to win national debate titles: in uneven years, when the national forensic fraternity, Pi Kappa Delta, would host a nationwide debate tournament, "Mac" would schedule a three-week barnstorming trip for the three debaters he intended to send into national competition. He would arrange for these speakers one debate every day, and sometimes three, against debaters in colleges on a regular route he had devised from the Twin Cities to Seattle to San Diego to Fort Worth to Omaha and home. The theory was that after such a trip, his debaters would have heard every possible variation, negative and affirmative, on the topic scheduled for the national tournament that year.

It is a measure of McElmeel's stature (and of the administration's flexibility) at St. Thomas that he could spring three of his students loose from classes for three weeks every other year to make this tour. The trio selected were his top two debaters, usually seniors, and one underclassman whose grade point average would tolerate his missing nearly a month of classes. As a second semester freshman, I was the number three man on the western swing in 1939. I filled in as a debater whenever either of the two principal speakers (Bob Short and Ed Larkin) was ill or tired.

Our coach was right. After two weeks on the road, we had heard all the possible "cases" affirmative and negative that we would be likely to meet at the national tournament. The dark side of that theory, however, and possibly the dark side of collegiate debate, is that it exposes eager practitioners to the pernicious fallacy that rhetorical skill, not solid evidence, determines the winners. Years later, in a seminary class in metaphysics, a professor icily informed me that I should not confuse the study of philosophy with the glib sophistry I had acquired as a collegiate debater.

On alternate years the St. Thomas debate team would host a visit from the English debaters of Oxford University. My father had taken me to this event on occasion before I entered college. Speakers on both teams wore tuxedoes for this elegant event. Confident that I would one day represent St. Thomas against Oxford, my parents, at Christmas my freshman year in college, presented me with a tailor-made tuxedo, complete with complementary white tie and tails. I never did debate the Oxonians on campus. But I got a lot of mileage out of my tux and tails. Later, at the seminary, I wore black trousers, with a grosgrain stripe down the side, under my cassock for two years. I hated to see those pants go. They were my last link with "the world." And I still love gardenias.

In my first year of college I first met Dorothy Day and Peter Maurin, cofounders of the Catholic Worker movement. Maurin, a creative, dynamic French peasant whose rapid-fire lectures talked of "communisma, capitalisma, and Catholicisma" (always with a final "a"), and Day, a zealous and dedicated convert from communism to Catholicism, had joined forces in New York to open a House of Hospitality for the victims of the Great Depression.

When they came to St. Thomas in 1939, they fired my imagination with their simple, radical explication of what it means to be a follower of Jesus Christ. On that occasion they were in town to locate and open a House of Hospitality in Minneapolis. As one eager volunteer, I helped them and Father Walter LeBeau, our professor of theology, wash the grimy walls and ceilings of a marginal old store building they rented on East Hennepin Avenue near Nicollet Island.

The next summer I made a pilgrimage to the original House of Hospitality on Mott Street in New York and felt honored to help serve soup and brown bread to a long line of what Maurin called "the ambassadors of Christ."

By the time I was in college the Shannon Cattle Company had offices in St. Paul, Minnesota, Fargo, North Dakota, Billings, Montana, Omaha, Nebraska, and Troy, Ohio. Father was in charge in St. Paul, Bill in Omaha, Pete in Billings, and Frank in Ohio. By then I was also old enough to be of some help in the business, usually in Montana during the summer when Father or Bill was contracting for the fall delivery of range cattle.

On horseback or in cars we would inspect as much of any rancher's herd as father considered necessary to see. He and the rancher would agree on a price (per pound or per head), a delivery date in early autumn, the place of delivery, and the number of cattle to be delivered. From his days in Ireland, father believed farmers and ranchers who have raised their cattle from calves tend to overestimate the weight their cattle carry. Many a rancher is surprised on delivery day, when his cattle are weighed, to learn that his check is smaller than he expected because his cattle are not as heavy as he assumed. Thanks to his early years with the "cow jobber" in Ireland, Father could regularly estimate the weight of range animals.

At the end of a trail ride at Wyola Siding in Big Horn County, Montana, in 1935, I once saw him demonstrate this skill. We were bringing a herd of yearling steers from range grass down to a railroad loading yard. The owner, wisely for him, had sold them to us by the head, not by the pound. But he still thought they would average 675 pounds. In a wager with the owner, before we reached the scales, my father wrote his guess (640 pounds) on a slip of paper and gave it to me as a stakeholder. When we had weighed all the cattle and averaged their weights they averaged 636 pounds each. I still have that slip of paper.

The summers in Montana and Wyoming, where we often worked long hours weighing and loading cattle, remain happy memories for me. That was the time that I was introduced to the American West. The grasslands and the mountains of the Rocky Mountain states still fascinate me. Some people are frightened by the open spaces of the West. Like Per Hansa's wife, Beret, in Ole Rölvaag's novel *Giants in the Earth,* they consider the wide open vistas of the West lonely, empty space. But like Willa Cather, I feel more free, more relaxed, more at ease in the West than I ever have in any urban setting. In her autobiography, Cather boasted that she would wake up in the night in the sleeper on the Burlington going west as soon as it crossed the Missouri River. She knew she was home again. I cannot match her remarkable intuition. But I do know what she meant.

At the end of my second year in college, I took the entrance examination for admission to the St. Paul Seminary. I was accepted but decided to stay at St. Thomas to complete my B.A. degree. Was I wavering in my vocation? Possibly. When classes resumed in September 1940, many of my classmates had left for the seminary. By taking some independent reading courses and telescoping my junior and senior years, I completed the graduation requirements for the B.A. degree in three years. In June 1941, as valedictorian of my class, I graduated *summa cum laude* and promptly enrolled for a summer course on the Great Books of Western Civilization at St. John's College, Annapolis, Maryland. Reading Plato, St. Augustine, Isaac Newton, and St. Thomas and sailing on Chesapeake Bay made that lovely summer pass quickly.

In September I enrolled at the St. Paul Seminary, at last a formal candidate for the priesthood. In spite of the warm and cordial camaraderie of my new classmates I felt uncomfortable in that new milieu. As a boy at home during the Depression, I was profoundly influenced by the role of the parish church as the helper of the poor. When farmers in the parish had no market for their potatoes, they dumped them on the parochial school playground where Father O'Callaghan and volunteers like me helped needy families shovel them into burlap sacks or cardboard boxes loaded on coaster wagons. But aside from these contacts, I had very little exposure to ecclesiastical life.

A true vocation, a calling, to the sacred priesthood is a mysterious process. According to Catholic teaching no one can be sure he has such a vocation until his bishop calls him by name on the day of ordination. Until that awesome moment, a candidate for holy orders remains — a candidate. He lives in hope that his years of prayer and study will merit for him the official "call" to holy orders.

CHAPTER FOUR

# ST. PAUL SEMINARY

The regimen of a diocesan seminary is designed to develop among its students the skills and virtues they will need as parish priests. There is an important intellectual element in this process but the ultimate objective is not intellectual. Daily meditation on the life of Jesus Christ and a regular effort to model one's life on that life are the central concerns of a seminary curriculum. Some seminary graduates turn out to be first-rate scholars. Some are tenors with perfect pitch. Some are eloquent preachers. Some are genuine saints. Some are good managers. Some become great money raisers. But these skills are incidental to the main purpose of a seminary: to graduate candidates for the priesthood who have developed the habits of prayer, industry, service, and purity of life they will need as pastors and teachers.

This objective makes life in a seminary far less competitive and vastly more enjoyable than life in other professional schools. Living in a regulated society with classmates who share one's values and goals, who are committed to the regular practice of Christian charity, and who regard the success of others as a sign that their community life is healthy is a most satisfying human experience. It was my good fortune to know such a life for six school years at the St. Paul Seminary.

That life revolved around the daily sharing of the Eucharist. We rose at 5:30 A.M. Morning prayers and meditation at 6:00 A.M. were followed by daily Mass at 6:30, breakfast at 7:30, and first class at 8:15. Planners of seminary curricula in those days placed great value on endless hours of classroom attendance, with relatively less emphasis on private study, writing, or research. One happy result of this tedious horarium was that every student was eager and chafing to play tennis, handball, hockey, softball, or touchball as soon as the last class ended at 3:00 P.M. If statistics were ever kept on such subjects, I dare say seminarians wear out more handballs per year than members of any other calling. Fine Christian gentlemen can, in good conscience, beat the hell out of a little rubber ball for an hour every day as part of their regular mental health program.

A hot shower at 4:30 following a vigorous workout is guaranteed to put healthy young men in the mood for nodding during the 5:00 P.M. daily lecture on the spiritual life. I recall some cases of minor injury by whiplash during those late afternoon lectures by our spiritual director. Dinner at 5:30, free time from 6:15 to 7:00, usually spent walking the perimeter of the campus, study time from 7:00 to 9:30, night prayers in common at 9:30, and lights out, with the "Grand Silence" from 10:00 P.M. till 5:30 the next morning. Wednesday and Saturday afternoons were free for shopping in town or for teaching in local parochial schools. One Sunday afternoon a month was visitor's day.

On that day families and friends were welcomed at vespers and for a short visit after that service. The official seminary view of families, however, was that fidelity to a priestly vocation mandated deliberate weakening of the ties with one's family. Somehow the pursuit of a priestly vocation called for putting a certain distance between ourselves and our families.

This view was as difficult for me then as it is now. It may be a re-action, in seminary folklore, to the European culture which encouraged extended families to move into the rectory with their son or brother once he achieved the status of pastor. Whatever its origin, it has always seemed to me counterproductive in the American culture where family ties are steadily eroded by our fondness for mobility and change.

The central event of the seminary week was the Solemn High Mass on Sunday. It was our principal liturgical celebration as well as an important training ground for the choir and for the younger students in minor orders still learning the rubrics of solemn liturgical ceremonies. I have never heard more inspirational music than the all-male, four-part polyphony and Gregorian chant we sang each Sunday in chapel at morning Mass and at evening vespers. To this day Gregorian chant sweeps me back to the days of my youth and to the special graces of life in the seminary. Is there such a thing as a holy sound? Or is our individual version of religious music the kind each of us learned to admire in our youth?

The camaraderie of seminary days is unique. Friendships made then are like no others. Before enrollment and after graduation from the seminary, a person competes for grades, achievement, recognition, or productivity, even in the ministry. But in the seminary the universal laws of competition among peers yield for a time to the pursuit of kindness, simplicity, and a sense of humor, the essential components, according to Thomas Aquinas, of the basic virtue of charity.

The common concern of seminary students is their trusting, mutual pursuit of the likeness of Christ in their lives. This shared objective makes them drop their guard in many ways in dealing with one another. There is an openness, a candor, a freshness about seminary life which make that campus community more cohesive and less fractious than any other fraternity. Friendships formed in this benevolent atmosphere have a strength and durability which contrast sharply with the ephemeral acquaintances so characteristic of our kaleidoscopic and transient society.

I cannot recall ever being rushed in the seminary. Bored maybe, but never rushed. There is time to pray, to ponder sacred scripture, to meditate, to be thoughtful, to be kind, to weigh the large questions of time and eternity, life and death, good and evil, and to decide how to build a life and a value system out of these elements.

The Latin word *seminarium* means a seed plot or nursery. Unfriendly critics have called seminaries hothouses where fledgling pastors are protected from the chill winds of the real world. This image can be overdone, but it has an element of truth. The seminary is not the real world. It leads from and to the real world, but it is a buffer zone, a staging area, where preparation is made over a considerable period of time for the intended career of service which lies ahead. In these years a deliberate effort is made by a student to place himself at arm's length from worldly affairs.

In our seminary parlance "the world," as used in the phrase "the world, the flesh, and the devil," was a wicked place, an occasion of sin. And yet "the world" is also the arena in which the future priest is called to serve. It is where God's people live, where they work out their salvation, where the priest is expected to help them bear their burdens and live and die with the dignity of the children of God. It is not easy to strike the proper balance between the world full of sin and the world to be saved.

In our seminary days we were not allowed to see daily newspapers or to have radios in our rooms. Radios and papers were considered "distractions." We could hear the evening news on one radio set in a crowded, smoke-filled recreation room. Those were World War II years. With no newspapers and only one "public" radio we got only the barest news of the outside world each day. One electrical genius in our day managed to defeat the system partially by fitting a small radio receiver into a one-pound Fanny Farmer candy box. He kept his illicit treasure beside his bed. It could be turned on or off by sliding a fingernail file positioned on its cover to make or break electrical contact. To tempt the rest of us, its builder connected it at night to the unused gas line in our old residence hall and gave some welcome night music at bedtime to anyone with a pipe wrench who was willing to unscrew the cap of the gas pipe jutting out of the wall above his bed. The sound was barely audible but the exercise held a kind of wicked attraction in a life carefully insulated from all the standard temptations.

The curriculum of the St. Paul Seminary in 1941 required that every first-year student complete a full-year course in elementary Latin *at the seminary*. Before I had left St. Thomas, my friend and mentor Father Frederic Bieter had suggested that I ask to be exempted from this requirement. By then I had studied Latin for four years in high school and majored in it at college.

In my first interview with the seminary rector, Father Lawrence Wolf, I innocently shared with him Father Bieter's suggestion. In a kindly but earnest fashion he then proceeded to tell me that this course was required of every student, that my request smacked of pride, and that a major purpose of seminary training was to help candidates for the priesthood learn the virtue of humility. I was off to a great start in my new career. I readily agreed to take the course.

Little did I know how uncomfortable that commitment would prove to be. The priest who taught the course followed a predictable elementary school pattern of calling on students to recite in alphabetical order in his class each day. It did not take long for my fellow students or me to catch on that he never called on me to recite. By Christmas it was clear that he had no intention of ever calling on me, and he never did. Over two semesters we had four written examinations. None of these was ever returned to me, and in both semesters he gave me a grade of F for the course.

The only explanation I could ever figure out for this pattern of "shunning" was that the rector had told the professor about my request to be excused from his course. Whereupon he decided to make that year-long experience a lesson in humility, not to say humiliation, for me. I never did learn whether he considered his pedagogical effort to humble me a success or not.

The first two years of the seminary curriculum at that time concentrated on the study of philosophy. Logic, epistemology, metaphysics, and natural theology formed the curricular bridge between the liberal arts and the "sacred sciences." The last four years of the seminary focused on dogmatic and moral theology, canon law, church history, and sacred scripture. In all six years of my seminary course, the classes were usually straight lectures. After five hours of lectures, back to back in one day, I often felt God owed me points. The sheer ability to keep coming back to class day after day for this mode of instruction says something about the endurance expected of seminary students in those days. Six years of this regimen does not mean a candidate has a right to priestly ordination, but it does document his earnest desire to be a priest.

To say that most of the classes were straight lectures is not to say that they were uniformly dull. Some were first-rate presentations by competent professors. But there was a deadly and predictable sameness about all those days in all those hard oak chairs, taking all those notes about all those sublime and marvelous realities, natural and supernatural. Later, as a curate at the Cathedral of St. Paul in my first year as a priest, I recall the sense of joy and relief I had in September on the day classes resumed at the seminary. I no longer had to return to those endless lectures.

Since Vatican II dramatic changes have come to seminary curricula. One result, I trust, is that candidates for the priesthood today are being prepared for lives of ministry and service with curricula which test their motivation but spare them at least some of the ennui once considered essential to form priestly character.

Professors in seminaries and pastors in pulpits enjoy a kind of intellectual protective shield. If their orthodoxy is unquestioned, they are often allowed to turn in consistently shoddy performances. Their doctrinal purity covers for their pedagogical deficiencies. The ideal, of course, for masters who would instruct novices, in the seminary or elsewhere, is that the master would know more than the students do about the subject and that the master would have the rhetorical skill to present that material as important and attractive. Unfortunately the mantle of a seminary professorship or of a canonical pastorate can give its possessor a false sense of security and could lead to early retirement, not from his tenured position, but from his youthful determination to develop the human skills necessary to complement the doctrinal orthodoxy he and the church prize so highly.

It is common practice today for some Christians to say that they are "born again." I am not quite sure what this term means. I know it refers to an experience of personal religious conversion. But I do not know the elements of which such a conversion is made, nor indeed, if it is essentially the same experience for all persons who claim it.

I can point to no such single event marking a sudden and dramatic shift in my spiritual life. I can, however, cite particular occasions during my seminary days when I felt that scales had suddenly been peeled from my eyes so that I could perceive old truths in a dramatically new and more impressive light.

One of these experiences came to me over several days as our spiritual director, Father Louis McCarthy, talked to us about the Psalms and their role in our prayer life. Citing particular Psalms in which David strives to express pure praise for the majesty of God, devoid of any petition or penitence or thanksgiving, Father McCarthy's commentary opened new vistas of light and understanding for me as I came to see that God deserves worship from a person because God is. David knew, and we should know, that prayers of petition, thanksgiving, or penance are good and necessary but that they are by definition inferior to the simple prayer of adoration. Persons climb mountains because the mountains are there. Persons worship God purely, and with no other motive, once they grasp that God is God.

Readers may smile at the naivete of these words. I was an adult, a college graduate, a priestly candidate for two or three years before the experience narrated here took place. And, all at once, this insight made an enormous difference in my life.

Everything seemed simpler after that. One's attitude toward material things, rewards, honors, even eternal salvation, changes when one comprehends what follows from the simple realization that Almighty God does exist, that God is all-merciful, all-knowing, and all-loving. From that point on, in my life, a lot of earlier concerns and anxieties seemed trivial. Prayer became a challenging and continuing effort to be aware of the presence of God in the world and with me. Somehow it then seemed out of place to use prayer as a complaint department or a shopper's list of needs. God knows our needs. God needs no list from us. God knows our sins and weaknesses better than we do. And God knows our good points better than we do. God wants from us the simple prayer of recognition, with all that that realization implies.

St. Teresa of Avila recounts in her journal that she would begin her daily prayers with the simple statement to God: "Your majesty, it is I, Teresa, your servant." That says it well.

The students called Father McCarthy "Big Lou, the High Priest." He stood well over six feet. He looms even taller in my book of memories. In my youth he helped me see for the first time that once you comprehend the full reality of God's existence and divine attributes, everything in life changes. It did for me. Maybe I was "born again."

Another experience similar to this in the seminary came from a book, Father Edward Leen's essays titled *Gifts of the Holy Spirit*. I used it for several days as the text for morning meditation. I had paid lip-service to the Holy Spirit for years in my rapid-fire daily prayers. But Leen's book made me see that if a person makes an earnest and habitual effort to remain open to the inspirations of divine influence, God can shape, guide, and enrich that life far more deeply than even the most disciplined human effort.

This insight is related to the earlier one about worship. Together, they transformed my life. Many earlier values, many achievements I once considered desirable, now seemed empty, compared to the powerful notion that an all-knowing and all-merciful God loves me and offers me, at every moment, all I need to know and to do to actualize whatever potential my life is supposed to achieve. This realization brought me an enormous sense of well-being, tranquility, and a better sense of humor.

On a less sublime but still important level, my life and thought were altered perceptibly by a series of lectures on psychology given to us by Dr. Rudolf Allers, a psychiatrist, then teaching at the Catholic University of America. As a young doctor in Vienna, Allers had studied under Sigmund Freud. The theme of his lectures to us was that much of everyone's personal unhappiness in life is homemade.

He cited examples from his clinical experience of persons who consume great amounts of precious personal energy trying to change unpleasant things around them which cannot be changed. He cited the law of gravity as a rule which has already been settled. To act as though we could repeal or reverse it is foolhardy. We learn to live with it. And the sooner the better. Allers stressed the importance of our understanding the essential unwieldiness of "objective reality." We imperil our mental hygiene if we act on the premise that "the world out there" should somehow accommodate itself to our moods and perceptions. I recall his example of a man who was habitually late for work. After being warned by his boss that his tardiness was endangering his job, he came to Allers for counsel. He also admitted that his marriage showed signs of strain. A few sessions with Allers revealed that the man's trouble all happened at the start of each work day. He was always rushed at breakfast, curt with his children, short-tempered with his wife, and often obscene to other drivers en route to work. By the time he got to his office he was mad at the world. And yet the man assured Allers that he liked his job, loved his wife, and had "great kids." So what was his trouble? Simple. He overslept every day, then expected others to make up for this indulgence on his part. Everyone else had to step fast to help him not be late for work. If they didn't, he boiled over in anger. Allers counseled him to get up an hour earlier every day. Surprise! It worked. Objective reality would not change for him. But he could change to accept as part of life certain things "out there" which were beyond his control.

Allers's message was two-edged. We should not worry about things we are powerless to change. But, conversely, we should worry about improving what can be corrected in our milieu. Allers's message complemented the lessons from Leen and the Psalms. We cannot leave all the work to God, simply because we believe God does exist and does influence our lives.

Allers was only one of several visitors who brightened our seminary days. Peter Maurin and Dorothy Day, making the rounds of their growing string of Houses of Hospitality, returned to talk to us when they were in town. The Baroness Maria Von Trapp and her talented children sang for us, in person, long before Julie Andrews played the baroness in "Sound of Music."

The seminary process made me more aware of God's presence in the world and in my life. It taught me to trust God's goodness, to rely on God's grace. It taught me how to pray. And it showed me that a life of service can be a life of joy.

In those six years of formation, I often thought the tempo could have been stepped up a little. But I have no complaints. I entered the seminary tentative and uncertain about my vocation, hoping God would enlighten me. The plan for my life then was still inchoate and vague. Six years later I left that closely knit community with a deep sense of assurance and confidence. I knew what I wanted to do with my life, and I was confident I had the natural talents and the supernatural graces to be a good priest and a faithful pastor.

The chapel of the St. Paul Seminary, recently remodeled, was in my day a handsome smaller replica of St. Paul's Outside the Walls in Rome. It was the scene, in my seminary days, of the richest liturgical experiences I have ever known. There were three hours of rehearsal every week to prepare for the solemn liturgy of Sunday. Two hours were spent rehearsing the music and one hour rehearsing the ceremonies for vespers and the Solemn Mass. The elegance, the symmetry, the color, the movement, the sounds of those Sunday liturgies created a world of beauty and majesty I had never known before and have witnessed all too seldom since.

As a seminarian, and even as a priest, I was aware that somehow I lacked the "ecclesiastical virtues." Many of my classmates could talk for hours about the Old Sarum Rite from Salisbury, or about the "O Antiphons" chanted in choir during Advent, or about that rare but never defined aura of *Romanità* which clings to clerics trained in Rome. I never had the eye or the ear for these peculiarly "churchy" concerns.

On the day we were ordained deacons by Archbishop John Gregory Murray, I was the deacon of the Pontifical Mass. My classmate Sylvester Treinen, later the bishop of Boise, was the subdeacon. The final task of the deacon at a High Mass (in Latin) was to intone the "Ite Missa Est." I had practiced that passage so often that I was over-trained. There are many Gregorian "modes" for this intonation. The most solemn form calls for four beats on the first syllable of the first word. At the proper time I turned to face the choir and began the chant. I gave the first syllable three beats, not four. I stopped and started over. Same error. I stopped and started again. I had Syl Treinen and the whole church humming. They were trying to give me the pitch. I had the pitch. It was the beat I was missing. After three false starts I made it on the fourth try. Everyone in the chapel had coach's nerves. Then, to make me feel even more embarrassed, the archbishop gave a short homily after Mass on the virtue of perseverance. In the course of it he praised me for mine. I am told by seminary raconteurs that my performance that day still ranks as the nadir for singing deacons.

My participation in the liturgical life of the seminary was often less informed than that of my classmates. Not less rewarding. Not less inspiring. Just less informed. I did it all (with the exception of the singing) reasonably well, but without the finesse of many of my classmates.

But the hours I spent in prayer in that quiet chapel made a great difference in my life. It has never been difficult for me to believe in the existence of God. Even as a child I considered the evidence for a benevolent creator overwhelming. But as a seminary student, working my way slowly through the gospels of the New Testament, I came to know Jesus Christ with a kind of personal intimacy vastly greater than the bond I share with most persons I see daily.

To this day when I kneel alone in the chapel of the St. Paul Seminary my Friend is there with me as truly as in the days of my youth. Since then I have prayed in many churches in many lands, but prayer in that chapel still has a quality of clarity and fitness that is, for me, unique.

One very good reason for the sheer length of the seminary course is that some candidates need time to decide whether their calling is or is not to the priesthood. There are a fortunate few who seem to have known early on, and with unwavering conviction, that they are called to the priestly life. I cannot say that I was one of these.

To be or not to be a priest was a serious question for me even in my final year of study. At one point, near the end of my fifth year in the seminary, unable to define precisely my own motives for seeking ordination, I requested and received a leave of absence. I had no desire to pursue any other calling. I had no desire to marry. I had no particular reason for leaving the seminary. I simply lacked the certitude I thought was imperative before I could present myself for ordination.

My leave lasted two months. I traveled. I studied. I prayed. And I finally concluded that what I wanted most in life was to pledge my talents and skills, such as they were, to the service of others, and to do this as a priest in the Catholic Church. When I shared this deceptively simple conclusion with Father Louis McCarthy, my friend and counselor, he calmly replied, "I told you so months ago, but you had to find other proof. I hope you're satisfied." I was.

In the last year of the seminary I no longer sought signs from heaven that I should be a priest. I was content with the simple syllogism that Almighty God had given me an abundance of blessings, that most of these had come to me through the Catholic Church and a Catholic family, and that I was free to pledge my life to the service of the church or to withhold that pledge.

My role models in the priesthood, and in society at large, were persons who generously "served" needs larger than their own interests. My old pastor, Father Jeremiah O'Callaghan, who helped his parishioners maintain body and soul and personal dignity in the Depression, was one of these. So was Father McCarthy. So was John Gregory Murray, archbishop of St. Paul, a prelate who had chosen as the motto for his episcopal coat of arms the words of the father to his older son in the Parable of the Prodigal Son: "Mea Omnia Tua" (All my things are yours).

The priests I admired most were men who were generous with their time and their talents in the service of others. They all appeared in my eyes as persons who had achieved a kind of personal equanimity and integrity which I found extremely attractive. Their lives seemed to demonstrate that a ministry of service brings to its practitioners a kind of satisfaction and a sense of fitness that self-serving persons never achieve. I believed then, and I believe now, that the Christian paradox really works, if we can be generous enough to take Jesus Christ at his word.

Acting on the simple premise that I wished to pledge my life to serve the needs of other persons, and trusting that the Holy Spirit would guide my judgment, I confidently presented myself for ordination to the sacred priesthood on June 8, 1946, a decision I have never regretted, and a decision which has subsequently brought me an abundance of grace.

# CHAPTER FIVE

# ORDINATION — IRELAND — MIESVILLE

In Catholic culture the ordination of a young man to the priesthood is an occasion of great importance and solemnity. His offering of Mass in his home parish for the first time, so long awaited, so carefully prepared for, so sacred and so central to Catholic life, is an event he can never forget.

Even at this distance, five decades later, my heart fills with gratitude to God, to the Catholic Church, to my marvelous family, and to all those teachers and friends who made it possible for me to offer the holy sacrifice of the Mass on Pentecost Sunday, June 9, 1946, in St. Augustine's Church in South St. Paul. Never before nor since have I known such a sense of being on the verge of great events. The prospect of a lifetime of service as a priest filled me with an enormous sense of excitement and expectation.

The acclaim given to a young priest by his family and friends is a pretty heady experience, especially if he should fail to understand that the honors and gifts heaped on him so lavishly are not rewards for his virtue or talent but signs of how highly his predecessors in the priesthood are esteemed by faithful Catholics.

One homely memory of the day of my first Mass is still fresh. The week before I was ordained my mother sent me a clipping from a story about a young priest named Oscar. He was the youngest child in a large family (as I was). Hence Oscar was always the child sent to the local store to get last-minute items needed for dinner (as I was). In the story, on the day Oscar was ordained his family had a reception for all his friends and relatives. In the midst of this joyous assembly, the young priest, standing in the receiving line, smiling and enjoying center stage, heard his mother's familiar call from the kitchen, "Oscar, I need a pound of butter and a dozen eggs. Hurry." He excused himself and went to the kitchen to protest. "Mother, please, all my friends are here. I can't run errands now." She replied: "Look here, my boy, you are the junior member of this family. Remember? We need eggs and butter and we need them right now. So move!"

On the day of my first Mass I got no such hurry-up call. But from that day until my mother's death her notes and letters to me always began "My dear Oscar."

The day after the first Mass my father, my uncle, Thomas Shannon, and his three daughters, Mary, Alice, and Frances, and I took off for a one-month trip to Ireland. It was the first visit back to Ireland for my father and my uncle in forty years and the first ever for my cousins and me. The era of trans-Atlantic air travel was just beginning. Hence the media and the airlines made quite a story out of our trip. We left New York on Pan American's *Clipper Shannon,* en route to Shannon Airport in Ireland. A Dublin paper carried our picture with the caption "Six Shannons, By Shannon, For Shannon."

That month in Ireland introduced me to all my Irish aunts, uncles, and cousins, gave me new insights into my Irish roots, and helped me see in action the bond which ties the Irish to their Catholic faith and to their priests. Visitors to the Emerald Isle quickly learn that the memory is still fresh in modern Ireland that priests were hunted down and executed because they continued their priestly ministry during the cruel penal days of the seventeenth and eighteenth centuries. The Irish continue to be grateful for past heroic services rendered by their priests.

Somehow the special status the Irish give their priests made me uneasy. I was cautioned by one friendly curate that my American style was too democratic. In his view, I did not keep sufficient distance between myself and the Irish people. Fortunately, the dilemma he posed seldom reoccurred. We spent all our days and many of our nights visiting with relatives who could not have been more hospitable. They were charmed to see the "little Yank priest" and to come to his "grand little Mass" each day in the village church in Hacketstown, County Carlow.

I suppose all people are proud of their national origins. I am immensely proud of mine. Coming to know the members of my father's family and being well received by them gave me a sense of solidarity with a cultural tradition I admire and treasure, the more so with the passing years.

Back in my home diocese of St. Paul my first assignment was to serve as pastor pro-tem in a small country parish at Miesville, Minnesota. It was heaven. I offered Mass and heard confessions each morning in a grand old Gothic church, cooked my own meals, attended to parish business, took long walks in the country, and once a week went to St. Paul by bus to see the pastor, Father Matthias Duhr, who was dying of cancer in St. Joseph's Hospital. He knew death was near and dictated to me each day a growing list of persons whom he wanted notified of his death. One name on the list was Pope Pius XII, whom Father Duhr had known in their seminary days in Rome.

The old priest was a marvel. He had a deep baritone voice and loved to sing. As we sat talking in his hospital room, he would often intone the opening words of the Gloria, the Sanctus, the Credo, or the Pater Noster from the ordinary of the Latin Mass. He knew that he would not ascend the altar again to chant these lovely phrases. But death held no terror for him. It meant only that he would finally be at home in the kingdom of God. He welcomed the prospect.

After each visit with him I had reams of notes on things he wanted done in the parish. One note was a warning that I was not to drive his car. He thought I was too young to be trusted at the wheel. I was twenty-five. The car was six years old.

One thing he forgot to tell me was that the hot and cold water in the rectory was contaminated. The "safe" drinking water was to be taken from a hand pump out in the yard. Water in the house came from a cistern, after it had run off the roof and through a half dozen birds' nests.

Each day as I drew the water to bathe and to shave I remarked that the local groundwater table had a lot of iron. Iron? As I was to learn, it also had high concentrations of decomposed animal and vegetable matter suspended in solution.

On the day of Father Duhr's funeral I had been drinking the bad water for nearly a month, but did not know why I had so little energy. That day I could hardly walk. Youthful pride kept me from telling the archbishop I was ill. After all, I had just had a full month's vacation in Ireland. It was time for me to do some work, not ask for sick leave.

The day following the funeral I was too weak to offer Mass. The next day I collapsed on the floor in the rectory and lay there alone from midafternoon until midnight. When I awoke in the dark I was frightened. I got to the phone and called my father. He took me to the hospital where I was unconscious for a day and a night. When I came to I was in room 333, Father Duhr's old room. My friend Father Harry Majerus, the hospital chaplain, was sitting in a chair beside my bed. He told me what had happened and said he had debated giving me the last rites. I recall thinking, "Is it time for me already? What a short tour of duty."

I slipped in and out of consciousness for a few more days. One of the interns was a college classmate of mine. He confided to me that he thought I had typhoid. He seemed pleased. "Typhoid is pretty rare in these parts. We seldom see it, at least in this latitude," he said. Each time he came into the room he pulled up my pajama top to see if I had any red blotches on my stomach, a symptom, he said, of typhoid. Sure enough, one day they appeared. My belly was a mass of red. He was delighted. I called for a second opinion. Sister Jane Margaret Flemming, C.S.J., was the nurse in charge of the floor. When she saw my blotches, she told the intern, "That's not typhoid. He's allergic. Cut the penicillin and he'll be okay tomorrow." One deflated young doctor. One grateful young priest.

Recovery was slow. A short walk down the hospital corridor left me exhausted. Archbishop Murray came to see me one day and said he was assigning me to the staff of the cathedral, where he lived. That way, he said, he could keep an eye on me and watch my diet. He assured me that the water at the cathedral was safe to drink. I was embarrassed at the brevity and the inglorious conclusion of my first assignment. But I was glad to be alive, glad to leave room 333, and charmed to be assigned to the staff of the cathedral.

CHAPTER SIX

# CATHEDRAL DAYS

The Cathedral Church of St. Paul is a massive Romanesque granite structure set squarely on the brow of the highest hill in the inner city, overlooking the Mississippi River. At the Louisiana Purchase Exposition in St. Louis in 1904, John Ireland, archbishop of St. Paul, taken with the strength and mass of the Renaissance pavilions designed by Emmanuel Masqueray, hired this French architect to design a cathedral for St. Paul which would compare with the great cathedrals Ireland recalled from his days as a seminarian in France.

Begun in 1906, plagued by a shortage of funds for construction, partially completed and opened for worship in 1915, the cathedral was not finished until 1958. There were those, including James J. Hill, who built the Great Northern Railroad from St. Paul to Puget Sound, who said John Ireland was too ambitious in his plans for a cathedral. The critics had a point. Completion of the cathedral, including the stained-glass windows, heroic statues of the four Evangelists, inside limestone finish, the pipe organ, and adequate lighting, took half a century. But in the defensive words of one old Irish pastor who sided with Archbishop Ireland, "The period of gestation for an elephant is two years. But when it comes, it's an elephant."

The Cathedral of St. Paul today is one of the great religious shrines of North America. John Ireland planned well. It just took a little time to work out the details of his grand design.

On August 15, 1946, I reported for duty as the junior curate at the cathedral, a position I was to hold for five of the busiest and happiest years of my life. In that span my "boss" was Father George Ryan, a gifted administrator with a light touch, who taught me much of what I know about how to be a good priest, about the art of administration, and about how to be happy while working hard.

The work schedule for the five priests then assigned to that staff was heavy. Keeping up with weekly convert classes, weddings, funerals, baptisms, counseling, confessions, daily Masses, and sick calls to the four hospitals in the parish meant long days and short nights. The first Mass on Sunday was at 5:00 A.M., on weekdays 6:00 A.M., followed by communion calls for an hour and a half every weekday at one of the four hospitals.

Conventional wisdom in the Catholic Church holds that a priest's first assignment shapes his ministry for life. Miesville aside, my formative years were spent in a busy, biracial, urban parish where the needs of the people, many of them poor, called for young priests with high energy levels.

On my first day there Father Ryan invited me into his study and explained the local ground rules: "This is a big parish. It has some rich families on Summit Avenue and some desperately poor families, some of them black, on Rondo Street. They all need all the help they can get from God and from this parish. You have the power of the priesthood. You can hear their confessions, heal their wounds, bring them the Eucharist, help them live and die with the dignity of children of God. You are just as much a priest as I am. I am a little older; if I can help you, I'm here. But I'll not tell you how to plan your days or spend your time. Come see me if you think I can help you. Say your prayers. Be a good priest. Ours is a great vocation."

George Ryan was what the Irish call "a lovely man." He had a rare combination of zeal and style. Being in his presence made everyone feel better. I never heard him say he was tired. My most vivid memory of those days is that I was always tired. On occasion I skipped lunch to catch a thirty-minute nap.

One of the chores I did not relish was "teaching" catechism to children in our parochial school every Wednesday. Little did I know how inadequate was my preparation for this assignment. I was scheduled to spend a half-hour in the seventh, fifth, third, and first grades once a week. The nuns in charge stood aside when I came in to "teach." I got along fairly well in the seventh grade. Less well in the fifth. I had real trouble in the third. I was a total failure, weekly, in the first grade. I had no idea how to present the material I wanted to share with those kids. They ran me ragged.

I finally asked the Sisters of St. Joseph, over coffee at recess one morning, whether I was doing any good by coming to their classes. They looked at each other and then at the floor. I asked them to be candid. One slowly replied, "To be candid, Father, it's awful. Just awful. When you leave, it takes me thirty minutes to get those children back to some kind of a decent learning experience."

We made a deal. I explained that Father Ryan wanted the children to know the priests and that weekly visits for that purpose were a must. But "teaching" these youngsters was clearly not for me. The nuns and I agreed that I would keep the same schedule, visit the classes weekly, but do so only as a courtesy call with a friendly greeting, and no attempt to "teach" anyone. The children and I became good friends. And the nuns were grateful.

That exposure to teaching in the primary grades convinced me that the highest pedagogical art is that of a good kindergarten teacher. The older the student, the more the subject matter of the class teaches itself. The younger the student, the greater the art required in the teacher. College and graduate level professors can get away with murder. But in kindergarten the teacher has to be an artist.

One assignment I did relish was that of scheduling and preparing for the liturgical functions in the cathedral. Archbishop Murray lived with us in the rectory, having abandoned his stately and lonely old episcopal residence in exchange for two rooms just like ours in the parish house. He frequently presided at pontifical functions in the cathedral. My job was to train the altar boys for these functions. I had a roster of seventy-two servers. The performances they turned in as acolytes, cross-bearers, miter-bearers, and assistant masters of ceremonies were the pride of my life. I had seventh graders on that staff who could guide elderly bishops or rusty monsignors through the intricate steps of a pontifical High Mass without a flaw. This was the cathedral, the mother church of the archdiocese. It was expected that the music, the ceremonies, and the liturgy would be models for the rest of the archdiocese. And they were.

The altar boys and I had the immediate satisfaction of knowing that Archbishop Murray and Father Ryan considered our work up to par. Compliments were seldom exchanged, but we knew we were good. We worked at it and liked our work.

A tangible reward for the boys was my season ticket to some of the home games of the St. Paul hockey team. It read: "This pass admits Father Shannon and 25 friends." I had a similar pass for the annual Shrine Circus.

Twice a year Father John Sankovitz and I would take half of our roster (thirty-six) to a Sunday smorgasbord dinner at the St. Paul Hotel. In white shirts and ties, *de rigeur* for that occasion (very few of them owned suits), our thirty-six "friends" worked over the buffet table like a horde of locusts. They vied with each other going back for "thirds" or "fourths."

With a little help from our friends, and occasional checks from Archbishop Murray, we also managed to get seventy-two servers to a summer camp for one week each year. On the day of departure they piled into a bus. I followed in a borrowed truck, loaded with their luggage and camp gear.

One year, on the evening of the first day of camp, just as I got back to the rectory with my empty truck, the phone rang. It was the camp director. I had not told him some of my boys were black. So what? "So they can't stay, that's what. You come and get these black kids right now or I'll put them on the next bus for St. Paul." This was the Catholic director of a Catholic camp. The year was 1948. I persuaded him to sit tight till morning. I needed some time. I was furious at his bigotry and at myself for getting those kids in a spot not of their making.

I went to the archbishop's room and knocked softly. He was still up. He invited me in. I told him my story. He asked a few questions and then asked if he might use my telephone. (He had no phone in his room.) He placed a call to the camp director, identified himself, and asked whether the camp still advertised itself as a Catholic camp. Informed that it did, he said that he found it difficult to reconcile a policy of segregation by skin color with Catholic teaching. The director tried to explain that the camp was a business. Having black kids there would hurt business. Coming quickly to the point Archbishop Murray said, "If you make a move to send any of our cathedral boys home from your camp because they are black, I will immediately revoke the appointment of your resident priest-chaplain and tell the public precisely why I have done it. I suggest that you consider carefully what that might do to your *business*." After a long pause the director said, "Okay. Tell Father Shannon the black boys can stay." The archbishop thanked him graciously and expressed the hope that the camp would enjoy a grand summer. The old boy knew how to play hard ball when the occasion demanded. None of our boys ever knew about this incident. The director at least had the good sense to display his bigotry only to me, not to them.

Urban blight had already infected much of the old housing stock of the cathedral neighborhood. Even on Summit Avenue, the grand boulevard of the city, several once-elegant mansions had become rooming houses, their big salons chopped into tiny one-room apartments. The proximity of the cathedral made these crowded, marginal lodgings attractive to elderly or infirm Catholics accustomed to attending daily Mass. Among these we had our fair share of eccentrics. One old gentleman came to the sacristy each morning to fill his plastic water pistol with holy water. We never asked how he used it and he never offered to tell us. But each day he needed a refill.

Another character, "Stanley," stands out from the crowd. He would come to church every afternoon to "make the way of the cross." This devotion calls for short prayers and a meditation on the sufferings and death of Jesus Christ at each of fourteen "stations" in the church. All Catholic churches have the stations, usually marked with pictures of Christ at different stages of his journey to death on Calvary. Modern churches often have only fourteen simple crosses on one or both walls of the nave to mark the separate stations. As Stanley piously moved from station to station, not satisfied with his own mental image of the sufferings of Christ, he would shine his flashlight on the figure of Christ in each tableau. He prayed aloud, but softly, as though he were engaged in personal conversation with Jesus. Visitors often reported him to the rectory. They thought he was balmy. We knew better.

Nursing homes for the elderly were not as common then as they are today. Older persons living alone on pensions in nearby rooming houses often died without any known relatives. I recall offering a funeral Mass for one of them in that enormous cathedral one day, when the only persons present were two undertakers, two altar boys, the parish organist, the soloist, and myself. No mourners. No family. No pallbearers. It was often the task of the priest on "house duty" to arrange with an undertaker for a free burial service and with the cemetery for a free burial plot for indigent persons.

Until I became a priest no one in our family and only a few of our relatives and friends had died. As a child I had often wondered when death would first touch our family and how it would affect us.

Both questions were answered on March 11, 1947. The early morning call from St. Joseph's Hospital in St. Paul came to me at the cathedral. My brother Pete, who never liked and never used his Christian name of Harold, had died suddenly the previous night of pneumonia, at age thirty-nine, leaving a young wife and two infant sons. At the time he was visiting Minnesota on business. It fell to me to call his wife in Montana and to tell my parents of his death. It took me more than an hour to summon the courage and to phrase the message for those calls.

Pete was the youngest of the Foxley children. I was the youngest Shannon. That junior status and our common interest in horses had drawn us together.

Death in the family is seldom welcome. When it claims a younger member it is doubly painful. Pete's death left me with an abiding sense of emptiness and loneliness for months. I tried not to show this, thinking everyone expected a priest to see death as a transition to a better life. I was confident that Pete was secure in the kingdom of heaven. But I was desolate at the loss of his presence in my life.

Following the old Irish tradition, my parents insisted that Pete's "wake" be held in our home. His friends were legion. They filled the house, the porch, and the yard. It was to be the last time that any member of our family was "waked" at home. After the funeral I went to Montana to close his business affairs and to help Fern and her sons move back to Minnesota, once more inside the family circle.

Because so many of our parishioners at the cathedral were elderly and because we had four hospitals in the parish, ministering to the dead, the dying, and their families was a great part of our daily work. It was not uncommon for one of our priests to be the only person present at the bedside of a dying person in one of the hospitals. In all of those vigils I cannot recall a single person who, at the end, was afraid to die.

There seems to be a particular grace available to persons about to die. I have seen it work. It makes the prospect of eternal union with God vastly more attractive than the alternative of continued life in this world, especially for those whose final days are filled with pain and suffering. I came to regard it as a special grace to be the priest who helped a dying person prepare for death.

I recall many nights when I walked back to the parish house from Miller Hospital in the middle of the night, alone, musing that I had just accompanied a believing Christian, strengthened with the Eucharist and the sacrament of reconciliation, to the threshold of eternity. I firmly believe that all those persons now know the peace and joy of eternal union with God. And I continue to pray that one day I might be so fortunate.

A sour smell marks the homes of the very poor. I know its peculiar pungency very well. It is always strongest in stairways and corridors. Cooking odors and body odors may disguise it in the living quarters. But it hits a visitor head-on just inside the entryway of a tenement. I came to know it intimately in my half decade at the cathedral.

My life these days seldom takes me to the tenements of the poor. But when it does that evocative scent tells me at once a lot about the lives of persons behind doors I have not yet opened. Thomas Aquinas holds that one of the arguments in favor of a benevolent creator is that the sufferings of the poor and the handicapped in this life demand an afterlife in which these manifest inequities will be righted. Whether it is my early Thomistic training or my days with needy families at the cathedral, I instinctively side with the poor today as soon as a speaker drops the code words "welfare chiseler." I am sure there are welfare chiselers.

I hold no brief for them. But I vastly prefer being taken as a patsy now and again to the alternative of always holding that the poor are poor because they are shiftless and that they relish their poverty.

On the night of March 31, 1947, at about 9:00 P.M. Archbishop John Gregory Murray, while crossing Summit Avenue at Selby Avenue, alone and on foot, was struck by a passing car. Walking back from Miller Hospital, I came on the scene minutes later. By then he had managed to crawl to the curb and was sitting with one arm around the base of a small tree. His glasses had been smashed. Blood from a gash on his forehead covered his eyes. A passing pedestrian offered to help him, but he would allow no one to touch him. I knelt beside him and said, "Archbishop this is Father Shannon. Please do not try to move. I'll get my car and come back in just a few minutes." I did so, and with the help of a pedestrian, lifted him onto the back seat of the car.

He forbade me to take him to the hospital and insisted we go to the rectory. I pleaded with him, but he was adamant. He also told me firmly that he wanted to be taken to the back door of the rectory and up the service stairway to his third-floor quarters, without being seen by any of our staff. With his arms around my neck I half-carried and half-pulled him up the stairs. In his bedroom I got him on the bed and removed his coat and shoes. Again he forbade me to call his doctor. With some warm water and a towel I sponged the blood from his face, forehead, and hands.

Fortunately, Father Hilary Hacker, the vicar general of the archdiocese, was at home. I alerted Hilary to what had happened and was immensely relieved to have him take my place in deciding what to do next.

The archbishop was just as firm with Hilary as he had been with me. No doctor. No ambulance. No hospital. The following morning he was scheduled to offer the funeral Mass for Father Donald Gregory, who had been his chancellor for several years, and for whom he had a strong bond of respect and admiration. The next morning, barely able to walk, he insisted on being the celebrant for Don Gregory's funeral Mass. We marveled at his incredible stamina, and at our inability to prevent him from putting his life at risk as he did.

However, once the funeral Mass was over, weakened and pain-ridden, even he agreed with Father Hacker's insistence that he be taken to St. Joseph's Hospital. We learned that day that one kidney had been injured and that major surgery was imperative. He was moved to the Mayo Clinic in Rochester. After surgery, therapy, and an extended recuperation, he did not return to the rectory until November. Soon after that he resumed his normal administrative and episcopal work schedule for almost eight years, until his death (from cancer) in October 1956. His durability and his dedication to his sacred ministry were wonders to behold.

World War II had delayed the marriage plans of many couples. The end of the war marked the start of a marriage boom that lasted through that decade. Diocesan regulations and canon law required that engaged couples review with their pastor, or another priest of their choice, Catholic doctrine on marital morality, contraception, and the duties of spouses. These "instructions" were minimal for Catholic couples but numbered six sessions for couples if one partner was not a Catholic. It was not uncommon for one priest to have a dozen couples under instruction at one time. These sessions regularly focused on that peculiarly Catholic fascination with sexual morality.

At the cathedral I first met members of a lay organization called the Legion of Mary. Founded in 1921 in Dublin, the Legion is a kind of a spiritual care block club. Its volunteer members, male and female, meet weekly to pray together and to plan visits to the poor, the sick, and the dying in their parish.

Members of the Legion were the eyes and ears of the cathedral parish in my day. Their distant early warning systems told us of current or impending distress in neighborhoods or families. Working with the priests and the parish staff, the Legion members linked our resources into a support system for persons who needed help of any kind. These volunteers were known, trusted, and welcome in the homes of the parish. They gave at least two evenings a week to their systematic visitation of homes.

Working with the Legion was my first sustained contact, as a priest, with lay leaders doing the apostolic work of the church. Without being aware of it, I had left the seminary with a subtle sense of clericalism. I had never been told that priests hold a proprietary interest in the church and its saving mission. But, implicitly, until I met the Legion, I had thought that those of us in holy orders could handle nicely all the work connected with the salvation of the souls in our parishes.

Little did I know. The clergy cannot do a fraction of the work in a modern parish. They need all the help they can get, first to discover the needs of their people, then to match the spiritual and temporal resources available to meet those needs. It was all I could do as a young priest to keep pace with the Legion members in our parish. They outdid me on every level, even in the quality of their personal spirituality. Our parish apostolate would have been a weak and limping program without their energy and zeal. With them it was a vigorous and expansive effort to share the good news of the gospel of Jesus Christ as widely as possible in a big urban parish.

Finding an apartment for a transient family, arranging treatment for an alcoholic, or helping black parishioners "crack" the skilled trade unions were tasks the priests and the Legion members worked at jointly. I learned that there is no boundary in these tasks to mark different zones for the work of the clergy and that of the laity. The task at hand regularly blurred the lines between what the priest did and the role of other serious Christians concerned about the welfare of their neighbors.

We also had access to a roster of lay persons, not members of the Legion, who were on call to help us from time to time when we needed particular expertise. With a phone call we could get free and generous assistance from nurses, doctors, lawyers, morticians, police, city administrators, secretaries, or bankers. Work at the cathedral was always steady, full employment; but it was also exciting and challenging.

In that busy parish I first heard the term "authority of service." Father George Ryan used it to distinguish the authority of appointment (which comes from the governor or the president or the bishop) from that more solid authority which good platoon leaders, good teachers, and good pastors earn, the progressive legitimation of their leadership roles by the positive and cooperative response of the persons whom they serve. The authority of appointment is only the prelude to the authority of service. Either of these two forms of leadership can exist separately. Ideally they exist together, with generous service continually establishing the legitimacy of earlier authority conferred by edict, appointment, or election.

The priest at the cathedral who best exemplified for me this blend of the authority of appointment and the authority of service was Father Joseph Bender. It is sometimes said that one can never impose on a friend, because a true friend places no limit on his generosity. Joe Bender was the most generous and selfless priest I knew. He heard more confessions, visited more families, counseled more troubled persons, and walked more extra miles than anyone else on that staff. He remains the best example I know of a priest whose canonical authority was confirmed by the authority of service.

Other priests who were my associates in those days offered me a variety of attractive role models. Archbishop Murray and his chancery staff, Father Gerald O'Keefe, and Father Hilary Hacker lived with us in the cathedral rectory. Their table talk about the affairs of the archdiocese and the Vatican gave us a window on the world much wider than the parish and brought to our table a fascinating stream of visitors from Rome, Washington, New Delhi, and London.

In his youth Archbishop Murray was a priest in Connecticut. To the end he remained convinced that God had stood in the middle of Hartford and created the world. Gerald O'Keefe is now the retired bishop of Davenport, Iowa, and Hilary Hacker was, till his death in 1991, the bishop of Bismarck, North Dakota. In my youth each of these good men helped me learn, empirically, that the authority of service in the church brings to its practitioners a kind of joy and satisfaction which may not be unique to the priesthood but which is abundantly available for those who will seek it there.

Life at the cathedral for five years made me a dedicated critic of the one-dimensional cardboard figures which pass in modern fiction and in television series for flesh-and-blood priests. Bland and colorless personalities like Father Mulcahy on M.A.S.H. ought to be reported to the Humane Society or the ACLU. Some day, please God, someone who can write and who knows the Catholic priesthood from the inside will capture on paper the vigor and vitality typical of this attractive fraternity which has been portrayed so badly so often by Hollywood and television as a band of mealy-mouthed simpletons made up of one part Cream of Wheat and two parts Ovaltine.

# CHAPTER SEVEN

# NAZARETH HALL

All during my seminary course I had deliberately kept quiet about the fact that my B.A. degree was in classics. I had found the study of Greek and Latin authors fascinating, but I had no desire to teach either subject. I also feared that someday I might be asked to teach in the diocesan minor seminary (four years of high school and two years of college), Nazareth Hall. Never having studied there, nor even visited the minor seminary, I somehow sensed that I would be considered an "outsider" if I were ever assigned to its faculty. So deep were these concerns that when a seminary retreat master, Father Paul Waldron, once asked us, prior to our ordination, to name the worst assignment we could imagine in our diocese, I knew my answer at once: to teach Greek at Nazareth Hall. I recall being very noble about it. I actually wrote it down and said that I would gladly accept even that "awful" assignment should it be given to me after ordination.

Two years after ordination, on August 15, 1948, the second anniversary of my joining the cathedral staff, Archbishop Murray asked me to meet him in the parlor of the rectory. The priests called this "The Trembling Room" because it was his favorite place for telling priests at the cathedral that they were being transferred to new assignments.

He began our visit by saying, "I have just appointed Father Louis McCarthy rector of Nazareth Hall. He has named four priests whom he would like assigned to that faculty. You are one of these. Would you like that assignment?" I replied carefully and truthfully, "If you wish me to go there I shall gladly do so." He not only wished it. He had the typed letter (somewhat crumpled) of my appointment in his trousers pocket. I was to join the faculty as a full-time instructor, but I was also to retain a part-time assignment on the cathedral staff and to keep my quarters in the parish house.

That afternoon I reported to Father McCarthy, who was as yet in his old quarters at the St. Paul Seminary. I still feared the new assignment, but going with him to our new posts made a great difference to me. I admired him and welcomed the chance to work with him. I inquired about my teaching assignments. He asked me to teach the

English literature course for fourth-year high school students and the freshman rhetoric course for first-year college students. I was pleased. Thank God, no Greek! We chatted briefly and I rose to leave. And then he said, "By the way, Jim, the instructor who teaches the college English courses also teaches first-year Greek. With your degree in classics that should be a breeze." Indeed. I assured him I would do my best.

I walked over to the empty chapel where I had prayed so often. I knelt at the edge of the sanctuary. I was numb. There were five hundred priests in our diocese. Only two of them taught Greek in the minor seminary. And now I was one of the two. The only job I had ever told God I did not want was mine. Then the humor of it all hit me. Never make deals with God. He listens and he remembers. The question was no longer whether I would accept my new position. The question was how well I would perform in a post I neither sought nor relished.

I had two weeks to prepare for my first classes as a college instructor. At least in those days, the Catholic Church assumed, in assigning its personnel to new positions, that zeal and obedience would compensate for lack of training. At my ordination I had promised obedience to my bishop. As I reported for duty at Nazareth Hall my obedience was in great shape, but my grasp of Freshman Rhetoric, English Survey 101, and Beginning Greek was so modest that I blush to recall my youthful temerity in accepting appointment as a college level instructor in these courses.

I quickly scrambled to enroll in at least one graduate course in English at the University of Minnesota. My first class at Nazareth Hall convened at 8:00 A.M. and my last class ended at 3:00 P.M. Hence I could enroll at the university only for courses taught after 4:00 P.M. Fortunately for me, that year at that hour Robert Penn Warren was teaching a graduate course called "The Technique of the Novel." It met once a week for two hours. I can almost repeat "Red" Warren's opening remarks to us.

"Ladies and gentlemen, the title of this course is 'The Technique of the Novel.' I suppose I should begin by defining a novel. I cannot do this. I have no definition for this literary genre. I have read several works called novels. I have even written a few. But I cannot define the genre. If you and I can go ahead on this basis, knowing vaguely what we mean by this term, I will be glad to share with you my insights on it."

Warren's classroom had two "no smoking" signs. He smoked constantly, lighting one cigarette from another, butting out the last one in the chalk-trough at the end of class. He assigned us one novel a week.

We met on Mondays to discover how little we and how much he had derived from reading the assignment for the week.

Without any qualification Robert Penn Warren is the best teacher I have ever seen in action. He was that *rara avis* on campus, the skillful artist who knows how to talk to novices about his art form in a way that has what Henry James once called the "density of specification." Warren never talked about literature. Only about what this author is trying to do, poorly or well, on this page in this chapter.

In his treatise on the art of teaching, Thomas Aquinas distinguishes the knowledge we acquire from others by instruction (*disciplina*) from that which we acquire by discovery on our own (*inventio*). *Disciplina* covers that mass of data passed by professors to students in lectures and by students back to professors in blue books. *Inventio* is what Galileo or Edison or Marconi discovered in their laboratories. And *inventio* is what Warren tried to make possible for us as we carefully took ten novels apart to discern the specific elements of craftsmanship which held them together. I learned more about the art of writing and of literary composition from Warren in ten weeks than I had learned in my previous twenty-seven years.

My twenty-one months on the faculty at Nazareth Hall were the toughest years of my priestly ministry. I welcomed the challenge of a teaching assignment and eagerly sought all the graduate courses I could get. That is, if they were taught after 4:00 P.M. that first year.

But I was also a part-time curate at the cathedral, assigned to teach the adult convert class one evening a week and expected for confessions every Saturday from 3:00 P.M. until 6:00 and from 7:30 P.M. until 9:00 and for Masses every Sunday all forenoon until 1:30 P.M. Every fourth Sunday at the cathedral I was also on house duty all day, taking sick calls at the hospitals and baptizing babies at 2:30 P.M. One Sunday I recall having twenty-five babies, accompanied by twenty-five sets of parents and twenty-five sets of sponsors, show up for baptism.

I liked everything I was doing in those years (except for Greek). The problem was that I was doing too much to do any of it very well. For the first time in my life I was consistently dissatisfied with the quality of my own work. My classmates at the university had weekends to read and to write papers, while I was on duty at the cathedral.

One day, in my second year of graduate studies, my faculty advisor at the university called me in to say he was troubled that I had three "incompletes" on my transcript of credits. I had finished the courses and done the reading, but had not yet written the papers on which my grades depended. He asked whether I was serious about a master's degree in

English. I assured him I was, explained my schedule, and promised that I would clear my transcript of the incompletes as soon as possible.

Ironically, that same week, Father Ryan called me into his study at the cathedral to say that he wanted me to take house duty at the cathedral every Sunday, not just once a month. I had been using the quiet of my free Sunday afternoons there to correct papers, prepare classes, and to work on my incompletes. Now even that precious piece of free time was gone.

My most vivid recollection of those two academic years (1948–50) is that I was always behind schedule and regularly uncomfortable with the quality of my work at Nazareth Hall *and* at the cathedral *and* at the university. The easy answer to my dilemma, of course, would have been for me to drop out of the graduate courses and pursue the M.A. degree only in the summer. The decision would have been mine to make. But I was unwilling to make it. It takes forever to get a graduate degree if one works on it only in summer sessions.

I did have a short and most welcome respite from teaching and from parish duties in the summer of 1949, when I enrolled at Oxford University to learn, first-hand, how the English tutorial system works. Life and study in England were a delight. Two months there passed all too quickly. I read English literature with two tutors and garnered six graduate credits, transferable to Minnesota. At that rate it would have taken me eight summers to finish the M.A.

My superiors, my fellow teachers, and my students at Nazareth Hall were gracious and supportive. The students even took up a collection one day to help me pay for a speeding ticket I got rushing between classes at the seminary and the university.

At that time a fellow priest of the archdiocese of St. Paul, Father Edward Klein, was in residence at Yale University, where he was helping edit the works of Thomas More. Father Klein and I were old friends. At his urging I asked Father McCarthy, rector of Nazareth Hall, and Archbishop Murray, whether I might apply for admission to Yale's graduate school to pursue studies for a doctoral degree in American history. (Thanks to Bob Fogerty at St. Thomas, American history was my first love.) Permission was granted, and I was accepted by Yale, for admission in the fall of 1950. In June of that year my assignment to the minor seminary faculty was officially terminated, and I was again assigned, full time, to the staff of the cathedral. The plan was for me to spend that summer at the parish and then to leave for New Haven in the fall. The prospect of going to Yale, and of being relieved of all other assignments, seemed too good to be true.

One evening early in September, shortly before I was to leave for Yale, the archbishop invited me to meet him after dinner in the parlor ("The Trembling Room"). I smelled trouble. I was right. He explained that the diocese was short of priests. Our diocese has always been proud of the record of its priests in military service. Several of them were then serving as chaplains in the Korean War. Cardinal Spellman had just asked all the bishops to send more priests to the armed services. Archbishop Murray said that, with regret, he had decided to cancel my plans for going to Yale. With regret? I was devastated. I even volunteered on the spot to answer the call for chaplains. No. He wanted me to continue the "fine work" I was doing at the University of Minnesota.

Of course, I accepted his decision. My obedience was still in good shape. But I was heartbroken. Never before or since have I known such a keen sense of personal disappointment over plans which were not to be. Yale was so attractive. And it was so close.

The next year, 1951, I had the consolation of having only one and a half full-time jobs. That winter on the morning of February 8 my orderly schedule of university classes in the morning and parish work at the cathedral in the afternoons was dramatically interrupted.

As I was about to leave the rectory for class the phone rang. The police were calling to ask that any available priests report at once to the main plant of the Minnesota Mining and Manufacturing Company in downtown St. Paul. An enormous explosion had just ripped through several floors of the main building. Several employees were dead. Many were dying. My car was ready. Father Joseph Kuncl joined me and we rushed to the plant.

The scene there was pandemonium. The explosion had wrecked the elevators and blown out the solid concrete stairways in the building. It was a bitterly cold day. By then the area around the plant was cordoned off to hold back the growing crowd of wives and family members who had heard the news on the radio.

Near the entrance to the shattered building a young, nervous fireman came over to me and said quietly that he was a Catholic and that he was new on the force. This was his first emergency. He was afraid to go into the building because the chief had told him that a second explosion was still expected, or at least possible, because of a ruptured gas line.

I tried to remind him of his special duties to serve the public, even at risk to himself. I said that he and I had to go where we were needed, not just where we were safe. Just then the fire chief came out of the building. On a bullhorn he announced that all firemen were forbidden to enter the building till further notice because it was unsafe. The explosion had torn out whole sections of solid concrete floors. Large pieces of these were still crumbling and falling inside the building. The young fireman smiled wanly. He had a reprieve, at least for the moment.

Then the chief turned to Father Kuncl and me: "Come on, Padres, follow me. There are some people inside who need you." As I pulled on a hard hat and followed the chief into the building the young fireman patted me on the back.

I climbed downstairs with the chief, through what had been a staircase but was then little more than a tangle of steel rods and dangling chunks of concrete. Father Kuncl and the assistant chief went upstairs. Broken water pipes had flooded the basement. The chief and I followed the sound of someone moaning until we reached a pile of rubble. A man was pinned, on his back, under a piece of concrete the size of a car. His face, exposed, was thickly covered with cement dust. I knelt and wiped his face clean with my handkerchief. He opened his eyes. I said I was a priest and asked if he were a Catholic. He smiled and said, "No, but I'm sure glad to see you, Father." He asked us what had happened. We explained and told him that a stretcher would come for him soon. I prayed briefly with him and moved on. Nearby was the body of a man who had been decapitated by the blast. As we discovered more persons pinned in the wreckage I gave the sacrament of last anointing to a dozen persons, some already dead, some still showing signs of life. Together that day Father Kuncl and I anointed twenty-six persons.

All the windows in the building and the heating system had been shattered in the explosion. It was as cold inside the building as outside, sixteen degrees below zero. By then water in the basement was over my shoes. I have never been so cold in my life. As I emerged from the building with the chief, my high school classmate and friend, Dick Hance, covering the accident for KSTP-TV evening news, signaled me to face the camera. That night I saw myself on television for the first time in my life.

As we walked to our car a Red Cross lady gave us each a cup of hot coffee and a hot dog. I was so cold I was ready to cry. When I told about our experience that evening at dinner at the cathedral, Archbishop Murray needled me that I should have refused the hot dog. It was a day of abstinence in Lent.

The sheer variety of pastoral experience at the cathedral has always made that parish an exciting assignment for priests. The passage of time and the excitement of being part of a busy parish that year soon made me forget the disappointment of not going to Yale. That winter I got my incompletes cleared at the university, passed the written and oral examinations, and earned a master's degree in English.

Graduation day was Holy Thursday, 1951. I arranged for my friend, Father James Lavin, to take my place in the confessional that night, and I went off to be graduated. I felt a sense of satisfaction and relief in receiving that diploma. I had no further plans for graduate study. It was enough to be a parish priest in a busy parish. I was glad that the frenetic university schedule was behind me.

Some weeks later Yale wrote to inform me that I was still eligible to begin graduate studies in the new class of 1951 and that I had been awarded a full tuition scholarship. Would I be able to accept? The war in Korea had not ended. The archbishop's supply of priests had not increased. It was pointless to ask him for permission to accept the Yale offer. I did not want to put him in a position where he would have to say no. And I did not want to get my hopes up again, just to have them dashed. I wrote to Yale, thanked them for the scholarship, and declined the offer. I told no one, save my parents and Father James Moynihan, my good friend and former professor, about this exchange of letters.

The summer of 1951 was a joy for me. I had no incompletes to worry about, no graduate courses to prepare, only one full-time job as a curate in a very dynamic parish. It was good duty.

At lunch one day near the end of September, Archbishop Murray asked me to meet him after lunch in the parlor. He began by saying that Father James Moynihan, the former president of the College of St. Thomas, had told him of my most recent correspondence with Yale. He asked if Yale had indeed offered me a scholarship. I confirmed that it had. He then asked whether it was too late for me to accept. I did not know but agreed to inquire. I telephoned the dean of the Graduate School and learned that I was still welcome if I could be in New Haven the following Monday. It was then Thursday. I reported this to the archbishop. He asked when I would be prepared to leave. I offered to leave on the spot, but agreed to wait until morning. One thing priests can do is pack in a hurry.

I was on the road with all my earthly possessions in my Plymouth coupe the next day, with my father beside me as a companion for the trip. By Monday morning I was in New Haven, on campus, and in my first history class in Yale's Hall of Graduate Studies.

# CHAPTER EIGHT

# YALE

It took a little time for me to realize that I was, at last, not only at Yale but actually part of it. It had never occurred to me that Yale might be too fast a track for me, until I met my classmates. Some from Oxford and Cambridge and some from Harvard, Stanford, and Princeton suddenly made me aware of my new role. For the next three years my work was to be judged against their best efforts.

It had been a long time since I had felt the challenge of personal competition. But on day one at Yale, I got that old feeling that I was being eyed and measured. I in my Roman collar and black suit, they in their tweed jackets with leather patches on the elbows. By the luck of the draw we were to be friendly adversaries in the battle of the books. No challenge was ever more welcome.

Even at this distance I can recall only good memories of Yale. Undoubtedly I had been conditioned, by the several conflicting claims on my time in the preceding three years, to appreciate any new position in which I would be able to devote my energy to a single endeavor. The prospect of reading, writing, and studying with that faculty and in the well-stocked library at Yale seemed to me the best of all possible worlds. Competition, high standards, demanding assignments were no threat. At last I had that most precious commodity — time. If the reading lists were long, if the papers to be written were numerous, what matter? I now had time and I was eager to spend it meeting deadlines which were no longer impossible.

Yale is a relatively small academic community. Its faculty and students have a close bond. My second day in New Haven two professors, Ralph Gabriel and David Potter, hailed me on the sidewalk, invited me to coffee, and told me that some of their best students had come from Minnesota. I was flattered by the compliment to my home state but flattered even more by the personal attention of two senior professors who seemed genuinely pleased to meet a new student and to talk about his native place.

In that company of scholars who were to be my associates for the next three years, two southern gentlemen stand out: Robert Penn Warren and David Morris Potter. Warren, my teacher and advisor at the University of Minnesota, had just joined the Yale faculty. His gracious introductions of me to his old friends and new associates at Yale made my first days there doubly pleasant. David Potter, then chairman of the Department of American Studies, took particular interest in me and convinced me to pursue doctoral studies in his department. Like "Red" Warren, Potter carried the courtly mark of the Old South in his diction and in his gracious manner. He remains to this day the most deeply courteous man I have ever met.

From the beginning I was aware of Potter's special attention to my work, but not of his reasons for it. It may have had something to do with my seeking his advice on papers I was writing. He had been the editor of the *Yale Review* and was reputed to be a demanding critic. Some students shied away from the rigor of his blue pencil. I sought him out because of it. Warren had told me at Minnesota that I could learn to write, but only if I would accept the discipline of working closely with a good editor. David Potter was to be that editor. He was always available to read what I wrote and to offer criticism and encouragement. Whenever he sensed that his editing of my stuff might hurt a little, he would say, "Never forget that criticism before you go to press is friendly criticism. After that it's just criticism." God rest him now. In a company of distinguished gentlemen and scholars David Potter was in the first rank.

The keystone graduate seminar in American History at Yale then was a year-long course, History 180. It offered an interminable reading list, was taught by three professors (Samuel Flagg Bemis, Leonard W. Labaree, and David M. Potter), and served as the litmus test for taking the measure of new graduate students. The purpose of the course was to give students an extensive view of the major American historians. In addition, each student was responsible for reading all the published works of one author on this list and for a "big paper" at the end of the year on this writer. I chose Frederick Jackson Turner. Drawing on the skills of textual analysis I had learned from Robert Penn Warren, I wrote about the influence of Social Darwinism on Turner's work.

The weekend before the final class in our first year, David Potter telephoned me to say that my paper had been chosen best paper of the year. He asked me to summarize its central theses for the class at our final session. That phone call gave one young scholar the assurance he had been seeking all year long.

After my remarks at the final class Samuel Flagg Bemis, the senior professor in 180, presented me with an autographed copy of his book,

*Guide to the Diplomatic History of the United States 1775–1921,* inscribed on the flyleaf "To Father James P. Shannon for the best paper read at the final session of History 180, Yale University, May 15, 1952, with friendly regards." Till that day I really did not know whether I could "cut it" in competition with good scholars. Bemis, Labaree, and Potter assured me that I could. I was grateful and relieved.

Yale was not all work and no play. Two afternoons a week I played handball against Father Paul Siegfried, S.J., or Father Richard Donovan, C.S.B., fellow graduate students, swam a few laps in the Yale pool, and headed home to St. Rita's parish house in Spring Glen, relaxed and convinced that I was enjoying the good life in its fullness.

The pastor at St. Rita's was Father William Downey. He and his two curates, Father Donald O'Leary and Father John Blanchfield, did not really need a fourth priest on their parish staff. I had met them shortly after I arrived in New Haven. A few weeks later Father Downey invited me to live at St. Rita's, with the understanding that in return for room and board I would offer one or more Masses for the parish on Sunday, be available in emergencies, and "house sit" on Sunday afternoons and evenings when the other priests visited their families.

I was delighted to accept. My scholarship at Yale took care of my tuition. Father Downey's offer took care of my laundry, room, and board. Books and car maintenance were my only regular expenses. During my three years at Yale I did not receive any support from the archdiocese of St. Paul, but considered myself well endowed with a handsome savings account of $2400, which I had squirreled away during my salad days at Nazareth Hall. As a curate at the cathedral in St. Paul I had received a monthly salary of $75 and as a seminary instructor a monthly stipend of $100. With a frugality which amazes me in retrospect, I managed to bank half of my income during those worldly years when I was collecting two such handsome salaries.

At St. Rita's after the last Mass on Sunday I had the parish house to myself. The phone seldom rang. Our affluent middle-class parishioners rarely had heart attacks (on Sunday) or domestic crises requiring the ministrations of a priest. With the Sunday *New York Times* in hand, the leisure to read it slowly, and a stack of 45 RPM Mozart recordings for background music, I enjoyed some of the loveliest days of Sabbath rest at St. Rita's that any person could ask for.

By necessity and by preference my social life in New Haven was modest. Deadlines for reading or writing assignments were seldom out of mind. I marveled at classmates who could meet them and still maintain the family schedules expected of them by their spouses or children.

My days were busy and full, but the demands on my time were manageable. The hectic schedule I had left behind in St. Paul conditioned me to appreciate life at Yale and to be aware that life would probably never again be any more pleasant or satisfying than it was there. It is nice to enjoy the good life. It is doubly nice to know at the time that it is a good life and to be grateful for it while it is happening.

Four families in New Haven contributed enormously to my sense of well-being in those years. Bob and Ann Asman, Chris and Elaine Buckley, Bob and Lucy Giegengack, and Albie and Mary Pat Lawton made me as warmly welcome in their homes as I was in my own.

Before settling down to the big business of writing a doctoral thesis, graduate students must cross the threshold of oral examinations covering the spectrum of their graduate studies. In May 1953 five members of my Yale class were scheduled for this ordeal in a single week, one of us each day. My day was Wednesday. The five professors who conduct the examination announce to the candidate shortly after the close of the session whether he or she has passed or failed. To my great discomfort the two candidates who preceded me on Monday and Tuesday had failed. Each of these candidates, in my mind, was a first-rate scholar. Within the next year each of them passed the examination. But on that fateful Wednesday in May I knew only that they had failed on their first try.

The examiners are free to ask any questions reasonably related to the candidate's field of interest. David Potter, as chairman of my committee, claimed the right to ask me the first question: "Father Shannon, can you tell us anything about the life or work of Ignatius Donnelly?" Potter was well aware that Donnelly was a populist folk hero in Minnesota history. The question was a softball pitch to put me at ease. I knew more about Donnelly than the rest of the examiners wanted to hear. One professor finally got the examination onto another track by saying that he had never heard of Donnelly but now felt that he had learned all he ever wished to know about him. By that time we were all smiling and I had forgotten about the fate of my classmates who preceded me at the round table on Monday and Tuesday. Potter had accomplished what he wanted. He got me to relax and enjoy the encounter. On the previous day he had given me two rules: in an oral examination never bring up a topic you are not prepared to discuss further; and never bluff. ("A simple 'I don't know' will suffice, provided you do not use it too often.") These are still the two best rules I know for candidates facing oral examinations.

After two hours Potter signaled the end of the questioning and asked me to step outside the room while the committee conferred. Five minutes later he came to the door, offered me his hand and said, "Doctor Shannon, won't you come in please?"

I have always been proud of my bond with Yale. But for pure satisfaction, few occasions in my life can compare with that moment, in a sparsely furnished room in Yale's Hall of Graduate Studies, when five professors each stood to shake my hand and to welcome me to their academic fraternity.

In my second year at Yale, influenced by the writings of Marcus Lee Hansen on the "push" and "pull" factors in human migrations, I had decided to write my doctoral thesis on nineteenth-century Catholic colonization in Minnesota.

At the time of the great migrations to the United States during the nineteenth century, people of good will on both sides of the Atlantic, aware that the immigrants were undergoing hardship in transit and after their arrival, formulated plans to alleviate their suffering. One leader in this humanitarian effort, Bishop John Ireland of St. Paul, never tired of reminding urban Catholics that "man made the city but God made the country." He helped establish, from 1876 to 1881, ten rural villages in western Minnesota (DeGraff, Clontarf, Graceville, Minneota, Ghent, Currie, Avoca, Iona, Fulda, and Adrian). In most of these colonies the land was furnished by land-grant railroads; in all of them the settlers were Catholics, recruited partly from Ireland, England, Belgium, Germany, or French Canada, and partly from states east of Minnesota.

My study of these settlements analyzed their distinctively religious features, their role as archetypes in colonization, and the reasons for their subsequent growth. To demonstrate that these colonies in Minnesota were successful called for study of comparable settlements which failed. To provide this comparison I traveled in the summer of 1953 to Virginia, North Carolina, Kansas, and Nebraska to examine the records and reconstruct the history of comparable religious communes established in those states during the last quarter of the nineteenth century.

The final chapters of this study were completed in the summer of 1954. I left Yale in August that year to return to my alma mater, the College of St. Thomas in St. Paul, to become an assistant professor in the department of history, where my old friend and mentor, Father Nicholas Moelter, was then chairman.

I was glad to be going home but sad to leave Yale and St. Rita's. As I packed my car, with the help of my friend Father John Sankovitz, who had come from St. Paul to accompany me home, I noticed that Father John Blanchfield of St. Rita's, whom I was about to leave, was busy at the windshield of my car. I assumed he was cleaning it. Not so. He was inscribing a message on the dusty hood with his finger. The message did not become legible to me in the driver's seat until much later that day when the setting western sun made the letters appear: "With Supreme Reluctance."

In due course I was notified that my thesis had been accepted and that I would receive the doctoral degree at commencement at Yale the following spring. In May I drove back to New Haven, accompanied by my mother, father, and my sister Helen. They had never visited Yale. We took a full day to traipse around the Village Green, the old campus, the Hall of Graduate Studies, and to visit the library carrels where I had spent the better part of three years. On graduation day it came as a surprise to me to learn that my thesis had been awarded the George Washington Egleston Prize for excellence in American History and selected for publication by the Yale University Press as volume one in the new Yale Series in American Studies. Considering the miles I had covered to get it written, David Potter, in making the award, called it the "most athletic piece of research" undertaken in history at Yale in his time.

CHAPTER NINE

# COLLEGE OF ST. THOMAS

Graduate students often feel like the carpenter who spent his life sharpening saws but never built a house. When the time comes they welcome the chance to cross the desk to try their skills as teachers. I was no exception. The College of St. Thomas was my alma mater. Its president, Father Vincent Flynn, and many of its faculty were my friends and former teachers. I was glad to be home.

In the fall of 1954 student enrollment at St. Thomas totalled 1356. As low man on the faculty totem pole that year I was asked by Father William Emmett O'Donnell, dean of the college, to divide my time three ways: teaching American history, teaching English rhetoric 101, and coaching the debate team. I would gladly have taught skydiving if he had asked me.

Even though my principal academic interest was American history, I was surprised to discover considerable satisfaction in teaching freshman rhetoric. Then, as now, many entering freshmen were innocent of any knowledge of how to construct a cohesive paragraph in their mother tongue. It may have been the shadow of "Red" Warren or David Potter over my shoulder, but I actually enjoyed helping the willing ones learn to speak and write in English.

Correcting freshman themes was a good starting place for a young professor. But history was my field. And church history was my particular delight. In the decade following World War II the Catholic Church in this country enjoyed a period of unprecedented vigor and growth. As a Catholic and as a historian I was eager to study this growth and to trace its roots.

Those years witnessed the publication of a considerable quantity of first rate books and monographs on American Catholicism, many of them by John Tracy Ellis, or his graduate students, at the Catholic University of America. Monsignor Ellis and Father Thomas McAvoy, C.S.C., of the University of Notre Dame had generously opened their respective archives to me while I did the work for my thesis at Yale. They had also taken a personal interest in my work and encouraged me to stay in church history.

My career as a history teacher was cut short in the summer of 1956 by the sudden death of Father Vincent Flynn, president of St. Thomas. Archbishop Murray, whose duty it was to appoint a new president, then lay dying of cancer in St. Joseph's Hospital. That spring Pope Pius XII had named William O. Brady, bishop of Sioux Falls, South Dakota, to become the coadjutor-archbishop of St. Paul and to succeed Murray. I had never met Archbishop Brady until the day in August 1956 when he invited me to visit him. He was known for quick decisions and no-nonsense administration.

His first question to me was "Have you had much administrative experience?" I replied that I had very little. He then jolted me with the brusque announcement: "Well you're going to get some. You are the new president of the College of St. Thomas." I tried to convince him that he had mistaken me for Father Thomas Shanahan, a professor at the St. Paul Seminary.

In saying this, I had overlooked the fact that Brady and Shanahan were old friends. No, he was not confusing Shannon and Shanahan. Acting after consultation with Archbishop Murray and the board of trustees of the college, Brady had decided that I was to succeed Father Flynn. I tried to think of all the reasons for naming someone else. My age. I was only thirty-five. Brady admitted that was a little young.

It was public knowledge that Archbishop Murray was near death. I suggested that a new president not be appointed until after Murray's death. I feared that my bond of friendship with the dying archbishop might influence his judgment in my favor. With more time to decide, I argued, Brady would be able to make his own decision and pick a president he favored. I also argued that the new president of the college should have the solid endorsement of a living archbishop, not the final blessing of an archbishop who was deceased. Brady had thought of these arguments and had answers for them. True, I was Murray's first choice, but Brady had checked widely with older priests, the senior college faculty, and the board of trustees. He was satisfied with the appointment and assured me that it was being offered to me jointly by the dying archbishop and by himself.

He quickly outlined to me his administrative style, promised to back me in public at all times, as long as my "batting average was over 500." When it dropped below that level he "would be forced, reluctantly, to back up a successor." I liked his candor and his breezy style. I liked him. He said he favored a five-year term for the appointment. At the end of that time he or I could, without explanation, terminate the appointment. If we both agreed, a second five-year term would follow, but no more than that. We agreed that ten years was long enough for any president to translate his grand plans into action. After that I could be appointed to a pastorate in the diocese as most earlier presidents had been. Fair enough.

I accepted the appointment, with a mixture of misgivings and eager anticipation. The visit lasted thirty minutes. Brady relished the role of bishop. He enjoyed the challenge of making big decisions quickly. As I left he shook my hand, told me I had lots of good friends, and that he wanted to be one of them.

The prospect of working with him intrigued me. Before being named a bishop in 1939 Brady had been a professor and then rector of the St. Paul Seminary. Hence he was well known to all the priests in our diocese who had been his students. They often joked about his cockiness and his omniscience. You could never tell him any news that would surprise him. He would act as though he had already heard it long before you did. In the parlance of the priests, he was "one of the wise men from the East," a reference to his place of origin, Fall River, Massachusetts. I liked him from the day I met him. That bond grew stronger with time.

Archbishop Murray died on October 11, 1956. He had been a principal influence in my life. As a student I had admired him from afar, especially his simplicity of style. He had no public "persona." He was always the same man, kind, gentle, modest, considerate, and totally dedicated to preaching the gospel. During the five years I lived in the cathedral rectory with him my admiration for him continued to grow. His episcopal motto, "Mea Omnia Tua," means "All my things are yours." It is the line used by the father in the Parable of the Prodigal Son (Luke 15:31) as he speaks to his older son who stays out in the field and refuses to join the celebration being given in the house for his returning errant brother. The father goes out to the son and tells him not to be angry at the cost of the celebration. "Remember," he reminds his son, "between you and me there is no mine and thine. All my things are yours."

John Gregory Murray lived by that motto. He did not draw a salary. He did not drive a car. He rode the street cars and the buses alone whenever he had business in the city. He was a man of great faith and simple tastes. Over a span of five years I served as his master of ceremonies at cathedral functions and occasionally drove him to ceremonies out state. He was, in Irish parlance, a lovely man. When it came time for me to choose an episcopal motto for my own coat of arms as a bishop, my choice was clear: "Mea Omnia Tua."

William O. Brady had gone to Sioux Falls as bishop of that diocese in 1939. The aftermath of the Great Depression and the drought of the '30s still held rural South Dakota in the grip of hard times. In his seventeen years there he acquired a reputation as a sound administrator and a careful money manager.

When he arrived in Sioux Falls some of his churches were threatened with foreclosure. He bargained with bankers, refinanced parochial and diocesan debts, cut costs, and, by the time he left Sioux Falls in 1956, that diocese was in excellent financial condition. He taught me a lot, very quickly, about the management of money.

We are all the product of our own education. Brady's early years as a bishop were spent on the edge of bankruptcy. He did, generously, whatever needed doing for the good of the church. In his formative years as a bishop it happened that financial survival was a critical issue. To rise to the occasion, he quickly mastered new skills that he had never before been called to exercise. If he had not been a priest he would have been an entrepreneur. And, I would guess, a happy and a rich one.

Archbishop Brady understood and practiced the art of management by objective. He believed in careful selection of his administrative aides. Then he would load them with all the authority and responsibility they could bear. He knew how to delegate. This mode suited me. The College of St. Thomas had many needs to be filled as quickly as possible. Brady was a providential leader on the scene for us at the right time.

In our first years together we moved quickly to increase faculty salaries at St. Thomas, to separate St. Thomas Military Academy from the college, to clear out the "Tom Town" temporary barracks left over from World War II, and to construct a new library, a new student center, and a new residence hall.

We financed the new student residence, named for Brady's friend and patron, Archbishop Austin Dowling, with federal funds. The student center, named for Archbishop Murray, was financed in great part by federal funds and by a gift from Ignatius Aloysius O'Shaughnessy, an alumnus of the college and a member of its board of trustees.

O'Shaughnessy was a legend among the independent oil producers of the country long before I met him. He had graduated from St. Thomas in 1906. His first job was that of business manager of the college. After one year in that post he moved to Texas, then to Denver, then to Wichita, where he struck it rich after World War I as an independent oil operator.

Until I became president of St. Thomas I had never met "I.A.," as all his friends called him. Our first meeting occurred shortly before my first session with the board of trustees of the college in October 1956. After that meeting he and I walked about the campus. He asked me what our most urgent need was at the college. Citing a recent faculty report, I told him we desperately needed a new library. He asked where we would build it. We walked to the corner of Summit and Cleveland Avenues. I told him it should be there and should connect with the science building (Albertus Hall) and the classroom building (Aquinas Hall). On the spot he told me to hire an architect and build the library. He agreed to pay for the building and its furnishings. That evening as we walked till dark he recapitulated for me his youth on that campus and told me he would always be grateful for the Catholic formation he had received there. Months later the public announcement of the new library was made on May 8, 1957, the day I was formally installed as president of the college. By then we had an architect's drawing of the proposed new three-story library. It was completed and furnished in 1959 at a total cost of $1.6 million, all of it a gift of I.A. and Lillian O'Shaughnessy.

I.A. in his lifetime was by far the most generous benefactor that St. Thomas had ever had. He helped make my decade as its president an era of building and progress. More important to me than his money was the warm, personal friendship he extended to me. Each year in March, he would invite Father Theodore Hesburgh, C.S.C., and Father Edmund Joyce, C.S.C., of the University of Notre Dame, and me to spend a week with him on his yacht, the *Marileen,* in the Florida Keys. In those days, before the new rite of concelebration of the Mass, we would have three separate Masses each morning on the *Marileen.* I.A. would serve as acolyte at each of them.

He was a great practical joker. He loved fun and had a way of making everyone feel good. Unlike many wealthy persons, he learned early in life to enjoy the satisfaction of giving money away. When Carol Channing appeared on Broadway to sing the lead in "Hello, Dolly," I.A. and I went to see her. On the way back to our hotel in the taxi, he remarked, "That young lady has the right idea. Money is like manure. It doesn't do any good unless you spread it around." God rest him. He spread lots of it around while he was still alive to see it and while he could enjoy the happiness he made possible for others.

Before joining the St. Thomas faculty in 1954 I had met Peter Drucker, who was then a lecturer in the management seminars for business executives sponsored by the American Management Association at the old Astor Hotel in New York City. As a novice in the field of

COLLEGE OF ST. THOMAS

administration I was impressed with what I learned from him. Back at St. Thomas I urged Father Flynn to consider for our campus some kind of postbaccalaureate program for business executives who already had their bachelor's degrees.

I can still recall the put-down I got for this suggestion. Flynn, always the dedicated liberal arts purist, said, "I would remind you, young man, that this is a college of liberal arts. It is not a service station. And while I am president there will be no refresher courses on this campus for tired executives." True to his word, he never allowed any management program to take root at St. Thomas.

One of my priorities after assuming the presidency was to explore the costs and benefits of a management center on our campus. With a grant from the Elizabeth Quinlan Foundation, John H. Farley, a professor in our department of business education, conducted such a study. With encouragement from Drucker, who gave us access to his file of Midwest clients, and to the University of Chicago, which offered us part-time faculty support, we organized the St. Thomas Management Center. John Farley became its first director. It opened for classes on June 1, 1957. With apologies to Father Flynn, the center grew steadily. Its graduates today far outnumber the graduates of any similar academic program in the upper Midwest.

Since the College of St. Thomas was founded in 1885 by Bishop John Ireland, every archbishop of St. Paul has continued to serve as the chairman of the college board of trustees. Most of the priests on the St. Thomas faculty are priests of the archdiocese. Lay faculty members, however, far outnumber the priests. The quantity and quality of this preponderant lay presence gave this faculty an academic distinction earlier than most Catholic colleges, which relied solely on priestly vocations to build their teaching staff. The voice of the lay professor at St. Thomas shaped academic policy and curricular development well before many clerics in other Catholic colleges were ready to relinquish their traditionally exclusive control of academic policy.

Clericalism is deeply rooted in the Catholic Church. Trusting the integrity and the professionalism of lay leaders, on campus or in parishes, is something the church has learned to do in recent years. At St. Thomas this welcome trend began in the presidency of Father James H. Moynihan (1933–44) and was encouraged greatly by Father Vincent J. Flynn (1944–56). Much of the academic distinction enjoyed today by what is now the University of St. Thomas has been earned for it by its lay professors.

To say this is not to minimize the scholarly or pedagogical talents of able and dedicated generations of priests on that faculty, but merely to record that, early on, this faculty developed a *modus operandi* whereby priest-professors and lay-professors worked harmoniously and productively in an atmosphere of mutual professional respect.

Professor Robert Fogerty of our faculty was fond of saying that the primary public relations person of any college is the person at the blackboard or the lectern. Following his counsel I adopted as a basic premise that my primary duty as president was to recruit, support, reward, and motivate the best faculty members we could find. I saw the faculty as my primary public.

Conversely, presidents who see the students as their primary public, without involving the faculty as an integral link in the collegiate chain, will be vulnerable, at least, to the charge that their priorities are confused, and possibly to the more serious charge that they court cheap popularity.

I do not mean to imply that the students are an unimportant constituency for the president. One of the joys of my years as a college president was my bond with the students. However, I learned, the hard way, that I could not continue to teach, even one course, after I became president. The demands on my time in or out of the office were no longer under my control. After becoming president, I had the notion that contact with the students would keep me alert to the real world. But I was forced to abandon the idea of teaching just one upper division history class, once a week, after I had missed three class meetings in a row. It was not fair to the students.

The contact I could and did keep with them was a column which I wrote every other week for the school paper, *The Aquin.* "The President's Corner" had no limits on its subject matter. Sometimes it was serious, on occasion frivolous, but always it marked out a piece of turf where the students, either through their letters to the editor or their visits to my office, and I could trade views and express our criticism or support for one another.

In addition to my administrative duties on campus at St. Thomas, I learned early on that the president of an urban college also has a variety of extramural civic duties as a member of several larger communities to which the college is somehow related.

In the last half of the decade of the '50s bond issues for capital improvements in public high schools in St. Paul had been rejected twice by the voters. Since St. Paul was then more than one-third Catholic and abundantly endowed with Catholic elementary and secondary schools, the ugly rumor gained credence that the Catholics, already heavily taxed to support their own schools, were responsible for the defeat of the bond issues for public education. Writing in the *Catholic Bulletin,* our diocesan weekly, I took issue with this opinion and said it was pure speculation to blame Catholic voters for the defeat of the bond issues.

A Committee of Citizens Concerned about Schools appeared in St. Paul early in 1959, asking that a survey be made by impartial professionals of the true financial needs of the local public school system. Chairman of the committee was Harold Wood, a respected St. Paul securities broker. I was asked to serve as vice chairman. With a grant from the Hill Family Foundation our committee retained the consulting firm of Cresap, McCormick and Paget to study our public high schools and to report whether and how much these schools needed money for repairs or new construction. During the year that this study was underway Harold Wood was killed in an auto accident. I inherited his role just as the Cresap report, which called for a bond issue of $23.5 million, was ready to be shared with the voters. Wood and I had agreed that we would take the Cresap report, once it was done, to every PTA in the city. The committee members and I kept that promise. We presented the report and fielded questions about it with every PTA in the city that would give us time on their program. For three months we pleaded the case for new taxes to support the bond issue. On election day, November 3, 1959, the bond issue won by a comfortable margin. I got a little flack from voters on both sides of this question. Some Catholics who heard my pleas for more taxes for public schools questioned my loyalty to Catholic education. And some public school advocates expressed the fear that I was some kind of an undercover agent for parochial schools, masquerading as a friend of the public schools. But, criticism aside, the bond issue passed and the new schools, including the St. Paul Vocational Technical Institute on Summit Avenue, were built with the proceeds.

As a Catholic priest, and later as a bishop, it pleased me to be asked to cooperate with programs in public education in Minnesota. Such invitations, to a Catholic priest, were a sign of enlightened public administrators, and also a signal that I was perceived as a friend and ally in civic affairs.

Early on the morning of January 27, 1961, I got an unexpected telephone call from my father, asking if I could come to see him at home "right away." When I walked into our family living room an hour later, I was surprised to see him all dressed in a suit and tie, with a small suitcase, all packed, waiting for me.

He explained that in the night severe chest pains made him fear he was having some kind of heart disorder. We called our family doctor who told us to meet him as soon as possible at St. Joseph's Hospital in St. Paul. We were there within the hour.

Dad's diagnosis was correct. He had had a mild heart attack. Later that day he had another one, much more painful than the first. Knowing that I feared he might be dying, he calmly told me that he was prepared to die, that in his adult life the only prayer he ever said on his own behalf was the "prayer for a happy death."

Although most persons probably consider this term an oxymoron, it has rich significance in Catholic parlance. It means that a person is alert as death approaches, is able to express sorrow to God for all the sins of his lifetime, and has the presence of a priest to administer the sacraments of reconciliation (confession), the Eucharist, and final anointing. That afternoon the hospital chaplain had administered all three sacraments to my father.

Secure in his confidence that his prayer for a "happy death" had been granted, he assured me that he was at peace, grateful to God for a long life, a great wife, "good kids," and that he was ready to enter eternity to meet his creator. That night he died in his sleep, January 29, the feast of St. Francis de Sales.

My long visit with him on the eve of his death, which I reported to the family, made his passing somewhat less painful for Mother, and for each of us in the family than if he had died, say, at the wheel of his car. But each of us has only one father to lose, and his passing must be for each of us a trauma that is unique. My father was a devout Catholic, a good friend, and a mentor whose wise counsel I treasured deeply. He was always "available" when I needed him. At his wake the night before his memorial Mass at St. Augustine's Church, hundreds of his business associates came to express their condolences. One of these plainspoken cattlemen grasped Mother's two hands firmly in his and said in a loud voice, "The cattle business has a lot of crooked bastards in it, Mame, but Pat Shannon was an honest and an honorable man." It was a fitting epitaph for this pious and gentle son of Ireland.

In 1963 the Minnesota legislature created a new statewide system of two-year community colleges and invited the eleven community colleges, then part of local school districts, to join the state system. Governor Karl Rölvaag named a five-member state board to oversee the new system and to carry out the legislative mandate of picking the sites for seven new junior colleges to be located at strategic points in the state. Frederick Deming, then president of the Federal Reserve Bank in Minneapolis, was named chairman of the board. I was named a member of this board in 1964 and became its third chairman in 1967.

The greatest single achievement of that board, in its early years, was the appointment of Dr. Philip Helland, then superintendent of schools in Willmar, Minnesota, to become chancellor of the new statewide system of community colleges. Helland is one of the ablest educational administrators I have ever met. Minnesota is fortunate that his firm hand and clear head guided its network of community colleges in the first years of this statewide system.

In 1955 Governor Orville Freeman appointed a task force to study the future needs of higher education in Minnesota. His charges to the members were to compile a census of the elementary and secondary school enrollments of the state and to produce a plan to accommodate these "war babies" in the colleges, both public and private, of Minnesota when they would reach college age. The report of the task force called for doubling the spaces for college students in Minnesota within the next decade. A secondary purpose of the study was to put the private colleges of Minnesota on notice that their help would be needed and welcome in providing for this enrollment boom.

Higher education in Minnesota, from territorial days, has been known for cooperation and mutual respect between the publicly supported and private colleges. The report of the Freeman task force came out of that tradition. Even before this report was issued, it became the occasion at St. Thomas for raising the delicate questions of separating St. Thomas Military Academy from the college and for relocating the academy on its own campus.

Our college faculty favored the separation of the two schools. Pressed by the need to expand the college, I also favored the split. But the faculty and the headmaster of the academy, Father John R. Roach, now the retired archbishop of St. Paul and Minneapolis, were, to say the least, cool to the idea. In the folklore of the diocese the academy always had a special status, treasured and protected by its alumni, many of whom were senior pastors in the diocese by 1959. The academy faculty did not relish the prospect of being forced off the forty-five-acre campus (the old William Finn farm) which it had shared with the college since 1885.

Again the steady hand and cool head (and deep pockets) of I. A. O'Shaughnessy guided the discussion. As a trustee of the college, O'Shaughnessy favored the separation of the two schools. Knowing the history of many other Catholic colleges, he realized that a secondary school and college on the same campus must eventually become competitors for the same limited funds. As president of both schools, I was finding it increasingly difficult to allocate our limited resources and personnel equitably between the two schools. As an alumnus of each I was in a fortunate position. Both faculties trusted my objectivity even when one of them differed with my decisions.

In the spring of 1959 the trustees of the college authorized a committee to prospect for a new campus for the academy. With assurance from I. A. O'Shaughnessy and Archbishop Brady that they would help finance the new campus, Father Roach gave his blessing to the project and became its most effective spokesman.

The need for public transportation dictated that the new campus be on a metropolitan bus line. Its need for acreage dictated that it be outside the city limits of St. Paul or Minneapolis. In the summer of 1959 Father Roach and I inspected a dozen possible sites. In the end we recommended the purchase of thirty-seven (later increased to fifty) acres on Rogers Lake, Mendota Heights, Dakota County. The board approved the purchase and Archbishop Brady bought the land with diocesan funds. The handsome new St. Thomas Academy (we dropped the "military" from its name) opened for classes in September 1965. On the day it opened it was debt-free, thanks largely to the energetic leadership of Father Roach and to the generosity of its alumni and I. A. O'Shaughnessy.

In my first year as a college professor, Father Flynn, then president of St. Thomas, had shared with me his definition of a college professor as a "person who always feels otherwise." The independent spirit which makes one a good artist or a good teacher frequently makes that person wary of consensus and often opposed to unanimity on principle. Competent teachers cherish their independence so much that professorial paranoia is often more intense than the garden variety which most of us exhibit daily. In learning to appreciate the intricacies of faculty politics, to grasp the intrinsic value of full disclosure and open debate on controverted issues, and to follow the occasionally scrambled circuits of the professorial mind, my greatest friend and ally at St. Thomas was Father William Emmett O'Donnell, dean of the college.

"Okie" O'Donnell had taught me history in my undergraduate days at St. Thomas. He was my senior by thirteen years. Throughout my decade as president of the college he became my best friend and most trusted counselor. In his scarlet doctoral regalia from Louvain University, he cut a striking figure in our academic processions. A man of impeccable integrity, his candor often made faculty members swallow hard, but none could ever fault him for being unfair. He called things by their right names, did his homework, met his deadlines, and expected others to do the same. When they fell below those simple standards he told them so. This directness probably cost him a few friends. It endeared him to me. I knew I could count on an honest answer, based on solid evidence, whenever I asked his opinion. Like Abraham Lincoln, he lived by the adage that people who tell the truth are spared a lot of pesky record-keeping.

He wrote clean English sentences and asked others to do the same. His brevity made his speech and memos fabled for their economy of diction. His wit was as constant as it was subtle. Pomposity is a vice to which clerics and professors often fall prey. "Okie's" native modesty protected him from this vice and kept his associates humble. When faculty members complained to me that he had belittled or overlooked their most creative suggestions for improving the college, I came to accept the opinion that "Okie's" position would regularly be supported by more and better evidence than the views of his critics or adversaries. There were, and possibly still are, some critics who held that his influence was too strong in my administration. I still consider him the best academic dean I ever met.

If the decade of my presidency at St. Thomas was, as I believe, a period of solid growth and development at the college, a major portion of the credit for the quality of that growth belongs to William Emmett O'Donnell, one of God's great men.

Archbishop Brady, stricken by a heart attack, died in Rome on October 1, 1961, where he was at work on the planning commission for the Ecumenical Council, Vatican II. In his five years as the archbishop of St. Paul and Minneapolis (renamed, from the archdiocese of St. Paul, by the Vatican at his request) he had given dynamic leadership to the diocese and to the several institutions it embraced. The College of St. Thomas and St. Thomas Academy benefited particularly from his ability to respond promptly to changing times and new needs.

Shortly after we met, Brady and I became aware that our administrative styles were complementary. I went to him for counsel only when I considered his help necessary. He prized brevity. I would lay out the problem, survey the available options, pick the one I favored, and offer my evidence. He would usually decide on the spot.

In the five years we worked together we had only one major disagreement. He wanted to build an expensive addition to the minor seminary, Nazareth Hall. Believing that minor seminaries were a thing of the past, I tried to persuade him to cancel these plans and in-

stead to build a new residence for young seminary candidates on the
St. Thomas campus and close the minor seminary. When I cited the declining enrollments at all minor seminaries, he told me that my faith
was weak. I had to admit that my faith in minor seminaries was, by
then, nonexistent. In the end he put $1.7 million into handsome new
facilities at Nazareth Hall. (In June 1970 Archbishop Binz made the
painful decision to close Nazareth Hall; and in November of that year
the school and its campus were sold.)

Shortly after Brady's death I received a phone call from James
Armsey, a program director of the Ford Foundation. Among college
presidents Armsey's name was well known. He directed the Special
Program in Education through which the Ford Foundation was then
making multimillion dollar grants to selected private colleges chosen
for the quality of their programs, on condition that the colleges would
raise two matching dollars for every dollar pledged by the foundation.

St. Thomas had made no overture to the Ford Foundation. Armsey's call was a surprise to me. We had been selected on the basis of
a secret study done by his staff. They had already checked our faculty
salaries, curricula, campus facilities, leadership quality, and the caliber
and track record of our graduates. Encouraged by this report, Armsey
invited us to prepare for his further review a detailed twenty-year budget for the college, covering the preceding decade (1952–62) and the
decade ahead (1962–72). It was a monumental task but our administrative staff, under the direction of Lloyd Rogge, completed it in two
months.

Work on this budget did two things for us: it showed the ascend-
ing curve of our salaries, assets, and programs for the past decade; and
it got our staff into the habit of viewing the future in five-year planning frames. On January 2, 1962, I delivered the study to Armsey in
New York. Two months later one of his assistants came on campus,
incognito, to interview students and faculty. We gave her the run of the
place for several days. She set her own agenda and interviewed whom
she would. We later learned that her mission was to uncover evidence
at St. Thomas of "reform and expansion of curricula, upgrading of
the faculty and student body, encouragement of independent study,
superior students, and adoption of cooperative programs with other
institutions."

In addition to the twenty-year budget, Armsey asked us to prepare a
statement answering the simple question, "Why should the Ford Foundation give money to the College of St. Thomas?" The rest of my
staff had worked overtime preparing budgets covering two decades.

I thought that I should write the essay Armsey requested. I did. It expresses my views on Christian liberal arts education today as well as it did then:

"The liberal arts are habits whereby we recognize and use effectively the elements of language, number, and form. Properly employed these arts free the mind from fear, fantasy, and ignorance.

"Such fundamental disciplines are not acquired easily or quickly. As habits they can never be 'taught.' They can only be acquired by novices and exemplified in action by accomplished practitioners.

"Consequently any school which seeks to further this process of exemplification must rely on teachers or tutors who are themselves recognizable liberal artists. Such persons need not be old, but they must be experienced. Furthermore, such teachers must be patient enough and interested enough to take the time necessary to lead undergraduates to see and to admire the essential worth and the vital necessity of the liberal arts as the means for acquiring a liberal education.

"Considerable evidence indicates that such experienced, patient, and stable faculty members prefer as the locus of their labors the campus of a small liberal arts college rather than a collegiate department in the shadow of a university research center.

"The liberal arts can be exemplified by educated persons in any place: on a log, in a field, in a classroom, in a small college, or in a large university. But they can be exemplified most effectively among groups (of interested persons) large enough to offer members the benefit of disagreement, agreement, or qualification by other members, and small enough to permit participation by every member of the group.

"Such groups should not only be of manageable size, they should also be composed of persons who share a common desire to spend the time and to acquire the discipline which are demanded of a liberal artist. Such persons seldom move and never function well in large flocks. Samuel Eliot Morison has said that the academic atmosphere most congenial to this pursuit is that of the 'small hilltop colleges of America.'

"With the present-day necessity for maintaining and extending our highly specialized technology and our expanding economy, our universities must constantly foster the basic and applied research on which our economy is based. External forces, such as the threat of communistic domination of the world, also increase this pressure toward specialization and professional education. To answer this crucial but transient challenge by sacrificing our education in the liberal arts would be a tragic blow to the Western civilization we wish to save.

"Hence we are committed to an increasingly serious effort to expand and improve the caliber of our liberal arts teaching at the same time that we expand our technology and our specialized research. Both tasks are necessary. The latter can best be accomplished in and through our splendid universities. The former can best be done by our colleges of liberal arts.

"For almost three decades the articulate voice of Robert Maynard Hutchins has reminded all educators who would listen that an education, as distinguished from a trade or a professional skill, must at least lead its possessor to some acceptable metaphysics, some reasonable system of looking at life and of bearing its burdens with dignity, and should at best lead its possessors to scientific theology in their efforts to reconcile the ways of God to men. The College of St. Thomas concurs wholeheartedly in this line of reasoning.

"We are aware that the opinion is abroad and is often expressed that the cultivation of the liberal arts and the systematic study of theology are mutually exclusive pursuits. This opinion we categorically deny. It is our earnest conviction that Hutchins, in spite of the number and the vigor of his critics, is right, and that the tragic fruit of present trends among liberal arts colleges that are deliberately moving away from their Christian theological origins will in time demonstrate this opinion beyond all doubt.

"In the best definition of an educated man written in our day, José Ortega y Gasset has said that an educated man is one who understands and appreciates the cultural tradition which produced him and who is willing to spend his time, his talent, and his training in order that that precious heritage might be preserved, protected, and perfected for the generations which will come after him.

"There is in modern or ancient literature no better definition of an educated person. It says everything. It looks to the past. It faces the future. It relates human rights to human duties and it demands that every man use all of his potential, that he recognize his debt to his forebears, and that he accept moral responsibility for the heritage he bequeaths to posterity.

"Unless there is a God and unless men are accountable to some standard for the morality of their conduct, it is ridiculous to speak of justice and honor among men or among nations. The liberal arts cannot solve the problems which frighten modern man. Only the sciences of philosophy and theology can supply these answers. Hence our firm conviction that the liberal arts lead their practitioners to laurels of dubious and ephemeral value unless they lead them to see more clearly and to bear with dignity the moral burdens of responsible free men under God.

"Under the constitutions of the several states and of the United States, as these documents are now construed, it is not possible to teach Christian theology in tax-supported schools. Hence the work of explicating the Christian view of man and human society can today in America be carried on only in private or independent schools and colleges. If these premises be true, they supply one more reason why the liberal arts college should exist as a separate entity and not as a program in a state university system."

•

Satisfied with all our written reports, Armsey asked for a special meeting with our board of trustees.

On March 25, 1962, the board met on campus to receive the formal proposal from Armsey. Quoting Henry Heald, then president of the Ford Foundation, Armsey explained the purpose of the Special Program in Education: "To build excellence, and realistic aspirations in a group of colleges with differing backgrounds, geographic locations, and plans for the future." Our new archbishop, Leo Binz, preferred not to attend this meeting on the grounds that his presence there would, implicitly, commit him to a program he was not ready to endorse.

Our board was impressed and eager to accept the offer of the Ford Foundation. I was charmed at the recognition implicit in the offer and at the prospect of rising to meet its challenge. The terms were that we would receive $1.5 million from the foundation, over a period of three years, if we could match each of their dollars with two new gift dollars from other sources. It was a dramatic opportunity for the college to achieve greater visibility in the academic community and to obtain new resources for its several programs.

By midsummer of 1962 I was well aware that Archbishop Binz had something less than galloping enthusiasm for the joint venture our college was planning with the Ford Foundation. Preliminary negotiations on it had been conducted by me with Armsey after the death of Archbishop Brady and prior to the appointment of Binz. I was, in a sense, operating during this period on my own, with no explicit authority from Brady or Binz.

Unfortunately, in my first business session with Binz, after his installation as archbishop on February 28, 1962, I had to report to him that the fund drive for St. Thomas Academy was stalled at midpoint, with pledges and gifts on hand of only $1 million, less than half of what we needed, and that the Ford Foundation gift to the college required both his endorsement and his promise of future support.

I expected some resistance from him. He had come to town a few months earlier, hearing glowing tributes still ringing in memory of his warmly admired predecessor. Brady had spent money and pledged future diocesan income on a grand scale. All these promises had to be kept by his successor. Frankly, Binz was afraid that his diocese was badly overcommitted. Hence my requests for his help to the academy and the college were, in his view, both untimely and unreasonable. The urgency and enthusiasm with which I presented them probably also worked against me. What I considered thoughtful programs, carefully designed and assured of success, he considered ill-advised and overambitious invitations to financial disaster.

Brady's aggressive style of administration and his buoyant optimism had spoiled me. I was absolutely unprepared for the careful curial style which Leo Binz would spend the next seven years trying to teach me.

In careful, polite, but crystal clear words, Binz patiently explained to me that he had no intention of pledging the credit of the diocese and his own credibility to back either the new academy drive or the ambitious program being planned jointly by the college and the Ford Foundation. When I said that it was unthinkable to call off the academy drive or to refuse the Ford Foundation offer, he calmly told me that these difficult decisions were vastly better than the twin debacles of public failure he could foresee for both efforts. I was amazed at his coolness. He never raised his voice, never said an unkind word about me or my plans, and seemed as relaxed as a cat on a windowsill in the sunshine.

It took me a few days to realize that he did indeed have a point. As a new chief administrator, he had an obligation to review the operation of the entire diocese, to retrench where necessary, and to make his own decisions about where he would commit his credibility to advance projects he considered worthy. I had rushed him. The urgency of my special interest had led me to think that my priorities should dictate his agenda. I don't think I ever made that mistake with him again.

With a little help from my friends I soon decided that my case for St. Thomas needed more and better evidence from me and less reliance on Archbishop Binz. Several senior pastors in the diocese and I. A. O'Shaughnessy had assured me of their support for the academy and the college. I went back to Binz with a new plan. This time I asked only that he agree to serve as honorary cochairman of our drive, with I.A. as the other cochairman, and that Binz send a letter to all the parishes in the diocese, giving his blessing to our efforts to raise the money we needed. This way his credibility was never at stake. Ours was. His letter of May 4, 1963, was one year in the making. It told the priests and their parishioners that St. Thomas was embarked on a drive of its own. That letter came to be known in the diocese as "Jim Shannon's hunting license." It is a rhetorical masterpiece.

Grateful for any kind of episcopal blessing, Father Roach and I agreed that he would assume full responsibility for fund-raising for the new academy and that I would be responsible for directing the effort at the college to match the Ford grant. We named the college drive the "St. Thomas Program for Great Teaching." Patrick Butler, a generous and dedicated board member, agreed to serve as the chairman of this important project, a role then being ably managed in the academy drive by alumnus Henri Foussard.

My friend and seminary classmate Father Terrence Murphy became executive vice president of the college to free my time for travel and fund-raising. I.A., always loyal and always available, pledged $1 million, half for the academy and half for the college. We broke ground for the new academy in Mendota Heights on September 27, 1963. And on May 1, 1965, Patrick Butler announced that the fund drive for the college had comfortably passed its goal with a total of $6,301,000 and qualified for all of the money promised by the Ford Foundation.

Some college presidents relish their role as money raisers. I never did. It was a necessary part of the job. I did it as zealously and effectively as I could. But in my heart I never enjoyed it. The challenge grant of the Ford Foundation and the caliber of our faculty and curriculum made my task as fund-raiser bearable. I was proud of the college, its program, its faculty, and its graduates. It was easy for me to recommend it warmly to would-be donors. The alumni and friends of the college responded generously. I never doubted that they would, but I was relieved and pleased when the drive ended. Archbishop Binz was also relieved. His worst fears had not come to pass.

Curiously, our success in meeting the challenge of the Ford grant played some part in the decision of Archbishop Binz to ask Rome to name me one of his auxiliary bishops in February 1965. I do not know precisely the reasons which led him to make this request. I only know that on February 2, 1965, I received a confidential letter from Archbishop Egidio Vagnozzi, apostolic delegate in the United States, informing me that I had been nominated to become a bishop and asking that I notify him at once whether I would accept the appointment, should it be made by Pope Paul VI.

The certified, confidential letter warned me that I could reveal its contents to no one, save my confessor and my archbishop, under pain of losing the appointment. That night I went to see Archbishop Binz at his residence. He told me that he had asked for me by name as his auxiliary bishop and that he wanted me to accept the appointment. It was then that he also told me that he had been favorably impressed by my administration of the Program for Great Teaching.

I was flattered and puzzled. Catholic tradition accords extraordinary respect and deference to bishops. I was not sure that I had the requisite qualities for this role. I told Archbishop Binz that I was not the type. He asked me who was. I replied that he was. Then I was embarrassed because I could not explain what I meant by this exchange.

Binz could not have been more kind. He urged me to pray over my decision and to send a wire the next day, accepting or rejecting the nomination. Though the final decision was mine, he expressed clearly the desire that I accept. It pleased me to learn that he wanted me as his assistant bishop. Somehow I had acquired the notion, after working with him at arm's length for four years, that given his own choice, he would not have picked me as his close associate. In the quandaries which beset a man prior to his ordination as a priest or as a bishop he can only pray and hope that he is doing the right thing by going forward when his name is called to approach the altar.

In our seminary days we had often heard Father Louis McCarthy tell us that we were being ordained "to do the work which the church needs done." The church was speaking to me through the pope's personal representative and through my own bishop. Both urged me to accept. I had no solid reason for declining the appointment — only a vague, wordless, highly personal intuition that I was not cut from the same cloth as the bishops I knew and admired.

After a sleepless night and many prayers, with no possibility to discuss my dilemma with close associates at the college, I sent the wire (in code) on February 3, accepting the nomination.

On March 31, 1965, amid all the color, sound, and splendor of episcopal ritual, in the sanctuary of the cathedral where I had been ordained a priest, at the altar where I had offered Mass hundreds of times, and near the confessionals where I had pronounced the words of absolution thousands of times, I responded "I am present" and stepped forward to accept ordination as a bishop in the Catholic Church. Was that decision a mistake? Should I have declined? On what grounds? In the words of Father McCarthy, I truly believed that every priest is ordained to do the work of the church, as that work is progressively revealed to him by his ecclesiastical superiors. Each of my superiors, my confessor, my archbishop, and the pope's representative, had counseled me to accept.

Since then I have often pondered that decision. Could I have justified to myself a decision to decline? I do not know. I made the decision in good faith, confident that divine grace would be available to me to enable me to function effectively and honorably for the rest of my life in the honorable and onerous role of a Catholic bishop.

On the day I became a bishop my lovely mother was still alive. It was her eighty-ninth birthday. In a chic new hat she sat in the front pew in the cathedral. My family and friends by the hundreds came from all parts of the country to celebrate that happy occasion with the joy and high hopes which mark the making of a new bishop. The outpouring of euphoria and benevolence at an episcopal consecration is the human expression of the hope, built on Christian faith, that the new bishop will use the powers of his full priesthood for a long time, to the benefit of the church and for the cause of Christ in the world.

At the time of my episcopal ordination I was in my ninth year as president of the College of St. Thomas. The understanding I had with Archbishop Binz was that I would continue in the dual role of president and auxiliary bishop until the end of my tenth year in the presidency.

My decade as a college president included most of the troubled '60s. The nation was mired in the war in Vietnam. Civil rights activists were challenging the establishment in Washington and on college campuses. Faculty and students at St. Thomas were deeply involved in both these issues. It is probably correct to say that their concern about civil rights was deeper than their anguish about Vietnam. During midyear and summer vacations, students and faculty volunteered to register voters in southern states. But there was only a modest movement on campus, in my day, to question our national involvement in Vietnam.

My own thinking, at that time, also followed this pattern. Early on, I was convinced that Martin Luther King, Jr., was right and that his several shrill critics were on the wrong side in the fight for racial equality and civil rights. But on the question of war in Vietnam as late as 1965, I was still writing in the campus paper that, presumably, President Lyndon Johnson had more accurate data than we had on which to base his judgment favoring the war. My view on this touchy topic was about to change dramatically, but by midpoint in the decade of the '60s, our campus community and its president still refused to join the ranks of those who were saying that our role in Vietnam was wrong.

Traditionally the Catholic Church in the United States has made patriotism a primary virtue. Immigrant Catholics, grateful for new lives of economic and social opportunity in the New World, have, with the exception of the short-lived Irish revolt in New York during the Civil War, prided themselves on their readiness to fight and die for their adopted country. There had been, until Vietnam, a kind of tacit understanding in Catholic culture that wars involving the United States are "just wars" and that criticism of our national military or foreign policy is simply not done by loyal Catholics.

A promilitary position was part of my own heritage. I was proud to be a graduate of St. Thomas Military Academy and proud to be president of a college that had a distinguished and quite visible Air Force R.O.T.C. program in its curriculum. As a child I had learned from my immigrant Irish father that I had a sacred duty of loyalty and patriotism to the country which had received him so generously in his youth. All these premises inclined me, during the first half of the decade of the '60s, to caution our students and myself about premature and unsupported criticism of the war in Vietnam.

Writing from Rome in November of 1965, where I was attending the final session of Vatican Council II, I reported to our students and faculty that on November 2, All Souls Day, I had accompanied Cardinal Francis Spellman, archbishop of New York, from Rome to the American cemetery at Anzio Beach in Italy, to offer Mass for the ten thousand American soldiers who gave their lives and who now lie buried there. In that report I said: "It is presumptuous for any citizen to think that he has more data, better military intelligence, more respect for human life, or more concern for our country than does President Johnson."

The next issue of the *Aquin* published a thoughtful and well-documented letter from a faculty member, taking the opposite side on this question. The dialog at St. Thomas was beginning to build. My own position was to change completely within another year. But for the record, be it said that when my decade as a college president ended in June 1966, I was still one of the silent observers who were unwilling to fault Lyndon Johnson or his administration for their role in Vietnam. I believe I am also correct in saying that this opinion, at that time, was the majority opinion, by a wide margin, among our students, faculty, and staff.

# CHAPTER TEN

# SELMA AND THE CESSNA 180

Before my ordination as a bishop I had reminded Archbishop Binz that my work as his assistant in the diocese would inevitably lessen the time and attention I could devote to my duties as president of the College of St. Thomas. He agreed with this opinion and told me that he had already decided to transfer me to a parish as soon as convenient so that I would acquire more of the pastoral experience every bishop should have.

As this anticipated conflict between my two assignments became a reality I took some solace from the knowledge that I was soon to receive a new assignment and from the hope that Father Terrence Murphy might be named president of St. Thomas. My first year as a bishop, the academic year 1965–66, was to be my last year at St. Thomas. That was a critical year for civil rights across the country. The Civil Rights Act of 1964, proposed by President John F. Kennedy and enacted under Lyndon Johnson, was the prelude to intense civil strife in states where the registration of black voters provoked violent reactions.

One month after the announcement of my appointment as a bishop, but prior to the scheduled ceremony of my ordination (on March 31), I received a telegram and then a telephone call from Dr. Martin Luther King, Jr., asking me to join him in Selma, Alabama, on March 15, in a memorial service honoring the Rev. James Reeb, a Unitarian minister and civil rights advocate who had been slain in Alabama while working for voter registration. I tried to explain to Dr. King that I was not yet a bishop. What he needed, in my opinion, was a senior bishop, a cardinal if possible, to join him and Walter Reuther of the United Auto Workers of America, Archbishop Iakovos of the Greek Orthodox Church, and the Reverend Dana McLean Greeley, president of the Unitarian Universalist Association, in their planned tribute to James Reeb. I proposed the names of Cardinal Joseph Ritter of St. Louis and Bishop Victor Reed of Oklahoma City. King had already called Ritter and Reed. Ritter was in Rome and Reed was in the hospital.

King clearly wanted the ceremony honoring Reeb to be an ecumenical service. But as we talked, on a Sunday afternoon, it was obvious to both of us that the ceremony, scheduled for the next day at 2:00 P.M., would go on without any Catholic speaker unless I accepted. I promised Dr. King that I would be there, if I could arrange transportation. That night I flew to Atlanta. On the plane I met three good friends, Father Harvey Egan, Father Anthony Louis, and Father Edward Grzeskowiak, fellow priests from St. Paul, also en route to Selma to honor James Reeb.

We arrived in Atlanta well after midnight and found that all flights to Montgomery were booked. We rented a station wagon, bought some orange juice, milk, and breakfast rolls, and headed for Selma. We drove all night and all morning. As we entered Dallas County, of which Selma is the county seat, we had picked up a tail. I was driving. If I speeded up, he speeded up. If I slowed down, he slowed down. When we stopped for gasoline, he pulled in beside us and asked me, "Where y'all headin', Reverend?" I replied "Montgomery." "That's just fine," he said. Within limits, I was telling the truth. My return flight was due out of Montgomery later that night. As we got underway, he pulled out and fell in behind us all the way to Selma. We got there just an hour before the 2:00 P.M. service at the Brown Memorial Chapel. As I walked with Father Charles Neice from St. Elizabeth's Rectory to the Brown Memorial Chapel, the streets were deserted. As we passed one house, a black man and a black woman, parishioners of Father Neice, rushed out to meet us. The woman kissed the priest's hand and said, "You take care. You hear. You take care." Then they rushed back into the house and locked the door.

The city block on which the chapel stands was surrounded by patrol cars on all four sides parked bumper to bumper. Persons entering that block had to climb over the bumpers of the squad cars. At intervals along the block police officers, holding German Shepherd attack dogs on leashes, stood guard.

The chapel was jammed. I have never been in a crowd so tightly packed. It took me ten minutes to work my way up a side aisle from a side door to the altar. In the sanctuary, Walter Reuther, Archbishop Iakovos, Reverend Greeley, and I found chairs, facing the people. Dr. King was not yet there. As we waited, watching and hearing the crowd in the nave and balcony, I became aware for the first time that we might be in some danger. The crowd, the warm day, the watch dogs, the armed guards, the tension in the air made me sense that we were close to a flashpoint. A spark could set off a reaction none of us could stop. Dr. King was late. My uneasiness began to mount. Just then, escorted by Jesse Jackson and Andrew Young and other members of the Southern Christian Leadership Conference, King arrived. His presence suddenly gentled the entire crowd. Without instructions we all rose, joined hands, and began to chant "We Shall Overcome." The earlier tension had passed. It was as though the arrival of the principal speaker had reassured everyone that all was well. Reuther, Iakovos, Greeley, and I spoke briefly, each citing in different ways the categorical imperative of Christian conscience which bade us protest the murder of James Reeb and the systematic suppression of the civil rights of black citizens. But King was *the* speaker of the day. His moving address uttered not one word of rancor. He praised the personal generosity and courage of James Reeb and told us that all members of the human family are equal in the eyes of God and equally deserving of all the civil rights promised by the Constitution. It was a healing message, full of hope and kindness. He was a powerful speaker but a most gentle man. Listening to him and his words of our concern for one another, I marveled that some police surrounding that chapel were even then wearing large buttons labeled with one ominous word: "Never."

That ceremony was not to be my last sharing of a platform with Martin Luther King, Jr., but it remains one of the moving experiences of my life. As I listened to his explication of the gospel of Jesus Christ that day, I knew that I was in the presence of a man of Christian faith and great personal courage. He could speak movingly about the gentle Jesus of Nazareth and about the nonviolence of Gandhi because he had disciplined himself to practice daily the difficult human conduct they espoused.

King made a lasting impression on me. Days later, back at the college, I could still sense the intensity of his commitment to social justice. I regard it today as an occasion of great grace in my life that I met and worked, even briefly, with Martin Luther King on behalf of human freedom and the cause of peace.

In January 1965 I was elected vice chairman of the board of the Association of American Colleges, with the understanding that I would be prepared, one year later, to accept the chairmanship of that board. The Association then had 873 member-colleges on its roster. Work on the Association over the next two years introduced me to two college presidents with whom I would have significant future contacts: Landrum Bolling, the president of Earlham College, Richmond, Indiana,

and Richard Weigle, president of St. John's College, Annapolis, Maryland, and Santa Fe, New Mexico. In executive committee meetings of
the Association I discovered that Bolling and Weigle and I regularly
ended up on the same side of controverted questions about the liberal arts in higher education. The classical curriculum of "Great Books"
at St. John's, the Quaker tradition at Earlham, and the Catholic tradition at St. Thomas often gave the three of us compatible premises
and similar conclusions, especially when the discussion centered on educational values. In January 1966 I became chairman of the board of
the Association, even though I knew then that my term as president of
St. Thomas was drawing to a close. When I shared this knowledge with
my associates on the board, they asked that I continue as chairman even
though I might leave college administration during the year ahead.

One of my duties as chairman was to represent the Association that
year in the ceremonies dedicating the new campus of St. John's College
in Santa Fe, New Mexico. On that occasion, walking in the academic
procession with actress Greer Garson, a patron of St. John's, as my
partner, I could not know that within four years I would become the
vice president on that very campus.

Once upon a time college presidents enjoyed a life of relative tranquility, with their books, their students, and their professional peers on
campus. That day is gone. Modern college presidents must be persons
whose own mental hygiene makes them comfortable with ambivalence and who have the skill to deal effectively, and often in quick
succession, with different constituencies, without losing their identity.
Presidents may use different vocabularies and employ varied meta-
phors to speak to the faculty, the students, the alumni, parents, donors,
or the legislature. But it is essential, whatever their diction, that the
substance of their position be the same with each of these different
"publics." Otherwise, their contradictory positions will inevitably lead
to coalitions of their critics whose common complaint will be that the
presidents are chameleons.

The American public, particularly its educational network, has an acquired fondness for listening to speeches, long or short, good or bad.
College presidents, eager to win new friends and recruit new students
for their college, feed this public craving by spending many hours on
the speaking circuit, urged on by steady pressure from the alumni and
the admissions office. I was no exception.

May and June, for me, were the cruelest months. One year I was
surprised to find that our admissions office had booked me to deliver
the commencement address at fifteen different schools. Driving home

alone on a sunny afternoon from one of these I dozed off at the wheel. As my car left the road and hit the coarse gravel on the shoulder, I awoke just in time to change course and miss a telephone pole by inches. I pulled off the highway to let my heartbeat slow down and made up my mind right there that I would learn to fly.

My instructor at Holman Field in St. Paul was a fellow Minnesotan with the well-known initials H.H.H. Howard H. Humphrey, no kin to our revered senator, was a crack pilot and an excellent teacher. After a dozen hours with him I soloed, got my student pilot license, and promptly told our admissions office that they could book me to speak any place which I could reach in three hours flying time from St. Paul's Holman Field, in a rented Cessna 180.

Thereafter I could work a half day at the office, take off from Holman Field at 1:30 P.M., be at almost any town in Minnesota, western Wisconsin, northern Iowa, or the eastern Dakotas by dinner time, deliver my speech, spend the night in the local Catholic rectory, and fly home the next morning. It was a nifty schedule and I enjoyed it thoroughly.

Bad weather could ground me and did occasionally send me back to the highways. H.H.H. had taught me never to fly in bad weather and to live religiously by the old maxim: "There are old pilots. And there are bold pilots. But there are no old, bold pilots."

Learning to fly was a brief and welcome diversion from my duties as president. But my principal occupation in my decade as a college president was my constant search for new and better ways to work cooperatively and productively with a faculty of 150 members. On balance that group of dedicated professionals taught me far more than I taught them about the importance of solid evidence, logic, candor, full disclosure, truth, fairness, courtesy, and good faith bargaining in the administration process.

Prior to my time as a college president I had espoused the garden variety liberal principles favoring openness and candor in the political process. But after my decade in the presidency I had empirical evidence that openness, due process, equal opportunity, and a forum for every variant opinion on an important, controverted question are essential requisites for effective academic management. The collegial process is tedious. It can be alternately boring, exasperating, or immensely satisfying. To chair meetings which seem endless, to insist that all sides be heard, to know that one has the power to cast the tie-breaking vote if necessary, and still to maintain silence about one's own opinion, lest that opinion, prematurely revealed, skew the discussion unfairly, is a solid learning experience for anyone who believes, as I do, that the benefits far outweigh the costs of this collegial process. The rules of academic management to which I subscribe date largely from that decade of my middle years when the faculty of the College of St. Thomas taught me to trust the collegial process, in spite of its flaws.

# CHAPTER ELEVEN

# VATICAN II

Pope John XXIII surprised the world, not to mention the College of Cardinals, by his sudden announcement on January 25, 1959, that he would convene an assembly of all the bishops in the world, an ecumenical council, the first since 1870 and the twenty-first in the history of the church. Councils are called ecumenical because they assemble bishops from every part of the inhabited world. (*Oikos* in Greek means a house. *Oikumenos* means any inhabited place.) Hence an ecumenical council, in theory, should represent all the inhabited parts of the world. Almost four years were spent in preparation for Vatican II. It opened in St. Peter's Basilica in Rome on October 11, 1962.

Pope John lived to see the first of four annual sessions of the Council completed. At the time of his election he had joked that even though he was overage and overweight to be pope, he was in fact the pope and intended to exercise the power of that office as long and as well as he could.

He died on June 3, 1963, after a reign of only five years. But he lived long enough to see the Council well begun and long enough to set for it a tone of confidence and optimism which would wax and wane but manage to last through the remaining three sessions. In response to his critics, prior to the first session, he had said, "The prophets of doom always talk as though the present, in comparison to the past, is becoming worse and worse. But I see mankind as entering upon a new order, and perceive in this a divine mandate."

Pope John admitted that he had sought no human advice before deciding to convene the Council. His own experience in the papal diplomatic corps, first as an envoy in Bulgaria, then in Turkey, then in Greece, and finally in France after World War II, and his confidence that the Holy Spirit was guiding him, had convinced him that the time was ripe for a wide-open dialog by the bishops of the world to review the role and to refine the methods for preaching the gospel of Jesus Christ in the modern world.

In his words, "The principal purpose [of the Council] would be to encourage the growth of Catholic faith, to renew the life of Christian people, and to adjust the norm of ecclesiastical law to the needs and thoughts of our times." He was fond of the term *aggiornamento* to describe the purpose of the Council. It means an up-dating or a bringing into step with the times. On one occasion he used another metaphor which will probably be cited forever to describe his tenure as pope: "We are opening the windows in the church to let the fresh air come in." Some of his critics now think that he invited a hurricane. His admirers, including this writer, regard Vatican II as an overdue, necessary, and painful effort by the Catholic Church to reexamine its divine mandate, its human weaknesses, the sources of its legitimacy, and its current procedural options in the modern world.

There were many stories circulating in Rome to illustrate Pope John's personal warmth and candor. One such tale, which cannot be proved but which has the ring of authenticity, relates to his first year as pope. The story says that early in his new role he invited the supervisors of all the administrative departments in the Vatican to visit individually with him to review the operations of their departments. One such visitor was the editor of *L'Osservatore Romano,* the Vatican daily newspaper.

John is alleged to have urged the editor to simplify the diction in the paper. For example, in that journal, references to the pope are often phrased in the third person, thus avoiding the necessity to attribute direct quotations to the Holy Father, and thus also providing a diplomatic loophole for him or the Curia if the comments attributed to him are later questioned or challenged. John asked whether the elaborate Vatican journalese which so often comes out as "His Holiness indicated that it was his opinion that..." could not be trimmed back to a simple direct statement, "The pope said...." The editor is reported to have listened respectfully and silently, confident that popes come and go but that the canonized rules of Vatican protocol endure forever.

Some weeks later, the story goes, Pope John visited a prison in Rome on Christmas Day. Talking to one prisoner the pope was overheard by the press to say, "I have sympathy for you, my son; a cousin of mine did time in prison." Horrors! How does *L'Osservatore Romano* report that a cousin of the Holy Father is an ex-con?

True to form, the Vatican daily came out the next morning with its cleaned-up version of the papal conversation: "His Holiness indicated to one of the unfortunate inmates that a distant relative of his, a long time ago, through a misunderstanding, was temporarily detained by the authorities."

That did it. The pope sent for the editor, pointed to the story and said, "This is a good example of the style I have asked you to correct. It was not a distant relative. It was my first cousin. It was not a long time ago. It was last year. It was not a misunderstanding. They caught him red-handed—poaching on a game preserve." There is no evidence that John XXIII ever persuaded the Vatican editor to clean up his prose. But the story, true or not, illustrates the welcome freshness which Pope John brought to an office which has been solemnized beyond the limits of reason or necessity.

Cardinal Giovanni Battista Montini, the archbishop of Milan, was elected to succeed John XXIII on June 21, 1963, and took the name Paul VI. John had set a tone and an agenda for the Council. Paul inherited the more difficult task of guiding the dialog which John had invited but which by this time many Catholic traditionalists considered dangerously innovative and entirely too responsive to the secular winds of change.

By the time I became a bishop in 1965 three of the four annual sessions of Vatican II had been completed. I was charmed at the prospect of being a voting member in the final session (September 14–December 8, 1965). At the age of forty-four I was one of the younger bishops in attendance.

En route to Rome for the opening session on September 14 I had paid a week's visit to my father's family in Ireland. While there I called on the James Rice family in Burnchurch, County Kilkenny, the descendants (on his mother's side) of Archbishop John Ireland's family. Ireland, the first archbishop of St. Paul, was born at Burnchurch in 1838, in a house still standing and still owned by his family. My visit to them was part of a plan I had conceived to build a permanent monument at the site of John Ireland's place of birth.

Burnchurch is not a village. It is merely a crossroads, with a few houses and a burned-out hulk of a "Fitzgerald" castle dating back to Norman times. No marker or tablet had ever been placed there to identify the birth site of an Irish-American prelate who is regarded in American history as one of the most dynamic leaders of the Catholic Church in the nineteenth century.

I asked the Rice family if they would approve the concept of some kind of a monument for John Ireland on their property. They readily agreed to the idea but assured me that they could not afford its cost. I told them that the cost would not be their problem.

Burnchurch lies in the Irish diocese of Ossory, whose bishop then was Peter Birch. Once I arrived in Rome for the Council I went to visit Bishop Birch at the Irish College, where the Irish bishops were staying during the Council. I told him of my visit to his diocese and of my plan and asked his approval. He already knew of John Ireland and was pleased at the prospect of erecting some kind of a fitting memorial to him. Birch, like the Rices, warned me that his diocese would not be able to sponsor any such memorial but would gladly oversee its construction if funds for it could be pledged by others. I assured him that finding the money would not be his responsibility.

During Vatican II Archbishop Leo Binz and his staff of three, including me, were quartered at the Michelangelo Hotel, a ten-minute walk from the Vatican. The three months we spent in Rome for the Council still stand as the most exciting and sustained spiritual and intellectual experience of my adult life.

Archbishop Binz, Bishop Leonard Cowley, Father Kenneth Pierre, and I would concelebrate Mass each morning at our hotel at 6:30 A.M. After breakfast we would review the agenda for the day's meeting, sent to our hotel each evening by special messenger, and then walk or take the bus to the Basilica of St. Peter.

There were 2392 bishops and abbots in attendance during the fourth session, all seated by seniority according to the date of their appointments. As a junior bishop I sat in the first row of a tribune (the first balcony) just to one side of the special altar which had been erected for the Council in the main aisle of St. Peter's. It was an excellent seat. I could see the entire span of that magnificent church each morning as we began the day's deliberation with a solemn pontifical Mass. My seat was directly above the section where half of the College of Cardinals sat and directly opposite the seats of the other half of the College of Cardinals. Cardinal Alfredo Ottaviani sat directly below me. I kept a close eye on him. He was reputed to be the most conservative voice in the Curia. But by then he was very old and rarely rose to speak.

From my vantage point in the balcony I could see below all the bishops in the world who were senior to me by date of their episcopal appointment. In my section, among the younger prelates, there were many black bishops. But among the two hundred ranking archbishops of the world, just below me, there were only a few black prelates and only two black cardinals, Rugambwa of Tanzania and Zoungrama of Upper Volta. The hierarchy of the Catholic Church, like the rest of modern society, had been racially segregated for centuries. But by 1965 it was trying earnestly to integrate its upper echelons.

Each morning at the opening of the Council, Archbishop Pericle Felici, or his delegate, would read aloud the name of any bishop in the world who had died the preceding day. Hardly a day passed that we did not pray for one or more deceased bishops. One day five deaths were announced. This fact had enormous impact on me. It made me realize for the first time the magnitude of the administrative task of the worldwide Catholic Church. Each bishop who died left a vacant diocese somewhere which then called for the appointment of a new bishop. No corporation, no other international organization, faces such a continuous demand on its procedures for naming new regional managers.

Historically, vacant dioceses have been filled by order of the pope within a few months, and the process never stops. Multinational corporations must from time to time replace senior vice presidents of different corporate divisions or subsidiaries. Coca Cola, General Motors, and IBM usually face this challenge only at carefully scheduled, predictable intervals. The Vatican has to do it, usually on short notice, year in and year out. Since attending Vatican II, I am often silent when others complain about the slow-moving administrative machinery of the Catholic Church. I would hazard the opinion that its process for naming new bishops is a model for large management systems which must constantly change while they maintain, within their respective structures, continuity of administration and coherence of policy.

(Admittedly, in recent years this process of naming new bishops has slowed down dramatically. At this writing one press report says that eighteen dioceses in Brazil, the country with the world's largest Catholic population, are and have been for some time awaiting the appointment of new bishops. Only time will tell whether this new slow-motion process is a permanent or a temporary feature of the Vatican's historic and admirable collegial *modus operandi* for naming new bishops.)

Another insight which struck me at the Council was the vital role played by the several scholars whose research and writing provided the substance for dialog at the Council. Many of these were in residence at Vatican II, usually as *periti* (experts) accompanying the bishops of their native dioceses. They were not entitled to vote, but their daily labors behind the scenes shaped and phrased the questions on which the Council fathers voted.

During the general sessions in St. Peter's, from which all outsiders were excluded, the *periti* were allowed to be present so that they could assess the debate and thus refine the documents under discussion to reflect the more promising oral opinions expressed in the daily debate.

The morning session of the Council each day was a general meeting of all the bishops, assembled in St. Peter's to hear papers, pro and con, on matters ripe for decision. As we finished the public discussion of each topic, we would vote by punching out tiny squares on computer-type punch cards: Placet (yes); Non Placet (no); Placet Juxta Modum (yes, with suggested amendments).

After lunch the various commissions, composed mostly of senior prelates, met to prepare the working papers which would be presented later at one of the general morning sessions. As a junior bishop I had no assignment to any commission. Hence for a period of almost three months I had free time every day from 1:00 P.M., the end of the general session, until the opening session the next day. In retrospect it looks as though I was surfeited with free time. Not so. The lovely sunny days in that beautiful city were never long enough for me.

Following the general session of the Council each morning, press briefings, in several languages, were held in different assembly halls near the Vatican. Father Edward Heston, C.S.C., of the University of Notre Dame, usually presided at the briefings for the English-speaking press. I attended these regularly and learned far more from his rapid-fire summary of each day's agenda than I had been able to glean from the position papers, all read in Latin, presented that morning in St. Peter's.

Almost every afternoon or evening there was a seminar or lecture by one or more of the *periti* somewhere in Rome. I sought out these sessions with the zeal of a graduate student. One of the best, by invitation only, met in a villa on Monte Mario, where Cardinal Leo Suenens of Belgium presided every Wednesday afternoon. The speakers were journalists, pastors, professors, and public figures selected for their ability to enlighten us on the large questions of religion, culture, and society then being debated as Schema 13, the catch-all final document of the Council.

Almost every day it was possible to hear first-rate presentations somewhere in Rome by theologians, philosophers, historians, anthropologists, sociologists, or scripture scholars of world renown.

It was like being enrolled in the University of the World. John Courtney Murray, Albert Outler, Barnabas Ahern, Anita Caspary, Jean Daniélou, George Lindbeck, Douglas Horton, Robert McAfee Brown, Godfrey Diekmann, Bernard Häring, James Norris, Cardinal Charles Journet, Luigi Liguitti, Cardinal Augustin Bea, Cardinal Franz Koenig, Cardinal Paul-Emile Léger, Roland Murphy, Dorothy Day, Mother Mary Luke Tobin, Barbara Ward, François Houtart, Karl Rahner, Pietro Pavan, Warren Quanbeck, Joseph Gremillion, Douglas Steere, Edward Schillebeeckx, Hans Küng, Patriarch Maximos IV were all in town for some or all of the fourth session of the Council. I learned the bus routes, the quick short-cuts, and the location of the best taxi stands as I went from meeting to meeting to hear these visitors to the Eternal City.

I recall many nights, back at my room in the Michelangelo, fresh from a lecture or seminar, when sleep would not come. I would lie wide awake, sometimes for hours, still excited by the discussions I had just heard, and by their future import for the church, the people of God.

There was no need for a car in Rome. Distances are short and taxis are abundant. On occasion my friend Father Vincent Yzermans, director of the Information Bureau of the American bishops, and I would rent a car for the weekend and drive to some quiet seaside village hotel where we would walk the strand, drink the local wine, and talk far into the night about the Council, the greatest experience of our lives.

It was not possible for all the bishops attending the Council to have a private audience with Pope Paul VI. But our archbishop, Leo Binz, having once been a member of the staff of the Vatican secretary of state, arranged for an audience for himself and his staff. In full episcopal regalia the four of us, Archbishop Binz, Bishop Leonard Cowley, Father Kenneth Pierre, and I met Pope Paul in his apartment. The picture of that meeting is one of my personal treasures.

Binz and the Holy Father spoke in Italian. The pope, courteously, spoke to the rest of us in his slow and careful English. Addressing me, he said, "I understand that the American clergy work very hard." I replied readily, "Yes, Your Holiness, that is true. We do work very hard." Later, in the taxi, the rest of our delegation ribbed me for "boasting" to the pope. They thought his question was merely a rhetorical gesture, to be answered by some kind of mild disclaimer. Not knowing the Roman protocol I had blundered ahead and simply told him the truth. He did not seem either surprised or amused by my response to his question. The fact is American priests as a group do work very hard. I was not about to sell them short during the one visit of my life with the Holy Father. My handling of this brief visit with the pope is probably a good illustration of my lack of that vital ingredient of episcopal style, *Romanità*.

A few days after our private meeting with the Holy Father he flew to New York to deliver his now famous address to the United Nations, his impassioned plea for world peace. The day after his return to Rome he addressed a general congregation of the Council and repeated his theme from the United Nations: all persons of good will and especially all Christians should agree that modern warfare has become too devastating to be considered any longer an acceptable instrument of foreign policy in any nation.

The war in Vietnam was escalating at that time but had not yet reached its peak. Many non-American bishops considered the papal message a direct reference to the war in Vietnam. But among the American delegation the papal address was generally considered a denunciation of wars in general, not of "our" war in Vietnam. The view was still strong in 1965, among the American bishops, many of whom had served as military chaplains in World War II, that the war in Vietnam was a "just war" being fought to protect the world from the spread of Communism.

Bishops and scholars were not the only visitors drawn to Rome by the Council. Major newspapers, the wire services, publishing houses, and the electronic media sent teams of writers to cover the Council and to report it in minute detail. One such visitor during the fourth session was Henry R. Luce, founder and publisher of Time, Inc. Born of Protestant missionary parents in China, Luce had a deep interest in the nexus between Christian tradition and human culture. He asked his American friends Father John Courtney Murray and Monsignor George G. Higgins to assemble a group of bishops for dinner one evening at the Flora Hotel to discuss the Council, its problems, and its prospects. It was my good fortune to be one of about eight guests that evening. I was impressed by Luce's intensity and by his extraordinary knowledge of political and ecclesiastical affairs in Africa, India, and the Far East. I had little to contribute to the dialog, but much to learn, from such guests as Denis Hurley, archbishop of Durban, South Africa; Angelo Fernandez, archbishop of New Delhi, India; Ernest Primeau, bishop of Manchester, New Hampshire; and Donal Lamont, bishop of Umtali, Rhodesia, from which he was to be expelled in 1977 because of his dogged opposition to racial segregation.

With the relentless curiosity for which he was known, Luce tirelessly picked the brains of everyone at the table. We all understood that his time was short, that his list of questions was endless, and that his clear purpose was to get as good a "fix" on the Council as his time and our knowledge would permit. We talked far into the night. Later, to unwind, I walked back across town to the Michelangelo, still excited by the range and substance of our table talk that evening.

As a young president of St. Thomas I had often met Maggi Vaughan, then a columnist-staff writer for the *St. Paul Pioneer Press* and the *St. Paul Dispatch*. In Rome I discovered that Maggi as a columnist for the *Daily American* was covering some of the Council and writing some free-lance features for other publications. Before she made the decision to leave a good job in St. Paul and head for Rome, a job awaiting her, she discussed her plans with me. I urged her to go. When we met by surprise at a press briefing I was charmed to learn that working in Rome was all she had expected. She was writing, painting, and in love with the place and the people.

Through Maggi I also met Helene Zelezny. Born in Silesia, Helene had come to live in Italy in 1919. A widow, teacher, and sculptor, she made her studio on the Via Margutta, a short walk from the Piazza di Spagna, available as a regular gathering place for artists, writers, and scholars in residence or en route. "Aunt Helen," as she was called, served tea once a week in her studio or garden for a few of her students (Maggi was one) and her galaxy of friends. The walls of her studio were lined with photographs of heroic sculptures she had done for sites in Paris, Vienna, Prague, Brussels, Rome, Venice, and the U.S.

I knew that Archbishop Binz was hoping to find a life-size, or larger, head-and-shoulders bust of Pope Paul VI to match one he already had of his old friend Cardinal Cicognani, who was then papal secretary of state. Somewhat apprehensive, fearing that she would turn me down, I asked Helene if she would consider doing a full-size head-and-shoulders of Pope Paul VI for me. Her eyes lit up and she accepted my offer on the spot.

With a few phone calls and a little lobbying by Archbishop Binz, we arranged for her to be admitted to a series of semipublic audiences with the Holy Father. In these sessions she took pictures of him from every angle and later used the photographs as models in her studio. The completed bronze likeness of the pope was not finished until the next year. It has a craggy texture, intended by Helene to convey a sense of strength and solidarity. I liked it, but since I had undertaken this project on my own, as a gift to Archbishop Binz, I was apprehensive that he might consider it too modern. It departed sharply in style from the bust of Cardinal Cicognani for which it was to be a companion piece. My fears were groundless. Binz liked it so much that he promptly ordered a second copy of it, which he then presented as a gift to his old friend Cardinal Cicognani, but forbade Helene or me to release (at that time) any details, either about the work or the artist.

It is said that many people know about Rome but that no one knows Rome. It is a city full of surprises. Free almost every afternoon, I walked endlessly in its avenues, gardens, parks, and cul-de-sacs. The Italian people know how to enjoy life, and in that lovely city there is abundant beauty to enjoy.

At the end of the day, Father Vincent Yzermans and I would often head for our favorite *trattoria,* overlooking the Piazza della Reppublica, to share a *cappuccino* and mull over the events of the day. In retrospect it is reassuring to recall that we were aware of the importance of what was happening around us. Each day was filled with a kind of intense intellectual excitement which I have never known, before or since. And the long warm evenings were welcome occasions, but never long enough for us to exhaust all we had to talk about.

By a personal decree of John XXIII all bishops attending the Council were required to wear full choir dress to each daily session in St. Peter's. Choir dress means a floor-length fuchsia-colored cassock, a six-inch fuchsia-colored cummerbund-type sash, a lace or linen surplice (called a rochet), with long sleeves and a hemline to the knees, a three-quarter length, sleeveless, fuchsia-colored silk cape (mantelletta), and a silk skull cap (zucchetto), topped off by a red silk box-like headpiece (the biretta). Trotting in the rain or bucking fall winds in these outfits in the Piazza di San Pietro, the bishops of the world gave the photographers of the world some great shots to share with the folks back home. My most unusual photograph from the Council shows Bishop Alphonse Schladweiler, of New Ulm, Minnesota, Bishop Leonard Cowley, Father Kenneth Pierre, and me in full choir dress on the steps of the Basilica of St. Peter, with me proudly displaying a copy of the *St. Paul Pioneer Press* from home which announced in a double banner headline that the Minnesota Twins had won the pennant that year for the American League.

The final session of Vatican II was, in many ways, the most productive of the four meetings because it saw the completion and promulgation of several documents discussed but not resolved in earlier sessions. What had been called Schema 13 in the original agenda of the Council was finally promulgated by Pope Paul VI, on December 7, 1965, as the Pastoral Constitution on the Church in the Modern World. Addressing such cosmic themes as the dignity of the human person, the universal community of humankind, the nexus between religion and human culture, marital morality, war and peace, economic development, political relations, and the community of nations, this constitution, by a wide margin, is the longest document to issue from the Council.

One section which occasioned spirited debate both before and after its promulgation is the section on marital morality. Prior to the convening of Vatican II, Catholic teaching concerning contraception or family planning was clear. In his encyclical *Casti Connubii* Pope Pius XI had stated, in 1930, this position explicitly: "Any use of matrimony whatsoever in the exercise of which the act is deprived, by human inter-ference, of its natural power to procreate life, is an offense against the law of God and of nature, and those who commit it are guilty of grave sin." Pastors and confessors the world over must have cited that passage thousands of times in the confessional and in pastoral counseling. I did.

Prior to Vatican II the bishops of the world had been asked to suggest moral, dogmatic, or canonical topics for the agenda of the Council. Many replies to this invitation recommended that the church reconsider its traditional opposition to every form of artificial con-traception. One bishop, writing from the Island of Mauritius, in the Indian Ocean, argued that the worst fears of Thomas Malthus (who wrote in 1798) had become reality on that tiny island. A rising birthrate and a declining mortality rate for infants (thanks to mod-ern medicine and pharmacology) had brought Mauritius a population which it could neither support nor contain.

News releases from Rome prior to Vatican II, understandably, did not highlight this episcopal plea for a more lenient Catholic position on birth control. But personal conversations among bishops attending the Council made it abundantly clear that many of them confidently expected the Council to mollify Catholic teaching on this issue.

The specific topic of contraception was never formally discussed in the general sessions of Vatican II. Pope Paul VI, in a letter to all the bishops, on his own authority, withdrew this precise question early on from the agenda to be discussed in public by the bishops, promising that in due time he would issue a papal (not a collegial) statement about it. Hence, as the college of bishops deliberated in the Basilica of St. Peter, their comments and their eventual decisions on this touchy topic were framed in the most general terms. Nonethe-less, a clear consensus was, implicitly, reached by the full college of bishops in their public debates. This consensus, in my opinion as an attentive voting member of that assembly, overwhelmingly favored a more lenient position in Catholic teaching on contraception. It was also my clear impression that the college of bishops, while respecting Pope Paul's reservation of this topic to himself, confidently expected that their views, phrased in general but understandable terms in the record of their debates in St. Peter's, would be reflected in any papal document or encyclical which Paul VI would eventually issue on this subject.

On September 29, 1965, Cardinal Paul-Emile Léger, archbishop of

Montreal, addressed the Council, asking that the traditional Catholic teaching on contraception be modified. He objected to the well-known, but limited, definition of marriage as an "institution ordained for the procreation and the education of the children." If this definition were to be retained by the Council, Léger argued, "The doctrine here proposed will not be of great help for the Christians of our time and I fear that it may disappoint their legitimate expectations.... For human persons marriage is not only an institution ordained for the procreation of children. It is also — it is above all — a community of life and love." This wider definition of the married state as a "community of love" was resisted by many fathers of the Council who favored the traditional formulation which limited the stated purpose of marriage to the procreation and the education of children.

In the end Léger's view prevailed. The text finally approved by the vote of the Council does not explicitly mention contraception as a permissible option for married couples but sections 48 to 51 of part 2 of the constitution were widely regarded, in the Basilica of St. Peter the day it was passed, and in the world at large, as a dramatic shift in Catholic teaching on marital morality. The passage cited most often in support of this "new" position is in section 51 of part 2. It reads: "The Council realizes that certain modern conditions often keep couples from arranging their married lives harmoniously, and that they find themselves in circumstances where at least temporarily the size of their families should not be increased. As a result, the faithful exercise of love and the full intimacy of their lives is hard to maintain. But where the intimacy of married life is broken off, its faithfulness can sometimes be imperiled and its quality of fruitfulness ruined, for then the upbringing of the children and the courage to accept new ones are both endangered."

Persons not familiar with the labored rhetoric of papal documents might search this passage in vain for some clear sign that it softens the strict earlier definition of the exclusive purpose of matrimony as the continuation of the human race. But the pastors of the world and the Council fathers in Rome knew that Cardinal Léger's plea for a wider definition of marriage had been heard and accepted, once the language of sections 48–51 of part 2 of the Pastoral Constitution on the Church in the Modern World became the official teaching of the Catholic Church on December 7, 1965.

The best evidence that a significant change occurred in Catholic moral teaching at Vatican II on the subject of marital morality is not printed in the formal report of the Council on Schema 13, but in the record of the amendments proposed and accepted or rejected by a special commission of sixty bishops who reviewed 484 separate proposed amendments given to them prior to November 15, 1965, when the Council, by a vote of 1596 to 72, approved the substance of what is now known as the Pastoral Constitution on the Church in the Modern World. Most of these rejected amendments favored the inclusion of language which would reaffirm the traditional total prohibition of contraception stated in *Casti Connubii*. By reviewing all, and rejecting most, of these amendments as contrary to the substance of the document already approved, the special commission was, in effect, supporting the liberal or modern position on marital morality for which the Melkite Maximos IV Saigh, the Dutch Cardinal Bernard Alfrink, the Belgian Cardinal Leo Suenens, and the Canadian Cardinal Paul-Emile Léger had spoken persuasively during the fourth session of Vatican II.

It is against this well-documented background that one can state categorically that it was the clear and deliberate intention of a majority of the bishops of the Catholic Church in their vote of November 15, 1965, to endorse within the church a new view of human sexuality and to enlarge for loving spouses the limits within which they could share their conjugal love and keep faith with the formal doctrine of the Catholic Church.

The "new" position did not recommend contraception. Nor did it abandon the longstanding prohibition against it. Rather it widened the possibility for Christian spouses to decide in their conscience the relative weight which they might attach on specific occasions to their obligation to use their procreative powers productively and the weight which they might attach to their correlative obligation to love, cherish, and console one another in what Cardinal Léger had called "the community of love."

The "new" position on marital morality still left Catholic couples with a serious moral obligation to use their powers of reproduction responsibly, but gave them some leeway in spacing their children, in protecting what the fathers of the Council called "the full intimacy of [their married] lives," and in planning the size of their families.

There was a clear sense of satisfaction among the bishops after the extended debates on marital morality were concluded. I shared that sense of achievement and looked forward to the opportunity at home of explaining the issues in the debate and the delicate balance of its conclusion. None of us could know then that the careful diction of the Council's decree on this subject would be shattered in July 1968 by

Pope Paul VI's encyclical *Humanae Vitae*, which restated the traditional position of *Casti Connubii*, against contraception, as the definitive teaching of the Catholic Church.

Near the end of the final session of Vatican II, Dr. Albert C. Outler, who had attended every session of the Council as an observer for the World Methodist Council, addressed the annual reception given by the Paulist Fathers at the Grand Hotel to honor the observer delegates and the American bishops. With that combination of light touch and solid scholarship for which he was known, Outler sounded the notes of achievement and challenge which many participants felt at the close of Vatican II: "Here we are, virtually at the end of the most epochal event in modern church history, already in the initial stages of a new era, on the verge of the enormous undertakings (and confusions) of the postconciliar era.... There will be no more meetings of this sort again in our lifetime. Our ways from here lie in a thousand directions all in God's keeping.... The splendors of Vatican II—this strange interlude when we have been so strangely one—will fade and be filed in the archives of our memories. But a new advent of the Holy Spirit has happened in our world in our time—an epiphany of love that has stirred men's hearts wherever they have glimpsed it incarnate."

Vatican II was solemnly adjourned by Pope Paul VI on December 6, 1965. The bishops of the world returned to their respective dioceses to explicate for their people and for the world the substance of the sixteen documents promulgated by that Council, covering the full range of Catholic teaching and setting a new agenda for the church in modern history.

One aspect of Vatican II merits particular emphasis. It was the most broadly representative democratic assembly ever held in the history of the world. True, there had been many ecumenical councils prior to this one, and many world conventions sponsored by governments or corporations. But this assembly explicitly invited and ordered every able-bodied Catholic bishop and abbot in the world to attend. If his resources were too meager to afford the trip, his expenses were paid by the Vatican. And thanks to the jet airplane, the invitees, young and old, accepted the invitation. Of 2908 eligible bishops and abbots invited to the Council, 2540 were in attendance at the opening session in 1962.

Each member of the Council had an equal vote. Each had the same right to prepare position papers, to be heard, to speak for or against any motion being debated. Thanks to the geographical organization of the Catholic Church, every inhabited place on the face of the earth is part of some diocese. And the head of every one of those dioceses, unless he was too ill to travel, was in Rome for the Council. The sheer universality of this worldwide assembly deserves a line in the Guinness Book of Records. Nothing like it has ever happened before. And nothing like it will happen soon again.

# CHAPTER TWELVE

# ST. HELENA'S PARISH

Before leaving Rome I met again with the Irish Bishop Peter Birch to assure him of my intention to construct a monument in his diocese at the birthplace of Archbishop John Ireland. We agreed that if the Rice family would provide a piece of ground next to the highway in Burnchurch for some kind of a monument, I would arrange for the design and fabrication of it, and for its cost.

Back in St. Paul I explained this plan to a dozen friends, including Archbishop Binz, all of whom shared my admiration for John Ireland and who were able to contribute to such a project. The memorial we chose is a massive gray, granite Celtic cross, which stands ten feet high, mounted on a granite pedestal eighteen inches high. The cross, cut and inscribed by artisans in St. Paul under the guidance of Joseph Osborne, was shipped to Ireland in July 1966, and on September 5 a delegation of thirty-six pilgrims from St. Paul flew to Ireland for its dedication.

We had arranged for the construction there of a rough-hewn elliptical stone wall eight feet high as a background setting for the cross, and a wrought iron railing to separate the site from the roadway. A large bronze tablet, with a likeness of Archbishop Ireland, was fixed to the wall next to the cross. On dedication day, September 11, 1966 (the 128th anniversary of the birth of John Ireland), Bishop Birch and I concelebrated Mass "in a fine soft rain" at a temporary altar erected in the middle of the macadam road which runs by the cross. The American pilgrims from St. Paul and a devout but rain-soaked gaggle of Rices and Shannons from Ireland offered the Mass with us.

In the summer of 1978 I had occasion to visit this handsome shrine once again. It is carefully maintained and weathering well. It is a tasteful and fitting memento to a prelate who is considered one of the strongest leaders the Catholic Church has produced in the United States.

On more than one occasion in Rome Archbishop Binz had reminded me that my days as a college president were numbered. His view was that additional experience in a parish would prepare me for the day when I would be named bishop of a diocese. This plan was acceptable to me. I had accomplished most of the tasks I had set for myself at the College of St. Thomas. The last of these, an extensive curriculum reform, was to be completed in the spring of 1966. The college was strong. My original understanding with Archbishop Brady had been that my tenure as president would last no more than ten years.

During my absence in Rome, Monsignor Terrence Murphy's strong performance as executive vice president of the college had earned him the right to be considered for the presidency. He was respected and admired by the faculty and the students. He was definitely my candidate to be the new president.

In the months following Vatican II an increasing part of my time was committed to trips around the archdiocese to bring the sacrament of confirmation to the parishes and to explain the meaning and the future import of the several decrees of the Council. These obligations took me away from the college with increasing frequency and convinced me that the faculty and students would be better served by the appointment of a new president who would not divide his time between their needs and those of the diocese.

In the spring of 1966, the end of my tenth year as president of the college, Monsignor Owen Rowan stepped down as pastor of St. Helena's parish in Minneapolis, a parish he had founded in 1911 when its territory embraced "the whole prairie south of Minneapolis, from Lake Street to the Minnesota River." I was honored to be named to succeed him at St. Helena's and gratified to learn that Monsignor Terrence Murphy was to be the new president of the College of St. Thomas.

I left the college on June 4, 1966, four days short of the twentieth anniversary of my ordination as a priest, to take up new duties as pastor at St. Helena's. I was a lonesome Irishman the day I left that lovely campus. My twelve years at St. Thomas had been years of growth for the college and me. The pain of leaving friends there was eased by my conviction that the college and I were both ready for a change.

As a rule, retired pastors move away from the territory of their old parish. Incoming pastors seem to appreciate a little distance between themselves and their predecessors. Contrary to this custom, Monsignor Rowan moved into a bungalow just one block from the handsome church he had labored twenty years to build. He continued to offer daily Mass there and to be an available, friendly, and generous counselor for the new pastor. In our three years together, we never had a cross word. He treated me like a son and insisted on taking me and my two associate pastors out to dinner once a month. On these occasions we always marveled at his regular practice of ordering a Brandy

Alexander *before* dinner and an extra dry Martini, straight up, *after* dinner.

Owen Rowan called his own priestly ministry "the workhorse variety" to distinguish it from what he called the "racehorse variety." His description of himself did not do justice to his seven decades of priestly service. He was a lovely man. He charmed us with his stories of the diocese and of St. Helena's in its early days. He deserves a chapter in some manual on how to be a good parish priest.

He was one of the persons to whom I wrote a longhand letter the day I decided to resign from the active ministry of the priesthood. He never answered the letter. A mutual friend told me it broke his heart. God rest him now. He remains for me a model of a good friend and a faithful pastor.

As a college president I had often thought that the life of a parish priest, in daily contact with his parishioners, would be a welcome change from the administrative burdens of the campus. At St. Helena's I offered Mass and preached a homily on the gospel each day for the parishioners, heard confessions regularly, and took my turn at house duty in the rectory as often as I could. But it soon became clear that my duties as a bishop, especially the diocesan confirmation schedule, my election to the administrative board of the National Conference of Catholic Bishops, and my duties as chairman of the Association of American Colleges and as chairman of the Minnesota State Junior College Board would never allow me the time to be as available to the people as Owen Rowan had been for a half century.

Fortunately, the parish had a strong staff. Delores Fladeboe, who had been my secretary at the college, came with me to St. Helena's. Her combination of brains, energy, courtesy, and charm made her as invaluable in the parish as she had been at the college. I was often away from the rectory. But she was there daily to respond with what can only be called administrative creativity to any needs or requests from the parish, the press, the kids, the nuns, or the neighbors.

She and Father John McGrath, my associate pastor, held up the sky over St. Helena's. John was as close to the people as I wanted to be. He was in the parish school every day, in the hospital whenever a parishioner needed him, and always available to share my load and to cover for my absence.

On Saturday mornings, when I was in town, I often celebrated Mass in the convent for the Sisters of St. Joseph who staffed our parish school. They would usually invite me to stay for breakfast. I usually accepted. These leisurely, and often extended, breakfast sessions are among the happiest memories of my two and a half years as pastor. Not able to visit the school, the hospitals, or the homes of parishioners as often as I wished, I suppose that my conversations with the sisters gave me some sense of being in touch with the parish and its needs. Nuns who staff parochial schools come to know their parish, through the children, with a specificity that any pastor could envy. Being close to the nuns gave me at least the illusion of being close to the people.

The sisters of St. Joseph of Carondelet, Father John McGrath, and Delores Fladeboe made up in great part to the people of St. Helena's parish for my frequent and regular absences from the parish. At this distance my recollection of my short tenure as a pastor is a bitter-sweet memory. In that role I succeeded, but did not quite take the place of, a venerable priest in a parish he had established and in which he could recite from memory the addresses and phone numbers of hundreds of families. I admired and genuinely desired to emulate Owen Rowan's pastoral style. But other duties continually claimed my energy and time.

I have no evidence to suggest that the parishioners of St. Helena's were critical of my performance as their pastor. The church and school were well maintained. The liturgical services, music, confessions, homilies, priestly ministrations, and participation in parish affairs by the parishioners were, I believe, well above average. Possibly the parishioners spotted me a few points because they were pleased to have a bishop as their pastor. Owen Rowan once told me that he considered it an honor to have a bishop named as his successor at St. Helena's. But in the back of my mind there was always the nagging realization that I was too much of an absentee pastor. No one ever said this to me. But I said it to myself, more than once.

One of my cherished memories of my time at St. Helena's is what I call a "blessed interlude" in 1968 when, thanks to Patti Kump of Minneapolis, I had the privilege of meeting Mother Teresa. Patti then served as the volunteer director of the Co-Workers of the Missionary Sisters of Charity. Mother Teresa was in town to consult with Patti on finding a Co-Worker in Europe to share this task with Patti. Patti invited me to be Mother Teresa's chauffeur while she was here. I was charmed. My two visits with her were brief, as I fetched her from the airport and later delivered her back there. I vividly recall her abiding benevolence for all other people, her gentle voice, and her heavy white wool sweat socks peeking out of her toeless leather sandals.

Recalling these brief visits with this heroic woman, I am reminded of an old aphorism: "No one has too many friends." Were it not for my friendship with Patti and Warren Kump, I never would have had the privilege of meeting Mother Teresa.

My appointment as a pastor had rested on the premise that parish experience would be good preparation for me on the day that I would be named bishop of a diocese. Ironically, however, my days as a pastor were regularly spent outside the parish or on matters only indirectly related to the welfare of the people in that parish.

All this is not to say that my pastoral period was unpleasant or unfulfilling. That was an era of growing concern for ecumenical co-operation. My neighbor and friend, Warren Nyberg, pastor of the Minnehaha Methodist Church, invited me to preach to his people and to share with them the insights I had gleaned from Vatican II. The editor of our diocesan paper invited me to write a weekly column in the *Catholic Bulletin* and opened for me a new apostolate in which, under different auspices, I was to be engaged for more than two decades. I chose the title for the column, "The Pilgrim Church," from the new translation of the Canon of the Mass, because it combined the transient, seeking, changing odyssey of the pilgrim with the permanent, settled, solidity of the church established by Jesus Christ. After my resignation from the active ministry I continued to write a regular column, but not under this title, in the *Minneapolis Sunday Tribune* for twenty years. It was a forum I appreciated and one I do not hesitate to call a continuing ministry.

My principal work as an auxiliary bishop was to bring the sacrament of confirmation to the parishes. I had two additional diocesan appointments, one as a diocesan consultor and one as the diocesan vicar for ecumenism. In the former role I met periodically with Archbishop Binz and the other consultors, on his call, to discuss diocesan needs and to review our procedures for addressing them. Consultors to the bishop serve in an advisory capacity. This role made few demands on my time or energy.

My appointment as the episcopal vicar for ecumenism sounded, initially, like an important new assignment. In a pastoral letter issued on October 11, 1966, Archbishop Binz announced the creation of this new position and named me to fill it. In those days, following Vatican II, hopes still ran high that a brave new era of ecumenical and interfaith cooperation was opening for all Christians and persons of other faiths. Archbishop Binz and I shared that sense of euphoria. We may also bear, jointly or separately, some of the onus for the failure of this brave new era to become a reality in our time.

I was to learn shortly that the diocesan ecumenical office was intended primarily as an agency to respond amicably to any overtures of good will from religious leaders in other churches, temples, or synagogues. It did not, at least during my tenure, have any strong, positive program to recommend to fellow Christians.

One episcopal task I especially enjoyed was the rite of confirmation. It took me all over the diocese, kept me in touch with my fellow priests, and introduced me to lovely children who came to be anointed with holy chrism to mark their formal, public commitment to following Jesus Christ.

As a child I had feared the coming of the bishop to our parish for confirmation. The nuns, the pastor, and my pious father had managed to convince me that the bishop was some kind of Grand Inquisitor and that our family name was riding on my ability to answer quickly and clearly any possible question he might ask me about the catechism.

To prepare children for this kind of a quiz game, teachers had traditionally favored crisp questions which permitted crisp answers. Most often the correct answer was a number or a series. How many sacraments are there? Name the seven capital sins. What are the three principal parts of the Mass? Determined to attack this unfortunate practice when I became a bishop, I resolved never to ask any of these old-line, sure-fire quiz questions. Instead I tried to engage the children in dialog by asking someone to volunteer to talk to me about what it means to be a Christian. Until the teachers and the pastors caught on to me, I found youngsters in many parishes who considered this a trick question. They were all primed to tell me about the seven gifts of the Holy Spirit, the three theological virtues, the four cardinal virtues, the holy days of obligation, or the ten commandments. They and their teachers thought I did not play fair when I asked the children to talk to me about what it means to be a follower of Jesus Christ.

I was determined to attack the established but artificial method of "teaching" the truths of the Christian faith and, in the process, to convince kids that bishops were not just overdressed monsters, sent out from the home office periodically to frighten them. When I discovered that some children were literally scared speechless when I addressed them at the confirmation ceremony, I began asking the pastors in the diocese to have on hand for me a "traveling microphone" with a very long extension cord I could use to cruise the length of the center aisle of any church to talk informally with the youngsters and, if possible, to allay their fear of "the bishop."

My most vivid recollection of these delightful encounters occurred May 11, 1967, in the Church of Christ the King in Minneapolis. As I talked to the class I paused in the center aisle, with my hand on the head of one little boy who sat at the end of his pew. I could feel that he was actually trembling. I leaned over and asked, "Are you afraid of me?" He looked up, swallowed once, and said softly into my microphone, "I'm not really afraid of you. But you sure make me nervous." He brought down the house. He also helped me make a point with all the adults, including the pastor, within hearing range.

After one such ceremony a senior pastor, Father Joseph O'Donnell, counseled me in a friendly fashion that my style as a bishop was much too informal and that it would, in time, lessen the "awe" in which a bishop ought to be held by the faithful. Father O'Donnell was a good friend. Even so, I had to tell him I thought he was wrong on this issue.

In one sense the best part of the confirmation season was the flood of handwritten letters I would get from children the week after they were confirmed. Most of these expressed great relief that the ceremony was finally behind them. Some of them are howlers. I still have them. One, illustrated with a crude drawing of me all in white vestments and miter, said "You look like a very clean man." Another expressed the wish that I would be "blasted with gases." The writer's teacher added a postscript to assure me that the writer meant, but could not spell, "blessed with graces." My favorite is the one that says jauntily, "Yesterday was my best day so far. Thank you."

I hope Father Joseph O'Donnell was wrong and that "out there" today some confirmed adult Catholics recall their confirmation as a good day and the bishop who confirmed them, for all his informal style, as a friend.

One of the mandates given to the bishops by Vatican II was to establish in every country a national conference of bishops, organized according to uniform administrative norms. One such norm called for the democratic election of an administrative board, analogous to a corporate board of directors, for each national conference. In November 1966 all the bishops of the United States met at the Catholic University of America in Washington, D.C., to reorganize what had been called the National Catholic Welfare Conference and to organize, in its place, the new National Conference of Catholic Bishops. At that meeting forty bishops were elected to serve on the new administrative board. Archbishop Binz was elected to this board. My election was a surprise, at least to me. I was the youngest of the forty members and one of the few auxiliary bishops chosen.

As an administrative board member, I was named vice chairman of the press department. In this role I quickly became aware that most bishops were paranoid about the press. Some were convinced that news personnel were the enemy. I had an entirely different perspective. I had never been betrayed by a journalist. I considered myself, after a fashion, to be one of them. Possibly my experience in dealing with a college faculty had taught me the importance of candor, openness, and reliable evidence in dealing with controverted questions.

In those days the bishops' conference meeting was never open to the press. No stenographers, or even tape recorders, were allowed in the sessions. My job was to make notes of each day's meeting, issue a press release at the end of the day, and field questions during press conferences at noon and at 5:00 P.M. daily. In these sessions I was not allowed to name any bishop as spokesman for any position, nor to attribute any direct statement to any bishop. My task was to summarize the topics of discussion during the day and to report any decision reached by vote, but not to disclose that there was ever a minority opinion.

I thoroughly enjoyed these sessions. Reporters often pressed me for information I was unable to reveal. But I had the clear impression that they trusted me and that they realized I had a difficult job. They would often smile at my answers to some of their tough questions. On occasion they laughed. Even after six such semiannual, hand-to-hand combats, I still felt the press treated me and the bishops fairly.

Many bishops did not share my cordial feelings toward the press. One, Cardinal Francis McIntyre of Los Angeles, came to believe that I was in collusion with the press to put the bishops and the church in the worst possible light. In any week that the bishops' conference was in session, I could expect to find Cardinal McIntyre waiting for me on at least one morning, holding that day's copy of the *New York Times,* and demanding of me an explanation of something in Ted Fiske's column.

These exchanges with McIntyre were always earnest but never violent. He thought I told the press too much. I thought I told them too little. But we maintained a level of courtesy in our exchanges, even as we both became aware that in our hearts we each considered the other dead wrong on matters related to the press.

I recall going to the microphone during one of our closed sessions to ask the bishops to consider opening at least some of their meetings to the press. In response, Cardinal McIntyre's question to me was, "What possible good would result from admitting reporters to these meetings?" My too-quick reply ("It would improve the caliber of the debate by the bishops") was one I keenly regretted as soon as I said it.

CHAPTER THIRTEEN

# VIETNAM

As a pastor I had the sad duty to offer memorial Masses occasionally for families who had lost a son, a brother, or a father in Vietnam. In seeking to console them I found that my earlier unquestioning support for the war in Vietnam was eroding. I could no longer, in good conscience, assure any of these good people that their loved ones had died in a worthy cause. The change in my thinking about the war took place over the summer and fall of 1966.

July 1 that year, Cardinal Lawrence Shehan, archbishop of Baltimore, issued a pastoral letter about the war in Vietnam and raised the question of the morality of American participation in that conflict. His letter made a strong impression on me. It contrasted sharply with the pro-war positions advocated by most bishops and especially by Cardinal Francis Spellman of New York.

As bishop of the military ordinariate, Spellman was in charge of all Catholic chaplains in every branch of military service. He took this assignment seriously, recruited new chaplains annually in all the dioceses, and went to Vietnam to offer midnight Mass for the troops on Christmas Eve every year of that war until his death.

On September 27, 1966, Pope Paul VI sent a special fact-finding mission to Vietnam to explore with the resident Catholic bishops there the possibilities for a new peace initiative. This effort coincided with the first anniversary of the pope's visit to the United Nations and his impassioned plea there to end all wars. In a papal letter issued for the same anniversary, the pope again called on world leaders to end the war in Vietnam: "We cry to them in God's name to stop. . . . A settlement should be reached now."

Three months later, on Christmas Eve, 1966, offering midnight Mass for the troops at Cam Ranh Bay, Vietnam, Cardinal Spellman replied to those who would fault the American presence in Vietnam: "This war in Vietnam is, I believe, a war for civilization. Certainly it is not a war of our seeking. It is a war thrust upon us and we cannot yield to tyranny. We do hope and pray for victory; . . . for less than victory is inconceivable."

A "high Vatican source" was quoted on the wire services the next day saying that "Pope Paul does not share Cardinal Spellman's view.... As an impartial observer the pope feels that a negotiated peace, rather than a military victory by either side, is the way to end the war."

The unwillingness of the American bishops to part company with Spellman on the issue of the war prompted Robert McAfee Brown, then a professor of religion at Stanford University, to accuse them in an open letter published in *Commonweal* (February 17, 1967) of failing in their duties as Christian leaders. By then my support for the war was all but gone. Nonetheless I felt obligated to defend the bishops and devoted one of my first "Pilgrim Church" columns to telling Brown that the bishops had no obligation to follow his style for protesting the war.

Good Christian and good theologian that he is, Brown responded to me by offering to change his style if by so doing he and the bishops could help end the war. He was clearly right. The issue was not one of style. It was one of substance. And on that question the Catholic bishops of the United States, with Cardinal Spellman as their leader, were on the wrong side, at least by their massive silence.

This exchange with Brown forced me to admit that he, a Presbyterian, was saying exactly what Pope Paul had been saying clearly for two years.

Stung by Brown and spurred by his public statements, I joined a group of Catholic educators and college presidents in signing an open letter asking all American Catholics to review our country's role in Vietnam. Citing "indiscriminate bombing, the needless destruction of human life," and massive injury to civilian populations, our letter, published at our expense in eight diocesan papers on Easter Sunday, March 24, stopped short of saying that the war was immoral, but clearly implied that it was.

Some of the other signers of that letter were Sister Ann Ida Gannon, B.V.M., president of Mundelein College in Chicago; Sister Jacqueline Grennan, president of Webster Groves College in Missouri; Father Colman Barry, O.S.B., president of St. John's University in Minnesota; Dr. George Shuster, assistant to the president of the University of Notre Dame; Monsignor John Tracy Ellis, professor of history at the Catholic University of America; and Father Joseph Fichter, S.J., professor of sociology at Harvard.

The publication of that letter marked a turning point for me. It put my opinion of the war into the public record, and it gave a signal to pro-war advocates that my academic confreres and I were fair game

for them. My friend and classmate Father John R. Roach, now the retired archbishop of St. Paul and Minneapolis, then the headmaster of
St. Thomas Academy, felt obligated to say in his school paper that our
letter was "a gross injustice" to the American traditions of patriotism
and loyalty. My friend and former student Father Marvin O'Connell,
who had delivered the sermon at my ordination as a bishop, writing
in his syndicated weekly column, labeled our carefully restrained petition "hysterical" and grandly told us that all it did was "muddy the
waters" of national public discussion about the war. I did not know
at that time that Cardinal Spellman and Cardinal McIntyre had, separately, called Archbishop Vagnozzi, apostolic delegate in the United
States, to lodge formal complaints with him about the impropriety of
my signing the Easter letter. On April 12, at the spring meeting of all
the bishops in Chicago, Cardinal Spellman, walking slowly and being
helped by his auxiliary, Bishop Terence Cooke, came up to me, put his
arm in mine as we left the meeting hall and said, "Young man, I deeply
regret that you and I are on opposite sides of the war in Vietnam."
I replied, "Your Eminence, your regret is no greater than mine." He
smiled, patted my shoulder, and walked away. I was touched by the
courtesy of the exchange.

Spellman and I were only acquaintances, not close friends. On November 11, 1965, during Vatican II, we had traveled together by car
from Rome to Anzio, where we concelebrated Mass to honor the
Americans who had given their lives on that bloody battlefield in World
War II. That visit was my longest and closest personal contact with
him. Francis Spellman was a decent man. He exemplified admirably
the virtues of loyalty and patriotism which my immigrant Irish father
and Spellman's immigrant Irish father cherished so deeply. He also respected each of his brother bishops in a special way. I believed him
when he said that he regretted our being on different sides of a moral
question we both considered important.

In the spring of 1967 I was invited by the chief of chaplains of the
United States Air Force to bring the sacrament of confirmation to all
the bases in the Fifth Air Force, which stretches from Hawaii to Japan.
Over a span of three weeks I confirmed and offered Mass at USAF
bases in Hawaii at Honolulu, in Japan at Yokota, Fucho, Nagasaki, and
Misawa, in Okinawa at Naha, in Taiwan at Tai Chung, at Clark Field
in the Philippines, in Guam and again in Honolulu. This trip through
the Pacific renewed my admiration for the pastoral ministries of military chaplains but opened my eyes to the enormous human costs of the
war in Vietnam.

On each base my days were usually free. The confirmation ceremony was most often an evening event, after duty hours for military personnel. At Yokota air base in Japan and at Clark Field in the Philippines I spent my afternoons visiting and helping to unload the giant C-130 hospital planes which flew casualties to these bases from Vietnam. At Clark I saw an entire hospital ward filled with blind veterans and one filled with soldiers who had lost one or both legs. By then I had concluded that the war in Vietnam was immoral and indefensible. Close contact with the casualties of that war merely reinforced my growing doubts about it.

My opposition to the war was by then well known. This fact set up some tension between me and a few of the chaplains who were my hosts. They were always courteous to me. After all I was their guest. I was also a bishop and, incidentally, a temporary GS-16 (the equivalent of a brigadier general), traveling under military orders with my own executive jet and two air force pilots to fly me around the Pacific. But on more than one occasion long lapses in our clerical conversations followed any chance reference to Pope Paul's opposition to the war.

As a matter of principle I never discussed my stand on the war with Archbishop Binz. I had the impression that he wanted it that way. Binz was a social liberal and an ecclesiastical conservative. When I went to Selma at the invitation of Martin Luther King, Jr., I never asked permission of Binz nor informed him of the trip in advance. On my return I sensed that he agreed both with my going there and with my not seeking his prior approval for the trip.

Whatever Archbishop Binz learned about my growing concern over the war he read in the papers. That way he was free to endorse or reject any of my views. But I must record here that he never once even hinted to me that he disagreed with my stand on Vietnam. He was much too careful an ecclesiastic to take a public stand on such a touchy topic. Binz had *Romanità*.

Sometime in April 1967, probably while I was flying around the Pacific, Binz wrote a confidential letter to the pope, asking that a coadjutor-archbishop be appointed as his assistant, with the right of succession, on grounds that ill health would probably force him to retire before the mandatory retirement age of seventy-five. I knew nothing of this letter. Had I known of it, I might have avoided some embarrassment that summer.

Early in June 1967 Rome announced that Archbishop Vagnozzi, apostolic delegate in the United States, had been named a Cardinal and would receive that honor at a consistory in St. Peter's on June 26.

Knowing that this elevation signaled the end of Vagnozzi's term as apostolic delegate in Washington, the American bishops scheduled a going-away dinner in his honor.

I was puzzled when Archbishop Binz asked me to take his place at this testimonial banquet in Washington. Binz liked testimonial dinners. Unaware that he, citing his recent and recurring illnesses, had asked Rome to name his successor, I gladly flew off to Washington for an evening of fine food and a few salubrious toasts at the Madison Hotel. About fifty bishops attended. It was a most pleasant evening.

Just before dessert one of the aides to the apostolic delegate came to my table to tell me that the delegate wished to speak with me privately after dinner. As the crowd left the dining room the delegate and I walked to the end of the head table and sat down. We were then the only persons in the room.

He began by asking about the health of Archbishop Binz. I assured him that Binz was in excellent health. He seemed surprised. I had seen Binz the day before and thought he was in great shape.

It soon became clear that the purpose of our little visit was not to discuss the health of my archbishop. Coming quickly to the point, Vagnozzi told me that Cardinal Spellman and Cardinal McIntyre were very unhappy about my public criticism of the war in Vietnam. I already knew that Spellman did not share my views on the war. But how did McIntyre get into the dialog? Vagnozzi told me that McIntyre had called him to say that my public statements on the war had embarrassed the bishops' conference and that I had to be silenced. I was appalled that McIntyre would say this and that the delegate would endorse it.

Vagnozzi made it clear that he was giving me a friendly warning. He had ordained me a bishop and may have felt some responsibility for me, but at that moment he was putting me on notice that any more public statements from me about the war would injure my future career as a bishop. In his words, "You could have a brilliant career in the church. You could become an archbishop. But you cannot afford to antagonize the cardinal archbishops of New York and Los Angeles."

Taking his arguments in order I said that I did not aspire to be an archbishop and that, in my opinion, the morality of the war in Vietnam was an entirely separate question from my future career as a bishop. Taking the initiative I reminded the delegate of the several specific instances in which Pope Paul VI had clearly spoken out against the war (at the U.N., at Fatima, in his encyclicals). Warming to my theme I told him that he had been misled by Spellman and McIntyre and that he should take his lead from the pope, not from them.

This response flustered him. He quickly denied that his views differed from the pope's. I said that I thought they did and that, in my opinion, more American bishops should challenge Spellman and McIntyre openly on the war. Clearly he had not expected such a reaction from me. He rose from the table and told me once more that if I persisted in my criticism of the war I would injure my future career as a bishop. I had no response.

We walked to his waiting car in silence. Cardinal Patrick O'Boyle, archbishop of Washington, was waiting for us at the curb. After Vagnozzi entered the car, O'Boyle turned to me, embraced me, and said, "Coraggio." Did O'Boyle know why Vagnozzi had taken me aside? Presumably he did. Otherwise why would he urge me to have courage?

On my return to Minnesota I reported to Archbishop Binz all that had happened. He carefully refrained from discussing further with me the admonition given me by Vagnozzi. I have always felt that my taking Binz's place at that testimonial banquet was a diplomatic method for the delegate to get me to Washington without summoning me and to deliver an oral warning to me without leaving any carbon copies.

I told Archbishop Binz that I was appalled at the delegate's linking my future promotions in the hierarchy directly with my future silence on Vietnam. In all this I knew I was making Binz very uncomfortable. By then I had come to believe that he liked me as a person and wished me well as a bishop. But he wanted no trouble with cardinals, especially McIntyre. Without intending it I was drawing him into a debate which he did not relish and in which one day he would be forced to take sides. That day was still more than a year away.

Within a month of my visit with the delegate I was invited to join a new national coalition, "Negotiation Now," organized to press for a settlement in Vietnam. Again, without telling my archbishop, I added my name to the list of clerics and laity who signed a full-page advertisement in the *New York Times* on July 9, 1967. This time I was not the only bishop listed. Bishop John J. Dougherty, president of Seton Hall University and auxiliary bishop of Newark, New Jersey, and Bishop Victor J. Reed, later archbishop of Oklahoma City, were cosigners. By then a new apostolic delegate, Archbishop Luigi Raimondi, had been named to succeed Vagnozzi. I was not anxious to be or to be perceived as deliberately disobeying the warning Vagnozzi had taken such pains to deliver to me in person. But, to my knowledge, Binz, Spellman, McIntyre, and I (and maybe Cardinal O'Boyle) were the only persons who knew of the warning Vagnozzi had given me.

In conscience, however, I felt obliged to challenge the popular opinion so explicitly stated by Cardinal Spellman at his midnight Mass on Christmas Eve, 1966, that victory was the only acceptable goal of our role in Vietnam. In my view victory in that endless war was no longer possible for either party. A negotiated peace was the only logical option, and the sooner the better. Pope Paul VI had already stated this view as his own on this question.

On August 15, 1967, Archbishop Paul J. Hallinan, archbishop of Atlanta, added his signature to the proponents of "Negotiation Now." Hallinan was then very ill with cancer and was to die within a year. His support for our petition gave us encouragement. The silence of the American bishops on the war in Vietnam at that late date was still deafening.

On August 4, 1967, the Vatican announced that Bishop Leo C. Byrne, of Wichita, Kansas, was to be the new coadjutor-archbishop of St. Paul and Minneapolis, with the right to succeed Archbishop Binz whenever he should choose to retire. The appointment was well received. Binz, Byrne, and I were then fellow members of the administrative board of the bishops' national conference. Binz was pleased at the prospect of turning over his administrative duties to Archbishop Byrne. I welcomed our new archbishop because of the energetic leadership he promised for the diocese and for the personal encouragement I hoped he could give me in my relations with superiors I had no desire to offend. On the day of his installation at the St. Paul cathedral, September 27, Byrne was asked by a reporter how he felt about my endorsement of "Negotiation Now." He smiled and told the reporter, "The situation is well in hand." I still do not know what he meant.

Wisely or not, I had decided to handle the war question with Byrne just as I had with Binz. Hence I never raised it with him in private, considering it prudent to leave him free to say that my views were not his and that I had never discussed them with him. He never took the initiative to discuss the war with me. Hence I assumed that he was comfortable with this arrangement.

On October 11, 1967, in the Caucus Room of the Old Senate Building in Washington I chaired a national meeting of "Negotiation Now," convened to present to any members of Congress who would listen our urgent plea for a negotiated peace in Vietnam. The meeting was well attended and widely reported in the press.

One never knows whether efforts like that have any effect. In reviewing the record now I can only say that, effective or not, I considered my testimony then to be a serious moral obligation. My friend

Father Marvin O'Connell felt otherwise. Writing about "Negotiation Now," he called the three bishops and the one archbishop who endorsed it "amateurs." We never claimed to be professionals. We merely said publicly what we thought in private about the war in order to face ourselves each morning in the mirror.

In January 1968 the national coalition Clergy and Laity Concerned about Vietnam (CALCAV), on whose board I served, invited me to take part in a prayer service in Washington, D.C., to be billed as a memorial to all Americans who had given their lives in battle throughout our history. Dr. Martin Luther King, Jr., Rabbi Abraham Heschel, and I were to be the speakers at this assembly, scheduled for February 6, 1968, at the Tomb of the Unknown Soldier in Arlington National Cemetery.

The day before this date we were notified by the Department of the Interior, the agency responsible for all national cemeteries, that our request for a permit to march and to pray at Arlington had been denied. The reason for the denial was the fear, among federal officials, that our speeches might be inflammatory and that our march might turn into violence.

We petitioned Interior to reconsider and promised to conduct the entire march in silence, if they would allow Dr. King, Rabbi Heschel, and me the privilege of announcing the beginning and the end of three minutes of silent prayer, once our marchers reached the Tomb. This permission was granted.

About three hundred persons gathered at the main gate of Arlington on the morning of February 6. We distributed handbills explaining the rules we had accepted for the occasion. In total silence and in good order we then marched, six abreast, up the hill to the tomb, led by two flag bearers carrying the Stars and Stripes, a rabbi carrying the scrolls of the Torah, a minister carrying the Holy Bible, and each marcher carrying a small American flag.

At the tomb Dr. King called out in a clear voice, "In this period of absolute silence, let us pray." After three minutes of silent prayer, Rabbi Abraham Heschel said, "Eli, Eli, Lama Azavtani," the beginning of the Twenty-Second Psalm in Hebrew, known to Christians as Christ's call on the cross, "My God, my God, why hast Thou forsaken me?" I then signaled aloud that our three minutes were ended: "Let us go in peace, Amen." Again, in a column of six abreast we slowly and silently walked back down the hill to the gate and into our waiting buses. The entire ceremony passed without incident.

Reviewing the record of the war and of our petitions to end it I have no regrets, either about the substance of our pleas or the style in which we presented them. This statement may smack of hubris to some readers. It is still my very firm opinion that active participation by the United States in the war in Vietnam was a mistake from the beginning of that interminable blood-letting.

## Chapter Fourteen

# CHANGING STYLES

Vatican II did not, in fact could not, alter fundamental Catholic doctrine. But it did call for dramatic changes in Catholic style — in the liturgy, in dealing with other Christians, in dealing with non-Christians, in addressing human culture, in missionary activity, in the role of bishops, in dealing with pluralism, diversity, and human freedom, in developing new ministries, and in expanding the role of the laity in the Catholic communion.

A change in style, for anyone, is not easy. Consider teachers who decide to alter their style of instruction, or parents who want to change the style of their relationship to their spouses or children. The easy part of such a change is the decision. The tough part is the execution.

The new style of religious practice called for by Vatican II put an enormous strain on even the most zealous Catholics. With very little notice they were asked to modify deeply ingrained traditions of piety and practice.

It is no exaggeration to say that the adjournment of Vatican II in Rome marked the beginning of the vastly more difficult second phase of the Council: making the decrees of that assembly intelligible and attractive to the clergy and laity of the world. This task proved to be far more complex than even the most farsighted bishops could have anticipated as they left Rome in December 1965.

A high priority in this second phase of the Council had to be some kind of extended dialog between the returning bishops and the clergy. In Rome the bishops had received a crash course on what the church expected from them. They in turn had to find new ways to share the insights they gained from this course with their priests and people back home.

One forum available for this dialog was the annual spiritual retreat of the clergy. For three or four days each year all priests are obligated by canon law to replace their usual daily routine with a regimen of quiet, prayer, and meditation on the duties of their priestly state. Most often this is done in a seminary or monastery away from their parish, campus, or office.

Acting on the premise that priests on retreat would be particularly well disposed for serious dialog about Vatican II, I devised a series of conferences, based on the decrees of the Council, to be the framework of a three- or four-day retreat for priests. Historically the regimen of most retreats called for four or five daily sermon-type presentations by the retreat master. The priests in attendance would use these talks as the basis for further private meditation on their own priestly ministry. In the traditional retreat there was little provision for exchange between the retreat master and the priests, except at mealtime or during one-on-one counseling sessions. Departing from this format, I devised a daily retreat schedule of four conferences, three of which were commentaries by me on selected documents of Vatican II, and one of which was an open discussion by all in attendance on any topics they would choose by ballot.

This concept was warmly received by most priests and bishops. Some did prefer the older "me and Jesus" mode of personal meditation and prayer, but invitations poured in to me once it was known that I was available as a retreat master. One retreat experience stands out in my memory. It took place at the lovely mountaintop Benedictine seminary, Mount Angel, Oregon, in the summer of 1966, at the invitation of Archbishop Edward D. Howard of Portland.

The day before the retreat began I explained to Archbishop Howard that the priests would decide by ballot each day what topic or topics they wished to discuss in the evening conference. But the next day when I informed him that the first topic chosen by his priests was celibacy, he expressed some reservations. The difficulty with my new retreat formula was that the retreat master was no longer in control of the entire process. He had to become a listener and a responder. Uneasy at the prospect of being drawn into a dialog on celibacy and not knowing the direction it would take, the archbishop said he preferred not to attend the session that evening but asked that I report to him later on what was said.

I would discover, after leading five such retreats for priests in the year ahead, that celibacy would be the number one topic chosen for dialog in each diocese I visited. But at Mount Angel in 1966 I faced this topic, as a retreat theme, for the first time. I shared some of Archbishop Howard's uneasiness about opening up a topic on which canon law was already firmly fixed and allowed no latitude for variation. But I also felt obligated to keep my word to the priests, to discuss any topic concerning their priestly life that they would choose.

That evening the discussion followed a pattern I would soon see in other dioceses: about 10 percent of the priests were firmly and deeply committed to the present discipline of mandatory celibacy as a necessary condition for ordination to the priesthood; another 10 percent were equally eloquent in their plea for celibacy as an option but not an essential condition for ordination; and the remaining 80 percent listened to both sides of the argument and said nothing.

As we came to the end of the discussion, a senior pastor, sitting up front in the chapel, rose to speak. Till then he had taken no part in the dialog. I knew at once he was Irish-born when he addressed me as "Your Lordship," a form of address to bishops sometimes still in vogue in Ireland. I also knew at once that the speaker was a favorite of all the priests in the chapel. Their eyes and their laughter quickly told me that they loved him as he addressed them with the salutation "My lads."

He began by describing his boyhood home in Ireland where neighbors were close and numerous, even in the country. Ordained "for the missions" he came straight to Oregon from the seminary and was assigned to an isolated mountain parish where he was so lonesome he would cry on occasion.

In the seminary he had been counseled to overcome loneliness by prayer, study, and pastoral visitations to his people. Turning to me he said, "Your Lordship, I did all of those things. I had lots of time to pray and I used it well. And I studied. And I can say that I learned more theology in the mountains of Oregon than I did in the Irish seminary. The lads here will tell you that I'm as well read as any of them (more laughter). And I visited — every parishioner, believer, nonbeliever, lumberjack, and sheepherder in that lonely mountain territory. I had no one to cook my meals or keep my house. I think the people I visited often thought I came by to get a home-cooked meal. And you know, sometimes maybe they were right.

"In the seminary we were taught to go to confession faithfully once each week and to cultivate the friendship of our neighboring priests. The nearest priest to me was a hundred miles away. In the winter, weeks would go by when I would never see another priest, much less make my confession.

"After three years in that parish I was promoted (more laughter). I went to a second parish almost as isolated as the first. And I got by there because I did what I was told to do in the seminary. I prayed, I studied, and I visited anybody who would let me call in. Your Lordship, for awhile there I even took to the drink. But I gave it up. I've got a weak stomach (more laughter).

"And now my time as a priest is nearly finished. I'm the pastor of a fine parish in a fine city. And I thank God for a long and useful ministry. But (turning to face the other priests) I put to you all a few questions, Where is Father Jimmy Ryan tonight? Or Joe Toolen, or Mike Mc-Grade, or John Flynn? [These names are fictitious]. Are they alive or dead? Are they drunk or sober? None of you know. And I don't know what's become of them since they drifted away from us."

The mood of the audience was suddenly serious. I knew that the speaker was naming absent priests who had abandoned their ministry. He continued, "I think it's time for the Catholic Church to consider the option of marriage for priests who choose to be ministers of the gospel and to be married. And I think the lads I've just named to you would be good, faithful, and sober priests sitting beside us in this chapel tonight if they had a good wife and a clean house and a warm meal to come home to at the end of the day.

"I think it's time for a change, lads, for priests who would find the ministry and marriage compatible. Ah, I don't mean myself. Sure who would have the likes of me? (very subdued laughter). But for some the choice should be given. And I think it's time for a change." He turned, bowed slightly to me, and sat down.

I never learned the name of the eloquent Irish speaker. When he finished the chapel was silent. There was nothing anyone could add to the touching testimony of this honorable and devoted pastor. We said our concluding prayer and adjourned in silence.

A year later at the annual meeting of the national conference of bishops, when the text of a proposed pastoral letter, written by Bishop John Wright, referred to priests who had left the ministry as "derelicts," I rose to protest the term and in so doing shared with the assembled bishops the essence of the monolog by the Irish pastor from Oregon. I think I embarrassed the bishops by retelling this story. As I walked back to my place in the hall, the chairman thanked me politely and moved quickly to the next item on the agenda.

# CHAPTER FIFTEEN

# "THE NEW AMERICAN CATHOLIC"

The Second Vatican Council prompted the media to increase their coverage of religion in general and of the Catholic Church in particular. In October 1967 the National Broadcasting Company decided to produce a one-hour documentary on the changes wrought within the American Catholic community as a result of Vatican II. Stuart Schulberg, then NBC's producer for Dave Garroway's *Today* show, was named to produce the documentary.

Bishop John A. Donovan, bishop of Toledo, Ohio, was then chairman of the Bishops' National Committee on Radio and Television. This committee maintained a New York City office, called the National Catholic Office for Radio and Television (NCORT), the purpose of which was to encourage liaison with producers working in the media, to insure that their coverage of things Catholic was accurate. NCORT had no production facilities. It was merely a Catholic resource for the networks and independent producers. NCORT, hearing of NBC's plans, offered its services to Stuart Schulberg and gave him a list of persons to consult in preparing the program. My name was on that list.

Schulberg and two of his writers came to see me at St. Helena's. We spent the better part of a day discussing Vatican II, its origins, and its results. As I commented on the different documents issued by the Council I would name the scholars or experts who had drafted these statements and others who, in my opinion, were best able to discuss them accurately on camera for NBC. In the course of that day's visit I probably named thirty persons, lay and clerical, male and female, whom I thought Schulberg might interview. In naming these persons I carefully identified spokespersons on both sides of any controverted questions.

At the end of the day Schulberg asked me to be one of the persons interviewed on camera about the Council. I declined and urged him to recruit some senior bishop, possibly Archbishop John Dearden of Detroit or Bishop Fulton J. Sheen of Rochester, New York, who were well known to the general public and credible spokesmen for the Catholic Church.

I admitted privately to Schulberg that I had a growing concern that my official assignment as press officer for the episcopal conference was giving me too much exposure and that I thought it prudent to cultivate a lower profile. I promised to continue to help him and his staff, and he withdrew his request for me to be interviewed on camera in the series.

Within the next several weeks I learned from my daily correspondence that some persons whom NCORT had recommended to Schulberg were being interviewed and that the production was moving along. Next I received a telephone call from Charles Reilly, executive director of NCORT, who reported that the NBC project was nearly finished but that it still needed some knowledgeable Catholic person to act as host or interlocutor to connect its different segments.

I could see it coming. Bishop Donovan and his staff were building their case to ask me to serve as the interlocutor for the show. Sure enough. Schulberg had told the bishop that I had been of great help to him and his crew and that they wanted me to present on camera the "bridge" between the different interviews. Schulberg had also told Bishop Donovan that I did not want this assignment.

John Donovan (now deceased) and I were good friends. I called him to discuss this invitation and jokingly told him that he was a stalking horse for NBC. To the contrary, he said that he was asking me to do this as a favor to the national conference of bishops. He thought I would do a good job, and he wanted to be sure that the episcopal conference could not be faulted for lack of cooperation with the network.

Again I proposed the names of Archbishop Dearden and Bishop Sheen. Donovan admitted that each of them had been asked and had declined. Hence I was at least NBC's third choice. When Donovan put his request to me a second time, on the grounds that some bishop had to do it and that he was asking me to do it on behalf of the episcopal conference, I could not refuse.

All smiles, Stuart Schulberg and his crew came back to St. Helena's the next week, this time with cameras. They televised part of our Sunday Mass and spent a day filming clips of me building verbal bridges between the several interviews which they already had on tape.

I taped my segment of the show one day in our rectory, without seeing any of the other interviews which would be the substance of the final narrative. I was impressed with the professional caliber of Schulberg and his staff. At no time did they try to slant or influence what I had to say. I knew that they had interviewed liberals and conservatives and that, on balance, they had recruited more exponents of change than of tradition. The original purpose of the documentary was to focus on change in the church. Its subtitle was "The Changing Church." Hence I saw my role in the production as that of a moderator, in the literal sense.

Titled "The New American Catholic," the show was first televised nationally on June 21, 1968. The next day Cardinal McIntyre issued a strong press release in Los Angeles criticizing the production as "erroneous, misleading, and unauthorized." Blaming me, by name, for my part in the production, he said, "Bishop Shannon was not speaking for the people of God." It did not surprise me that McIntyre did not like the show. Before, during, and after Vatican II he was repeatedly on record warning the church of the dangers inherent in any kind of change. Writing in 1964, John Cogley, then religion editor of the *New York Times,* had said of McIntyre: "He has been described by more than one Vatican observer as the most reactionary prelate in the church, bar none — not even those of the Curia."

What did surprise me about McIntyre's criticism of the NBC show was that he found it so offensive that he denounced it and me by name in a press release issued explicitly for this purpose. There is a well-observed fraternal code of mutual protection among the bishops. Cardinal Spellman, I had learned, respected it. McIntyre did not.

Because of scheduling conflicts, KSTP, then our local NBC station in Minnesota, did not broadcast "The New American Catholic" until July 7. Forewarned by McIntyre's criticism of the show, I watched it with great care and with a note pad and pencil at hand. It did, as I expected, focus on changes among American Catholics occasioned by the dialog and the decrees of Vatican II. But it was, in my opinion, a balanced, accurate, lively production. I could see nothing in either its matter or its manner which would offend even the most conservative Catholic. The reviews were favorable.

John Dart, reviewing it for the *Los Angeles Times,* in lavish terms that would return to haunt me, said, "The Spirit [of excitement and spirituality] was captured superbly in 'The New American Catholic....' The narrator was articulate, straightforward Bishop James Shannon, another hero. The auxiliary bishop of St. Paul and Minneapolis has emerged as the most sought-after liaison between the U.S. Catholic hierarchy and the public. The choice for narrator could not have been better." George Gent, a Catholic, reviewing it for the *New York Times,* implied that he held personal views opposing some of the changes occurring in the church, but also said, "The closest thing to a balanced perspective was provided by the Most Reverend James Shannon ... who spoke of the current tensions from what might be termed a moderate position." Good enough. I had defined my role as that of a moderator in a serious dialog on which different persons held different but legitimate positions.

After weighing the question I decided not to respond personally to Cardinal McIntyre's criticism. After all, he had not sent it directly to me. I did not know precisely what he found objectionable in the separate segments of the show. And I knew I would be seeing him shortly at a scheduled meeting in Washington, D.C., of the board of trustees of the Catholic University of America, of which he was a member and to which I had just been elected in April of that year.

Bishop Donovan wrote and Father Theodore Hesburgh sent a telegram to tell me they thought the show was well done and to thank me for doing it. Their kind words and the favorable reviews balanced, in my mind, the criticism from Cardinal McIntyre.

What I did not know then was that on June 24 Cardinal McIntyre had also sent a stinging letter to Archbishop John Dearden, president of the National Conference of Catholic Bishops, denouncing me and Bishop Victor J. Reed, then the bishop of Oklahoma City–Tulsa, for our participation on camera in the documentary. That letter also went to the apostolic delegate, to every archbishop in the country, and to all the bishops in California. I first learned of it from Bishop Donovan, who received a copy of it because of his role as the bishop in charge of NCORT. No copy was sent to me, but each of my archbishops, I was to learn some time later, had received copies. They did not share these with me.

The letter faulted the program for statements on authority by Father John McKenzie, S.J., then a professor at the University of Notre Dame; for statements on celibacy by Donald J. Thorman (a layman, the publisher of the *National Catholic Reporter*); for a joyful liturgical service at the Catholic Community of John XXIII in Oklahoma City, which the cardinal considered "grossly lacking in ... reverence and respect"; and for a "considerable segment [which] showed pictures [filmed in Los Angeles] of the Immaculate Heart Community's departure from religious tradition and its obvious defiance of regulations and directives issued by the Sacred Congregation for Religious." McIntyre was then deep in confrontation with this much admired religious community headquartered in his archdiocese.

The letter reserved its heaviest blows for me:

"While Bishop Shannon, as commentator, did not directly advocate a definite opinion on any of the divergences or deviations from ecclesiastical precedent and tradition which were presented, the mere fact of his participation, and that of Bishop Reed, constituted open approval of these deviations as far as the viewing public was concerned.

"It was evident that the very title of the program and its mode of presentation, with its emphasis on the word 'new,' and its consequent implication of a split between the 'old' or 'traditional' church and the 'new' church, was an initial attempt to suggest to the public mind a spirit of schism in Catholic belief and practice, and an implicit appeal for public support of such a schism.

"I feel that the participation of two Bishops in this program was an exercise of exceedingly poor taste and judgment. They assumed the right to speak nationally on matters and issues upon which they had no authority to speak nationally. Surely, from their presence on the program, the ordinary listener would assume that the program was authentic and deduce that it represented the mind of the bishops of the nation and had their official approval.

"Accordingly, I ventured to issue a statement to the secular press here, a copy of which I enclose herewith. Frankly, I am shocked at Bishop Shannon's participation in this program, particularly since for all practical purpose at the St. Louis Conference of the United States Bishops, he appeared to be the authorized press spokesman for the body of the bishops. In fact, he has been very active with the press; the Religious Editor of the *Los Angeles Times* recently stated that Bishop Shannon 'has emerged as the most sought-after liaison between the United States Hierarchy and the public.' Leaving aside the question as to the source of the authority upon which he has assumed this role, the fact remains that his participation in this program, at least in the mind of the press, is interpreted as authentic, authorized and representative of the position of the bishops of the United States.

"I would maintain that the program induces schism. It should be disapproved by the Bishops as a body. It was not authorized. In fact, the opinions and ideas promulgated in the program were not in accordance with votes and decisions of the National Conference of Bishops on the matters therein treated. They were not in accordance with the pronouncements of Pope Paul VI on the matter of celibacy. They were not in accordance with the regulations of the Sacred Congregation for Religious on the matter of the Religious discipline and the holy habit of nuns.

"Therefore, why should not the false impressions created by this program be corrected?

"You are free to use this protest as you may see fit. I consider the situation as serious — very serious in its potential effects upon the faith and spiritual tranquility of our people. I regret that I am compelled to express my views on this matter so strongly and positively but the circumstances seem to justify action."

Archbishop Dearden asked Bishop Donovan's help in framing an appropriate response to Cardinal McIntyre. On July 1 the NCORT staff, at Donovan's request, prepared a memorandum reciting the history of the NBC production and of their and my respective roles in it, a copy of which was sent, through Dearden, to McIntyre. That memorandum reads as follows:

### BACKGROUND MEMORANDUM CONCERNING RECENT NEWS SPECIAL ENTITLED "THE NEW AMERICAN CATHOLIC"

In early October, 1967, the staff of the National Catholic Office for Radio and Television (NCORT) learned that the NBC News Department was planning a TV special on changes within the church. For this venture it was using as a consultant a St. Louis priest, familiar with broadcast production efforts, who was no longer exercising his ministry (and who entered an invalid marriage in November of 1967). Further information came to NCORT that this contemplated Special would involve to a great extent ex-priests, ex-nuns, secretly married priests and discontented laity who had left the church. The theme was to be that the church was suffering great losses because it was no longer relevant to today's people and their needs. This information was at least partially confirmed by a news item which appeared in the *New York Times* of October 26, 1967.

Disturbed by these developments, NCORT contacted the producer and suggested a meeting, to which the producer agreed. He disclaimed the contents of the article referred to above and said he was open to suggestions. It was recommended to him to do the program on the basis of changes *within* the church, ignoring the views of those who had left. Vatican II, it was pointed out, was actually being soundly implemented by the church in the United States without any attack on its doctrinal foundations.

At the meeting of the hierarchy in November of 1967, arrangements were made for the producer to interview a number of bishops. (Unfortunately, these interviews were omitted from the show's final version). After this was done, the producer asked for the names of some dioceses where changes were notably taking place. Oklahoma-Tulsa was mentioned and he made his own contacts. He also inquired about the I.H.M. controversy in Los Angeles and was referred to His Eminence, Cardinal McIntyre, Bishop John Ward and Father John Urban, the archdiocesan director of radio and television. Their addresses were given to him.

The producer became acquainted with Bishop Shannon at the hierarchy's meeting referred to above. Sometime later, at his request, NCORT put him in touch with the bishop and arrangements were made for him to interview Bishop Shannon in Minneapolis. The latter's comments were then threaded throughout the News Special. The Bishop, of course, in no way considered himself to be a spokesman for the church, nor did the producer. In fact, the bishop did not actually see the remainder of the program until it appeared on the network. This is standard procedure in this type of producing.

It is well to remind ourselves here that the editorial area of any show of this nature cannot be invaded without charges of attempted censorship. Even if NCORT was aware of the total composition of this Special (its only information came through News Releases) and judged it to be one-sided, it could at most only offer suggestions and those in a very delicate manner. Otherwise it would act counter to one of its own publicly stated nonfunctions: it will not serve as a censorship office.

A rereading of this memorandum suggests a possible interpretation by readers that NCORT is unhappy with its participation in the preparation of this News Special and disowns any encouragement given to Bishop Shannon to have a part in it.

This is completely untrue. NCORT is convinced that it acted in the church's interest in the circumstances. It feels that Bishop Shannon's comments were realistic, moderate and perceptive. It is persuaded that despite the differences which separate so many members of the church today, this News Special will in the end benefit the church immensely.

It must also be remembered that a producer does not control the news releases of his network. To build up a show, the Public Relations Department of a network may unfortunately attribute to a participant a competence or delegation he does not possess. There is need of actual proof before stating that a participant personally claimed such a status or led others to believe that he was so empowered. NCORT, for instance, never entertained the thought that Bishop Shannon spoke for the entire hierarchy—for that matter, neither did Bishop Shannon—but it did regard him as a willing, knowledgeable, articulate and personable — TV-wise — commentator on the current church scene.

McIntyre was still not satisfied. He wrote to Dearden on July 8 and called the "unsigned" memorandum "inadequate, incomplete...(and not responsive to) the obvious points of my complaint." This time he explicitly told Dearden what kind of action he wanted: "I respectfully petition that a definite place be given on the agenda of our next meeting of the Coetus [i.e., the Conference of Bishops] to the study and discussion of this happening, its deductions and the possibility of consequences that can be most injurious. The impression received by the public with regard to the thinking and policy of the Bishops of the country is at stake. Are we advocating a 'New Church'? Are we rebuffing the Holy Father in his attitude on celibacy? Are we depriving ourselves of the authority of our respective offices and of our corporate body? We must provide against the repetition of this showing, and, further, against any similar programs."

On July 12 Archbishop Binz received a copy of McIntyre's letter of July 8 (his second) to Dearden and a copy of the NCORT memorandum of July 1. Binz called me at once and asked me to come to his home to discuss this correspondence.

Binz was concerned that this matter had escalated to the point where it would be on the agenda for the next meeting of the administrative board (i.e., the executive committee) of the National Conference. I was convinced that McIntyre's charges were so illusory and so unsupported that the bishops could not possibly take them or him seriously.

McIntyre was then eighty-two, seven years above the age at which Pope Paul VI had asked every bishop in the world to submit his resignation. I told Binz that I could not take McIntyre's defense of tradition and loyalty to Rome seriously in the light of his own obstinate refusal to comply with an explicit Vatican decree which bishops in every other nation had readily accepted.

I tracked through with Binz the separate allegations McIntyre had made in his two letters against the NBC show and against me. Each charge fell into one of two categories: either McIntyre had his facts wrong, or his unyielding allegiance to pre-Council customs (e.g., about nun's wearing apparel) blinded him to the legitimacy of several nondoctrinal changes in the church. In my zealous defense of NBC I came on a little too strong for my archbishop. I recall saying "McIntyre is a silly old man." Binz, always the archbishop, chided me, "Jim, you should not speak that way about him. He is a prince of the Holy Roman Church." Some prince!

At this point Binz decided to take me into his confidence on another related but more serious matter. As the archbishop of St. Paul and Minneapolis, he was the ranking prelate in the ten dioceses of Minnesota, South Dakota, and North Dakota. Typically, the appointment of a new bishop in any one of these states had to have his approval. His key role in this process gave him great but not final authority in deciding who would be named ordinaries (i.e., presiding bishops) in vacant dioceses.

It was public knowledge that Francis J. Schenk, bishop of Duluth, was then seriously ill. Binz then told me that Schenk's illness was terminal, that he had submitted his resignation to Rome, and that the process was underway to name his successor. As archbishop of the three-state province, Binz had then submitted my name to the apostolic delegate, with his personal recommendation that I be named coadjutor-bishop of Duluth, with the canonical right to succeed Schenk.

All this was a surprise to me. Everyone who knew Schenk liked him. It saddened me to learn that death was close for him.

I was not then particularly eager to be named bishop of any diocese. In spite of my periodic bouts with McIntyre I enjoyed my work and found the role of an auxiliary bishop satisfying. Binz and I were on cordial terms. Nonetheless I realized that after more than three years in that position it was probably time for me to move on.

Then Binz dropped the other shoe. In response to his endorsement of me, he had been told by the apostolic delegate that I could not possibly be promoted to Duluth because of the serious and repeated complaints McIntyre had lodged against me. My advancement in the church, he felt, would be an insult which McIntyre would not tolerate.

Binz assured me that he had done everything he could to help me. I believed him. He was clearly embarrassed to admit that the cardinal archbishop of Los Angeles had a veto power over the recommendations of the archbishop of St. Paul and Minneapolis on episcopal appointments within the state of Minnesota.

After a long silence, I asked, rather lamely, "Can McIntyre really do this to us?" Binz replied: "He's already done it. Archbishop Raimondi (the apostolic delegate) has told me that he cannot risk antagonizing McIntyre by approving your move to Duluth. A new bishop will be named there within the month, and whoever it is, it will not be you." I asked Binz how long McIntyre's veto power might last. He could not guess. He did say, quoting Raimondi, that my chance of being named to head any other diocese was negligible as long as McIntyre stayed in office and did not change his mind about me.

In retrospect it is chilling to recall that McIntyre did not resign until he was eighty-five, a full decade beyond the retirement age set by Pope Paul VI, and that he did not die until 1979. Only God knows whether he ever changed his mind about me.

I knew that Binz was reluctant that day to admit that McIntyre could and would override a senior archbishop and trample a junior auxiliary. Binz would never fault another bishop by name. He was appalled by McIntyre's ruthless style and he was embarrassed to let me glimpse this seamy side of ecclesiastical politics. As I left his home that night I felt more anguish for him than concern for my own career. Binz had to swallow hard to take McIntyre's heavy-handed intrusion into church affairs in Minnesota. Nonetheless he spoke not one negative word to me about McIntyre, then or ever.

The apostolic delegate announced on July 24, 1968, that Father Paul Anderson of Huron, South Dakota, was to be the new bishop in Duluth. I was delighted. Paul Anderson, now deceased, was the kind of bishop Jesus Christ had in mind when he put together the original team.

As the date for the administrative board meeting in Washington approached, it gave me some solace to realize that Archbishop Binz, Archbishop Byrne, and I were all members of that body. We could make some kind of joint defense against whatever attack McIntyre would mount. Granted, we were only three out of forty members. But Bishop John Donovan was also a member. I knew I could count on him to explain that I had become involved in the NBC project specifically at his request and on behalf of the episcopal conference.

Before we left for Washington Archbishop Binz asked me if I was prepared to defend the NBC production with the bishops and to answer McIntyre's specific charges against me. I assured him that I was. I knew then that one of the charges was that I had encouraged schism in the church. I did not know that McIntyre would raise the more sinister charge of heresy against me at our meeting in September.

In retrospect it is clear to me that Archbishop Binz was doing all he could to warn me not to take Cardinal McIntyre too lightly. In his heart Binz knew that McIntyre was abusing his authority and coming down much too hard on me. But Binz also knew that it was unwise for any bishop, young or old, to go one-on-one against McIntyre, no matter what the issue.

At 9:00 A.M. on September 17, 1968, the executive committee of the bishops' national conference met at their headquarters building in Washington. As usual, we were arranged classroom style, according to the alphabet, from front to back. The agenda scheduled Cardinal McIntyre's motion for discussion as the first item following our break for lunch.

At lunch Archbishop Binz called me aside and said that he had not slept well the night before. He asked if I would object if he returned to the hotel to rest instead of attending the afternoon meeting. My heart sank. He did not need my permission to leave the meeting. He was pulling out on me because he did not want to antagonize McIntyre by any defense he might offer of my part in the NBC program. I assured him that I would understand if he went back to the hotel to rest. He thanked me and said, "I have talked to Archbishop Leo Byrne. He will be at the meeting this afternoon to speak for you, if necessary."

After lunch Binz left for the hotel and the afternoon session was called to order. Archbishop Dearden, as chairman, recognized Cardinal McIntyre. I noticed at once that Archbishop Byrne was not in his place. I scanned the room. He was not there. For the first time the thought occurred to me that Binz and Byrne had decided, jointly or separately, that it was too risky, politically, for them to side with me against the cardinal.

McIntyre carefully recapitulated his objections to the NBC production: he had not given NBC permission to take any pictures in Catholic institutions in Los Angeles; he had refused their request for an interview with him; the sequence showing nuns at Immaculate Heart College in Hollywood, singing and wearing brightly colored dresses "at Mass," violated the rule of the sacred liturgy; the title of the documentary smacked of the heresy of "Americanism" which had been condemned by Pope Leo XIII in 1899; and furthermore, the second nationwide showing of the NBC documentary on August 30 in prime time "in response to public interest" was a deliberate insult to the Catholics of this country. The cardinal ended his remarks by asking the bishops to condemn the NBC documentary as subversive to the Catholic faith and to censure me for my youthful temerity in having participated as a bishop in such a damaging production, although the motion under discussion did not mention me by name.

Binz was right. McIntyre was a deadly adversary. I never dreamed he would raise the specter of heresy, nor that his oral remarks would focus so personally on me. When the cardinal was finished Bishop John Donovan rose to my defense. He urged the bishops to vote against the motion for two reasons: the NBC production presented a favorable and accurate image of American Catholics and legitimate changes in the church after Vatican II; and I had taken part in the production at his urgent insistence, against my own preference.

Archbishop Byrne was still not in the room. I continued to hope that he might arrive in time to help me. Bishop Fulton Sheen then asked to be recognized. I knew that he had been asked to act as narrator for the NBC documentary and hoped he might say a kind word for me. I was mistaken. His remarks focused on how demanding the television medium is for performers, especially for novices who are not acquainted with the skills and techniques necessary to be effective on camera and to fend off hostile interviewers. Till then no one had criticized my voice, gestures, or rhetorical style. He was doing so in such a way that, without reaching the charge of heresy, he was signalling his intention to vote in favor of the motion. His voice in that group, as with the public, carried great weight.

When no one else asked to speak, I rose to plead my case. In defense of the show, and in my own defense, I recapitulated the early and final stages of the production, stressing the scrupulous fairness of its producer, Stuart Schulberg, and his associates and my own desire to do a good job that would reflect favorably on the church.

I reminded the bishops that the so-called heresy of Americanism, by which Catholics in this country in the late nineteenth century had allegedly put their devotion to their country ahead of their devotion to the church, was recognized by historians as an illusion of anti-American French and Italian Catholics and that no definition of that "heresy" had ever been formulated by any of its critics. I also explained, directly to Cardinal McIntyre, that the sequence in the show picturing the singing nuns in bright colored dresses at Immaculate Heart College was not shot during Mass, as he had inferred, but during their community recreation period.

In closing I asked what purpose the motion under discussion would serve. Was it to put NBC on notice that any future production about Catholic life would require an imprimatur from some Catholic censor? We had no authority to make such a demand. Was it to warn viewers who had already seen the show that it taught what Cardinal McIntyre considered heresy? Or was it to make some kind of record to illustrate what Cardinal McIntyre considered my youthful temerity or my heretical proclivities? Later evidence would seem to show that having such a record to use against me was part of his plan.

As I was concluding my remarks, Archbishop Leo Byrne entered the room and took his place near the front. In closing I did not beg but I asked the bishops most earnestly to vote against Cardinal McIntyre's resolution.

As I sat down I hoped that Archbishop Byrne would ask to be recognized. He did not. As Archbishop Dearden prepared to call the question, I asked, as a courtesy to me, if the bishops would vote by raising their hands, not by their usual voice vote. Dearden agreed. McIntyre's resolution won by a vote of 13 to 7, with 8 abstentions. Archbishop Byrne did not vote. He explained, for the record, that he felt obligated to abstain because he had not been present to hear the discussion.

My great pride in being an American Catholic bishop suffered a blow that day from which it has never recovered. I could not know what was going through the minds of all the bishops in that room. One bishop who was there wrote me the next day, calling the discussion and the decision on McIntyre's resolution "the shabbiest performance" he had ever seen. As we moved through the rest of our agenda that afternoon my mind was not on it. Shortly before the time set for adjournment I left the meeting alone and walked back to the Mayflower Hotel. I was hurt, puzzled, and angry.

McIntyre's intemperate and vindictive conduct no longer surprised me. But the deliberate failure of my own archbishops to help me, or to warn me in advance that they would not help me, shattered my great respect for both of them. These two good and honorable priests crumbled under McIntyre's iron fist. I was as sad for them as for myself. Thomas Aquinas says that weakness in a leader is as heinous as malice in a subordinate. The weakness of my two archbishops, demonstrated publicly that day to a select group of their peers, strengthened my conviction that promotion or position in the church, purchased at the price they were willing to pay, is worthless.

Binz, Byrne, and I were scheduled to take the same taxi to the airport. Binz was flying to Chicago. Byrne and I were booked for the same dinner flight to Minnesota. We met at the appointed time in the Mayflower lobby. When the taxi arrived I asked them to go on without me. Traveling together that night, I explained, would be difficult for each of us. I took the next cab and changed my reservation at the airport so that Byrne and I would have no need, in flight, to review any of the painful events of that afternoon.

In fairness to the bishops who voted for McIntyre's resolution that day I must say that they were not aware of the cardinal's running vendetta against me. To my knowledge Binz, Byrne, and I were the only bishops present that day who knew of his effective intervention with the apostolic delegate against my being named to head a diocese. Our earlier awareness of McIntyre's anger toward me made his resolution, in my eyes, more ominous than it was to the other bishops who read his motion at its face value as a blast against NBC.

Some support for my position came to me on October 10, 1968, when Bishop William Connare, of Greensburg, Pennsylvania, wrote me to apologize for his "aye" vote on September 17. His gracious letter said, "I voted without being fully aware of the implication of my vote. I should have at least had the presence of mind to abstain."

I have never been certain why McIntyre considered me such a dangerous person. Was it my anti-Vietnam position? My growing visibility as a press officer for the bishops? My favorable writings about John XXIII, Vatican II, and the spirit of change? Or a combination of all of these positions, so different from his own? I have a theory that the NBC documentary was merely the occasion, not the cause, of McIntyre's determination to silence me.

He was never able to accept the openness, the confident sense of freedom, and the wholesome nondoctrinal changes in the Catholic Church which John XXIII and Vatican II considered necessary and long overdue. McIntyre's early training on Wall Street qualified him eminently for the demanding task of managing large amounts of money and of overseeing vast church and school building programs in Los Angeles after World War II, but he simply could not comprehend the premises which led to the convocation of Vatican II or to the conclusions reached by that assembly.

It was pathetic to watch him at the postconciliar sessions of the bishops. When all the bishops assembled for their semiannual meetings, the cardinals sat at a head table on a raised dais facing the rest of the hierarchy. Rank-and-file bishops wishing to speak would walk to the nearest aisle microphone. But table microphones were placed between every two cardinals and were within arm's reach for anyone at the head table. McIntyre could and did use this handy medium to interrupt at will or to cut off discussions on the floor which challenged his clear-cut categories of orthodoxy and acceptable practice in the church. His rasping voice and quaking anger could intimidate all but the most stout-hearted speakers. No democratic assembly in the world would have tolerated the high-handed manner in which he habitually handled dissent or expressions contrary to the norms he considered clear, fixed, and unchangeable.

Theoretically the vote of each bishop in the national conference has the same weight. But in practice, the vote of a cardinal, at that time, must have counted as a hundred votes by ordinary bishops. And the vote of two cardinals was usually enough to decide the issue, no matter how many votes there were on the other side. Maybe all this has changed since I was a part of the process. I hope so.

Even though my name was never mentioned in the resolution offered by McIntyre on September 17, I feared that its passage would give him a solid piece of evidence to use at his convenience in the future to document his conviction that I was, to use his phrase, "an incipient heretic."

On September 24, 1968, a news story about me in the *Minneapolis Star*, quoting the *National Catholic Reporter*, carried the caption: "Bishop Quiet on Reported Criticism by Cardinal." When I read it my first thought was the concern it might cause my mother. I called her to invite myself home to dinner. She had seen the story and asked me if it were true. Without divulging any more details than necessary about my embarrassing exchange with Cardinal McIntyre, I admitted that the story was essentially correct. Fortunately, the story did not seem to disturb her deeply.

After dinner I overheard her talking to my sisters in the kitchen as they dried the dishes. Her marvelous comment, offered, I am sure, to allay any fears they might have about my difficulties with the cardinal, was a line I shall always remember, "I've read about that old man in California. He was in a lot of trouble before he got in trouble with Jim." Thank God for mothers. They have an instinct for coming down on the side of their children, no matter who the adversary, no matter what the issue.

# CHAPTER SIXTEEN

# BIRTH CONTROL

In response to the original questionnaires sent out prior to Vatican II, many bishops asked that the Council review the church's traditional prohibition of contraception. Implicit in these requests was the hope that some way could be found to soften the long-standing Catholic opposition to all forms of birth control, save rhythm and abstinence, for married couples. Aware of the considerable public interest in this topic, Pope Paul VI early in his tenure (1964) notified the Council fathers that the special papal commission on family life (established by Pope John XXIII in 1963 and chaired by Cardinal Ottaviani) would continue its review of this matter, with the understanding that it would eventually report its findings directly to the pope. In effect this decision removed birth control from the agenda of the Council and hindered any collegial decision which might modify traditional Catholic teaching on contraception.

Respecting the pope's wishes, the Council fathers concluded their very general discussion of marital morality in November 1965 without making any specific comment about birth control. The existence of the papal study commission, but not its composition, was public knowledge. It was confidently assumed by the Council fathers that Pope Paul would at some time issue a papal statement on his own authority on this critical subject.

In November 1964 Pope Paul had added several new members to the papal commission studying family life. Cardinal Julius Doepfner, archbishop of Munich, Archbishop Leo Binz, and three married couples, including Pat and Patty Crowley of Chicago, were among those named to the commission by Pope Paul. One must write and speak carefully about this commission, its members, and its work product. Its operations carefully avoided any publicity. Archbishop Binz never admitted, even to me, that he was a member of it, even though I regularly substituted for him at parish confirmations while he was in Rome for the week-long meetings of the commission. On June 25, 1966, Doepfner presented the final report of this committee to Pope Paul.

Neither the content nor the recommendations of this committee were then made public.

However, it has long been known that the final report of this eighty-member international commission contained a majority report urging relaxation of the traditional prohibition against birth control and a minority position affirming the traditional prohibition.

Mrs. Patrick Crowley (a member of the commission and of the majority view) has revealed that the "majority opinion...said that the condemnation of birth control in *Casti Connubii* was not infallible teaching. The tradition leading to that encyclical was not of apostolic origin nor was it an expression of universal faith.... According to the majority, humanity had a right, and even a duty, to intervene in nature and shape it to good purposes. That right extended to one's reproductive processes. It was far more in keeping with men and women's rational nature to control conception than to leave it wholly to chance. As to the method of doing so, that was up to the conscience of individual couples."

Historically, within the Catholic communion birth control has been viewed as essentially a matter of private or personal morality, not as an element in the larger moral question of world population and its consequences for human society. While the pope and his commission studied the morality of birth control, pressure on him was mounting outside and inside the Catholic community. The rising birth rate in the world and the new Malthusian fear that world population might outstrip the resources necessary to maintain it increased scholarly and popular discussion of whether and how human population could and should be controlled.

In November 1966 John C. Bennett, then president of Union Theological Seminary in New York, and eighty-five world leaders, including twenty-one Nobel Prize winners, presented a petition to Pope Paul asking him "to take the lead in forging a new consensus on the need to combat the population explosion through the regulation of birth." This request was predicated on the expectation that whenever the pope would issue his statement on birth control it would, in some way, soften the traditional Catholic prohibition of contraception.

A year later, in October 1967, the first international synod of bishops, elected by their peers from many nations, met in Rome to address some of the administrative questions occasioned by the decrees of Vatican II. By this time Pope Paul had still not issued his statement on birth control. But in welcoming the bishops who were delegates to the synod he asked them, as individuals, to submit to him in writing any suggestions they had on this topic, but cautioned them once more that this subject was not on their agenda for public discussion at the synod. His original reservation of this topic to himself was still in effect.

While Pope Paul and his chosen advisors continued to study contraception in the abstract, millions of married Catholics, often acting on the advice of their pastors and confessors, were making up their own minds about whether and when contraception was a permissible moral option for them and their families.

As a pastor and as a confessor during the three years following Vatican II, I was regularly asked by Catholic spouses whether they could in good conscience practice birth control. My answer to each such question was guarded and qualified. I tried to help the questioner shape his or her conscience with due regard for a balance of the personal and conjugal rights and duties involved in this decision.

In my role as a confessor I was aware that my counsel, no matter how carefully phrased, could be cited in the parish and the diocese, with the prefatory remark "Bishop Shannon told me..." The seal of the confessional binds only the priest, not the penitent.

Hearing confessions and administering the sacrament of penance, or the rite of reconciliation as it is now called, had been for me over the years of my priesthood an occasion of great consolation. Even in my early days at the Cathedral of St. Paul, when the lines of penitents before Christmas or Easter stretched the length of that enormous church, the hours I spent in the confessional were a source of considerable personal solace to me. The priest as confessor, assuring the penitent of God's love, mercy, and forgiveness, is functioning near the peak of his sacerdotal powers.

Prudent confessors, mindful that the strict prohibition of contraception in traditional Catholic teaching had not yet been explicitly modified by any papal pronouncement, were walking a careful path in their pastoral counseling immediately after Vatican II. They knew that the Catholic tradition then firmly in place prohibited contraception. They knew that Vatican II had given clear signals that it was time to review and soften this sweeping prohibition of contraception. But they also knew that Pope Paul would some day speak to this issue, on his own authority. His public endorsement of the principle of collegiality led many, including me, to assume that when he did speak he would move more boldly and farther along the path toward leniency marked out so cautiously but clearly by the bishops at Vatican II.

As a bishop I felt a serious obligation to phrase my comments on birth control carefully, and usually only in the privacy of the confes-

sional or in direct personal counseling. I felt that the delicate balance
needed to discuss this topic fairly could not be handled well in a public address. Hence in my speeches about the Council I did not treat
this topic as part of my text. I would respond to questions about it.
But even in answering questions I was brief, careful, and restrained. In
the confessional or in the rectory, talking to a single penitent or a married couple, I was less guarded. There I tried to compress what I had
heard the bishops in Rome say: the purpose of marriage is twofold,
the procreation of children *and* the mutual consolation of the spouses.
Hence, on occasion, for sound reasons, husbands and wives can practice contraception without sinning. What constitutes sufficient reason
for practicing birth control differs from couple to couple and from
time to time. In every instance that I gave this kind of counsel to a
penitent or to parishioners I noted that continued, habitual contraception can be so selfish that it is morally wrong for a married couple if
they deliberately, for a sustained period, thwart the natural process of
child-bearing in their family.

Admittedly, there was an element of risk for me or for any other
priest then giving this kind of counsel. We were assuming, on the basis
of Vatican II, that when the pope did issue his statement it would
follow the liberal trend of the collegial consensus expressed by the
Council. In this assumption we were mistaken.

On July 25, 1968, Pope Paul VI finally issued his encyclical entitled
*Humanae Vitae* (Of Human Life). Adverting to the currents of public interest on birth control and granting that the traditional Catholic
position puts a heavy burden on Catholic spouses, the long-awaited papal letter came down squarely in favor of the traditional teaching: any
form of contraception, in every instance, is forbidden. In the words of
Pope Paul, "...each and every marriage act must remain open to the
transmission of life."

By not issuing this encyclical as infallible papal teaching, Pope Paul
left an opening, even for devout Catholics, to endorse an opposing position, on the grounds that if the pope were absolutely certain of his
position he would have defined it as infallible doctrine.

Public reaction to the encyclical was instantaneous and worldwide.
A group of seventeen theologians at the Catholic University of America signed a public statement telling married Catholics that they could,
in good conscience, practice birth control on occasion. Archbishop
Denis Hurley, of Durban, South Africa, issued a pastoral letter expressing disappointment with the encyclical. John Cogley, whose syndicated
weekly column on things religious appeared in dozens of Catholic

diocesan papers, announced that, because of the encyclical, he was discontinuing the column.

With his usual candor and courtesy, Cogley said that the encyclical had caused a spiritual crisis for him. In his final column he explained further: "I am ready to be a dissenter, even a dropout. I do not, however, believe in using the hospitality of a diocesan paper to infiltrate with ideas formally rejected by the church that publishes it....[To do this] would not be fair to the bishop-publishers, the priest-editors or the trusting readers of these papers who are turning to the Church for guidance." In an interview Cogley added that he had difficulty reconciling the advice of those dissenters to *Humanae Vitae* who would say, "The teaching should be ignored by those who in good conscience cannot accept it" and of the supporters of the encyclical who would say that "it should be accepted in a spirit of humble submission."

Archbishop Leo Byrne issued a clergy bulletin in our diocese calling on all Catholics to accept the encyclical in a spirit of humble submission to the official teaching of the church. Bishop Thomas O'Gorman, of Dallas, issued a warning to all priests in that diocese to stop giving penitents any advice contrary to the teaching of the encyclical.

I was in a quandary. Like Archbishop Hurley of Durban, I had confidently expected the encyclical to liberalize Catholic teaching on birth control. Like Cogley, I was also writing a syndicated weekly column which reached thousands of Catholics in a dozen dioceses. And like the confessors in Dallas, I was a regular confessor at St. Helena's, telling the penitents that, under certain circumstances, contraception was morally permissible.

As a bishop, however, I was unwilling, once the encyclical was promulgated, to make any statement, public or private, which would even *seem* either to question or to contradict formal papal teaching. A bishop's first duty is to protect the purity of Catholic doctrine. There was, however, one thing I could do — stop hearing confessions.

There were, in all, four priests at St. Helena's every weekend. With a little reworking of their calendars three of them could handle the schedule for confessions comfortably. Using the excuse that my duties outside the parish were mounting, I asked my three associates to take my name off the schedule for confessors. I was unwilling to admit, even to these close associates, that I had serious problems with the encyclical. By deciding not to hear confessions I at least protected myself from the danger that a penitent might quote me as endorsing a position contrary to that of Pope Paul, a risk I had cautiously taken prior to

*Humanae Vitae,* but which I was unwilling to take after the pope had spoken to the contrary.

I continued to write my weekly column but said nothing in it about the new encyclical. That deliberate silence bothered me. I cancelled several addresses I was scheduled to give at parishes in the diocese, lest I be forced in the question period to take a stand for or against the encyclical.

Archbishop John Murphy, of Cardiff in Wales, issued a pastoral letter in August of 1968 which said, "Now that the Holy Father has spoken let no man be so rash as to disobey or to *lead others to disobey*" (my italics).

Acting as a group the conference of British bishops announced their intention to take "disciplinary action" against any priest who would dare counsel penitents that contraception can be morally permissible.

To quiet some of the dissent against the encyclical, all twenty-seven bishops in New York State signed a letter to Pope Paul, expressing their complete and unanimous support of his position on birth control.

However, in other countries, several national episcopal conferences issued pastoral letters which put some distance between them and the new encyclical. On September 27 the Canadian bishops issued a pastoral letter which said, "We must make every effort to appreciate the difficulty experienced by contemporary man in understanding and appropriating some points of this encyclical.... Since they are not denying any point of divine and Catholic faith nor rejecting the teaching authority of the Church, these Catholics should not be considered, or consider themselves, shut off from the body of the faithful." The Canadian statement accurately reflected my thinking on this matter.

The strict interpretation of the encyclical would follow a syllogism something like this: every contraceptive act is seriously sinful; persons living in mortal sin may not receive the Eucharist; therefore married Catholics who practice contraception may not receive the Eucharist unless they confess their sin and promise to abandon contraception.

Addressing this dilemma, the bishops of Austria issued a joint pastoral letter which advised Austrian Catholics that they could, in good conscience, act contrary to the encyclical and still "receive Holy Communion without having confessed."

Adopting a similar position, the bishops of Belgium issued a pastoral letter on August 30 telling their people that the papal letter was not "ex cathedra" (i.e., infallible) and that sound Catholic moral teaching would allow the ultimate decision about contraception to rest on the conscience of married couples who would take into account all the moral factors affecting their family and the love spouses share with one another.

The pastoral letter of the bishops of Scandinavia, issued on October 17, was the most liberal of all. It read: "If someone, from weighty and well considered reasons, cannot become convinced by the argumentation of the encyclical, it has always been conceded that he is allowed to have a different view from that presented in a noninfallible statement of the Church. No one should be considered a bad Catholic because he is of such a dissenting opinion."

On November 11, 1968, the bishops of the United States assembled in Washington for their annual meeting. The principal task of that session was to draft a joint statement in support of *Humanae Vitae*. In its final form this statement assured the Holy Father that the American bishops were united in collegial solidarity with him in their denunciation of contraception as an objectively sinful act.

On the day the American bishops approved their pastoral statement and released it to the press I was promptly asked by the press how marital morality for Catholics could differ from country to country. I had to admit that I could not reconcile the statement by the American bishops with similar letters issued by European and Canadian bishops.

Just as different national conferences of bishops expressed different interpretations of the encyclical, different bishops within the same conference responded to it in different ways. When seventy-two priests in the archdiocese of Baltimore signed a public statement expressing reservations about the encyclical, their archbishop, Cardinal Lawrence Shehan, met quietly with them and reached some kind of unpublished agreement on how they and he would interpret the encyclical in that diocese. When ninety-one priests in the archdiocese of St. Paul and Minneapolis signed a public statement in the late summer of 1968 saying that they could not accept the "pastoral implications" of the encyclical, none of them was suspended or even reprimanded. But when forty-four priests of the archdiocese of Washington, D.C., signed a statement of conscience expressing their reservations about the encyclical, Cardinal Patrick O'Boyle, their archbishop, summoned each of them to a private hearing, denounced their position, and stripped several of them of their priestly faculties (to preach, teach, or hear confessions).

As the archbishop of Washington, Cardinal O'Boyle also served as the chancellor of the Catholic University of America. In response to a letter signed by seventeen professors at the university, dissenting from the encyclical, O'Boyle issued a forty-page statement supporting the papal letter and called for a meeting of the university trustees to take disciplinary action against the professors who had signed the letter. On September 6, the trustees met at the university to review the evidence by and against the seventeen (by then twenty-one) professors who had published their dissent. By this time six hundred other Americans, claiming professional status as theologians, had also signed a separate letter of dissent from the encyclical.

At the trustees' meeting I was most uneasy. I listened in silence as Cardinal O'Boyle stated his case against the theologians. Hearing the position advanced by the dissenting theologians I had to admit to myself that their carefully worded comments on the encyclical corresponded to my own reservations about it. During the discussion I did not speak. When it came time to vote for a full-scale investigation of the propriety of the professional conduct of these professors, I did not vote. Nor did I dissent. It was a voice vote. I merely kept silent. A unanimous vote for the inquiry was recorded in the minutes of the meeting. I was ashamed of my silence. But I was certain that any comment by me that day on behalf of the beleaguered theologians would have done no good for them or me.

Before our trustees' meeting ended we voted to ask the university to name a special committee to investigate what response the trustees should make to the dissent expressed by faculty members to the encyclical *Humanae Vitae*.

A few weeks after that committee began work, its chairman, Professor Kirby Neal, addressed a list of questions to the board of trustees, asking more explicit guidance on what the board expected from the committee. I was invited to serve on a small subcommittee of the board to draft a response to these questions. This subcommittee met for a full day at the residence of Cardinal John Krol, archbishop of Philadelphia. At the end of the day I was given the task of drafting a statement which would reflect the consensus of our discussion and which would respond to the questions sent to us by the faculty committee. I was being drawn deeper into a dialog which I preferred to avoid.

Still later I was asked to represent the board of trustees in a special meeting with the theologians and their attorneys. During and after that meeting I considered myself a hypocrite of the first order. The candor of their replies to my questions contrasted sharply with my careful and evasive replies to their queries as I tried to reflect accurately the mind of the Board without revealing my own serious reservations about the encyclical.

At the meeting of the administrative board of the bishops on September 17 the principal topic under discussion was how the bishops should respond to the widespread dissent being expressed to Pope Paul's new encyclical. Bishop Alexander M. Zaleski, bishop of Lansing, Michigan, as chairman of the Bishops' Commission on Doctrine, presented a report on the loyalty which faithful Catholics owe to papal teaching and some guidelines for persons who find assent to such teaching difficult.

Zaleski, a professional theologian, listed seven such guidelines:

1. It is possible that a person in good faith may be unable to give internal assent to an encyclical.

2. As a loyal member of the church such a person must beware of voicing dissent in the wrong way.

3. Dissent can be expressed but it must be done in a manner becoming to a docile believer and a loyal member of the church.

4. Such dissent must show that it is an expression from a believing person — a person of faith.

5. Such dissent can only be expressed in a manner which does not disturb the conscience of other believing people.

6. Dissent must be accompanied by an open mind and a willingness to alter one's view in the light of new evidence.

7. Such dissent must be brought to the proper authorities in the proper manner and quietly.

As I listened to Bishop Zaleski I realized that his comments spoke directly to my concerns. Till then I had made no effort to reveal my difficulties with the encyclical to any of my superiors. The appropriate person for me to tell was Archbishop Binz.

The occasion for telling him was, in a sense, forced on me. One afternoon while I was on house duty at St. Helena's, a woman, who had made a previous appointment, asked to see me. I had never seen her before. She told me that she was a Catholic and had come to see me in the hope that I could give her some helpful counsel. I agreed to try.

She was in her late twenties, married, the mother of two small children. She was a graduate of a Catholic high school and considered herself a devout Catholic. Her husband, also a Catholic, had only a grade school education. He had a modest job with an adequate income for their needs but little prospect of future promotion because of his limited education. She praised him as a good husband and father. They had been married about four years.

Because of their small income they had agreed to hold off starting a family and had mutually agreed to follow the "rhythm" pattern of having sexual intercourse only during her infertile periods. To their surprise she became pregnant within a year of their marriage. They were very much in love and, surprise or not, were both pleased at the prospect of a baby. When it arrived it was a fine healthy baby and they were delighted.

Another year passed. They tried carefully to keep to the rhythm cycle. Then she became pregnant again. One baby was fine. But two babies were a heavy burden on their tight budget. The second child was also healthy and strong. The mother was obviously proud of her babies and pleased to be a mother. But after the birth of the second baby the attitude of her husband toward her changed. She sensed that her fertility and the demonstrated unreliability of the rhythm schedule for her were constant worries for him because he could not foresee how they could afford any more babies.

They had discussed contraception but she firmly, and he reluctantly, concluded that birth control was a sin and not an option for faithful Catholics. She was aware that the warmth and generosity of their love in earlier years had declined sharply.

The occasion for her visit to me was that the previous day was her husband's birthday. She had prepared a special dinner for him, all his favorite dishes. She had wine and candles and had fed the babies early. When he came home from work, evidently pleased with her festive preparations, he came up behind her, put his arms around her, and kissed the back of her neck. She burst into tears, ran to their bedroom, and cried herself to sleep. He ate his birthday dinner alone.

She had come to me because some friend said I could help her. Could I? She had read the encyclical. Was it possible for her to use some regular mode of birth control, other than rhythm, without committing sin? My answer was an unqualified "Yes." All my caution evaporated.

I explained to her the logic which led many reputable Catholic theologians to say that persons in her position could in good conscience use birth control. When I told her that some bishops also held this position she asked, "Would Pope Paul agree with them?" I could only say that I hoped he would, given the same facts she had shared with me. She thanked me warmly, dried her tears, and left all smiles. She had the assurance of a bishop that she could take precautions to prevent pregnancy, without fear that she and her husband were living selfish lives of sin.

For the first time since the promulgation of *Humanae Vitae* I had openly counseled a devout Catholic spouse that her circumstances justified a course of conduct explicitly rejected by that papal letter. As she went out the front door of our rectory I went out the back door, got in the car, and drove straight to see my archbishop.

As always he received me most cordially. I told him the story I had just heard and explained that I had come to share it with him because I did not want it to come to him, third-hand, that his auxiliary bishop was counseling Catholic spouses that they could in good conscience, under some circumstances, practice birth control.

I probably unloaded more on Binz that day than I intended. But once started I told him of my sense of hypocrisy at the bishops' meeting and especially of my uncomfortable role as a trustee judging dissenting theologians at the Catholic University.

Binz did not ruffle easily. When I finished my long tale he asked what I thought he could do for me. I replied that I did not expect him to do anything, except hear me out. That he did. I felt relieved that I had finally shared with him the anxiety I had kept bottled up inside me for almost two months.

The Catholic prohibition of birth control posed no problem for Archbishop Binz. Furthermore, he could not see why it should disturb me, in light of my public promises as a priest and as a bishop to endorse and defend all the teachings of the church. In his opinion any intellectual difficulties I might have in accepting *Humanae Vitae* should be manageable if my earlier professed allegiance to Catholic teaching was still intact.

I tried to explain that my faith in the teachings of Jesus Christ was firm but that my experience as a pastor and as a confessor made me balk at the rigidity of *Humanae Vitae*. I never said that I thought the pope was wrong. I merely said that I could not, in good conscience, give the internal and external assent to this papal teaching which the pope expected of all Catholics, most particularly of all bishops. One paragraph of the encyclical, addressed specifically to bishops, urged them to "consider this mission [i.e., promoting the Catholic teaching on contraception] as one of your most urgent responsibilities at the present time."

The interview with Binz gave me some relief. At least I had admitted to him what I had been unwilling to admit to the conference of bishops or to the trustees of the Catholic University. In telling him this I knew I was putting a new burden on him. Could he, in good conscience, thereafter vouch for my orthodoxy or recommend that greater authority in the church be given to me? Probably not. Making him privy to my qualms about the encyclical lessened my anxiety but must certainly have added to his worries.

In sharing my concerns with Binz I also told him that I had felt a sense of hypocrisy during the meeting of the administrative board on September 16 and 17 while Cardinal O'Boyle listed his grievances against the priests in Washington who had publicly dissented from *Humanae Vitae*. Binz as much as told me that he could not help me with this dilemma. If I felt strongly about that issue I should have told O'Boyle, not Binz. Otherwise, I should somehow learn to bear my burdens like a man. Binz did not lecture me. But he did say that every adult has certain unresolved questions with which one must simply learn to cope. Obviously the encyclical was one such dilemma for me.

Catholic belief in papal infallibility rests on the premise that the chief teacher in the church cannot mislead the faithful in doctrinal or moral matters. Prior to the appearance of *Humanae Vitae* it had never been difficult for me to accept this belief.

Granted, Pope Paul VI did not claim infallibility for his encyclical *Humanae Vitae*. But its publication gave many Catholic spouses, pastors, and teachers their first serious doubts about the inerrancy of papal teaching. The worried mother who asked me if Pope Paul VI would agree with the counsel I had given her, permitting contraception, identified precisely my own concern about the encyclical. What I had learned at Vatican II, my experience as a pastor, my reading of sacred scripture, and my nonprofessional grasp of human psychology combined to prevent my giving the assent to *Humanae Vitae* which that document asked of all faithful Catholics.

After sharing with Archbishop Binz the dilemma posed for me by the encyclical I realized that my problem went deeper than my fear of being quoted (accurately) by a penitent. I was afraid to admit, even to myself, that my public promise as a bishop to support, endorse, and defend the official teaching of the Catholic Church had already been breached, quietly and privately, but breached nonetheless.

Pastoral letters issued by the bishops of Canada, Belgium, and Scandinavia were small comfort to me. In spite of their careful diction these statements gave counsel diametrically opposed to the counsel of Pope Paul VI on a moral question of great importance. No matter how cautiously the draftsmen of such letters phrased their arguments they were rejecting the central thesis of the long-awaited papal encyclical.

At the end of my visit with Archbishop Binz he cautioned me that, *as a bishop,* I had no alternative but to accept the papal encyclical. Only later did it dawn on me that my inability to give that assent went to the very heart of my continuing to serve as a bishop in the church.

Loyalty to the papacy is a necessary quality in any bishop. Pope Paul, on the recommendation of Archbishop Binz, had named me a bishop. Binz must have had second thoughts, maybe even regrets, when I told him that I simply could not deliver the loyal endorsement of *Humanae Vitae* which Pope Paul had a right to expect from the bishops.

It weighed on my conscience that I had lacked the courage to reveal to anyone but my own archbishop the conflict I experienced over the new encyclical. In the week following my visit with Binz I resolved to share with Pope Paul himself the crisis posed for me by his exhortation to all priests to give "loyal internal and external obedience to the teaching authority of the Church" on the issue of contraception.

After much editing and rewriting, I drafted the following letter to Pope Paul on September 23, 1968:

> Your Holiness:
>
> Since the publication of your encyclical letter *Humanae Vitae* on July 29 I have prayed fervently and studied carefully, striving, as one of your loyal and devoted sons, to give in the exercise of my priestly ministry loyal internal and external obedience to the teaching authority of the Church.
>
> This effort has been earnest and prolonged. It is now nearly two months since the encyclical appeared. In that time, because of my promise of loyalty to Your Holiness, I have not revealed in my sermons, instructions, or counseling to penitents my own great intellectual difficulties with that portion of the encyclical which teaches that of necessity "each and every marriage act [*quilibet matrimonii usus*] must remain open to the transmission of life."
>
> In my pastoral experience I have found that this rigid teaching is simply impossible of observance by many faithful and generous spouses, and I cannot believe that God binds man to impossible standards. In seeking to counsel such persons I have found myself resorting to all sorts of casuistry and devious kinds of rationalization, in the hope that I might both keep faith with Your Holiness and with the people of God who seek my help.
>
> I must now reluctantly admit that I am ashamed of the kind of advice I have given some of these good people, ashamed because it has been bad theology, bad psychology, and because it has not been an honest reflection of my own inner convictions....
>
> Your Holiness, I firmly believe that I am a man of faith, and I hereby solemnly reaffirm my faith in the teachings of Christ and his church.... [But] I cannot in conscience give internal assent, hence much less external assent, to the papal teaching which is here in question.
>
> I have prayed earnestly and pondered long the consequences for Your Holiness and for me and for the Church of this statement on my part. I am, under God, and with faith in Christ, prepared to accept these consequences. I take this awful step, Your Holiness, with the greatest possible reluctance, but with a conviction and a certitude which I have seldom experienced previously in my adult life.
>
> I would be deeply grateful if Your Holiness could favor me at your earliest convenience with a response to this letter. It is sent to you as my father

in Christ after weeks of anguish, days of prayer, and hours of fear. I seek your counsel and assure you that it will be eagerly awaited and received with gratitude.

In closing I promise my earnest and continuing prayers for Your Holiness in these trying days of renewal and reform in the Catholic Church. I beg also for your prayers for me now and in the future.

Devotedly your son in Jesus Christ
Our Lord and Saviour,

*James P. Shannon*

(Most Rev.) James P. Shannon
Auxiliary Bishop of the
Archdiocese of St. Paul and Minneapolis

Before mailing the original of this letter to the pope I sent copies of it to Binz and Byrne. When I mailed the letter to Pope Paul on October 2, with separate copies to Archbishops Binz, Byrne, Dearden (president of the conference of bishops), and Raimondi (the apostolic delegate), I still hoped that, somehow, my ministry as a priest could continue, but I knew that my ministry as a bishop would never again be the same.

When the bishops gathered in Washington for their regular fall meeting on November 11, their principal task was that of drafting a pastoral letter to support Pope Paul's encyclical. John Wright, the bishop of Pittsburgh, was editor-in-chief. At noon and 5:00 P.M. each day it was my task to brief the press. But following the usual practice, I could issue no release on the pastoral letter until the conference had voted on a final version.

The press had copies of the pastoral letters issued by other national hierarchies and queried me all week for some sign of the direction the American pastoral would take. I knew that it would be an endorsement of the encyclical but could say nothing about the discussion until the end of the week. As I fielded questions from the media I felt like a man treading water. And sure enough, Cardinal McIntyre issued his customary blast against the news media for their "inaccurate and unfair" coverage of the meeting and of the pastoral letter.

One confidential report given to the assembled bishops told them of the review then underway at the Catholic University of America, by a faculty committee, of the twenty-one professors who had publicly stated their reservations about *Humanae Vitae*. Several reporters, correctly assuming that the bishops would be discussing the Catholic University investigation and knowing that I was on the university board of trustees, did their best, but to no avail, to get a lead or a quote from me about the investigation.

Each night during the conference Bishop John Wright invited me to join him and the small group of bishops who were editing the proposed pastoral letter. Wright was determined to fashion a statement which would be free of any of the qualifications voiced by other national hierarchies. I tried, repeatedly but without success, to introduce into the text some such words of qualification. Wright would have none of it. The final draft was a total endorsement of *Humanae Vitae* ("in collegial solidarity with the Successor of St. Peter"). When it was finished I asked Wright if he would introduce it to the press and answer questions about it. He readily agreed and went on the next day to do his usual marvelous job with words. I watched it all on television from my hotel room. I was glad not to be on the firing line with the reporters.

As I watched Bishop Wright on camera that night I was sure that he would soon be a cardinal. I was also sure that I would soon be a nervous wreck unless I could resolve the dilemma of my private doubts about the encyclical which my brother bishops had just glowingly endorsed.

The next morning I rented a car and drove to St. John's College in Annapolis, Maryland. Dr. Richard Weigle, president of St. John's, and I had served together on the board of the Association of American Colleges. I did not know him very well. But I trusted him. With no appointment, I took two hours of his time to recapitulate the story of my unsuccessful efforts to reconcile my duties as a bishop with my reservations about Pope Paul's encyclical.

Weigle's father, Dr. Luther Weigle, had been dean of the Yale Divinity School. Hence the younger Dr. Weigle had more than ordinary insight into the ecclesiastical process. He listened carefully to my narrative. When I finished he asked whether I would be interested in a position on the faculty or the staff at St. John's College. On the spot he assured me that I would be welcome, either at the Annapolis campus or in Santa Fe. I had not asked him for a job. But I did hope that his response to my story would be an offer of some kind of assistance or counsel.

I had no clear plan at that time for my future. But I was relieved to learn that an honorable academic position was open to me, if I chose to accept it. I thanked Weigle and promised to accept or reject his invitation before Christmas. Leaving his office I felt that an enormous burden had been lifted from my shoulders.

Back home I shared this conversation with my confessor, who urged me not to reach any decision on the matter until I had thought and prayed for at least a week over the invitation. I agreed to follow his advice.

By the end of that week I had concluded that I would accept Weigle's offer to teach in Santa Fe, if Archbishop Binz would grant me permission. I had also decided that I would submit my letter of resignation as a pastor in the diocese and ask to be relieved of my duties as an auxiliary bishop.

Pastors resign every day. But the resignation of a bishop is a far more serious matter. My letter to Archbishop Binz, on November 23, two months after my (unanswered) letter to Pope Paul VI, offered my resignation and asked for a leave of absence, "to stay with friends in Santa Fe for several weeks of rest and study." By return mail Binz acknowledged my letter, assured me of his earnest prayers for me, and instructed me, without answering my requests, to carry on all future correspondence about my proffered resignations with Archbishop Byrne. Binz had a strong personal bond of affection and respect for the papacy. I think that my letter to Pope Paul in September had made him so uneasy that he wanted no part in any further discussion of how or why his auxiliary bishop could possibly persist in differing with opinions expressed in a papal encyclical.

Byrne and I accepted Binz's directive even though I regretted my loss of personal contact with Binz. From that time forward he and I steadily lost touch.

Between Binz and me the warmth of friendship never entirely disappeared. Between Byrne and me the warmth of friendship never had a chance to develop. Binz always received me as a friend in his upstairs sitting room. Byrne always received me as a caller in the formal downstairs parlor of his very formal residence.

Byrne was by nature a warm and gracious person. Our first two years together were cordial and friendly. The first sign of trouble between us occurred the day he abstained from voting on the resolution of Cardinal McIntyre to censure NBC and to reprimand me. The Sunday after that meeting I went to see Byrne at his home. I told him candidly that his abstention from voting, after Archbishop Binz had told me that Byrne would speak for me at that meeting, was a damaging blow to our friendship. Understandably, after that painful exchange he and I found it difficult to revive any sense of the camaraderie we once shared.

In the first of our "parlor" visits Byrne reminded me that I had what he called a "great following" in the church. In order not to scandalize these good people he suggested that I could, in good conscience, with-hold internal assent to *Humanae Vitae* but express external assent for its teaching. He could not understand why I found this double standard totally unacceptable.

At the end of our visit he asked whether I would consult a theologian whom he would choose to counsel me. I readily agreed to do so. The next day he called to say that he had made an appointment for me to see a professor of theology at the Catholic University of America whom he knew and respected.

I made plane reservations and prepared to leave for Washington the next day. That evening Byrne called again to say that he had second thoughts. Would I be willing to change my plans and seek the advice of a different theologian? I assured him I would. The new counselor-to-be was a theologian who happened to be a friend of mine. The next day I flew to the East Coast and spent an afternoon, an evening, and a leisurely morning explaining my views on the encyclical to a friendly theologian whose experience in the confessional had made him a good listener.

Archbishop Byrne confidently expected that a session with such a solidly orthodox theologian would set me straight once and for all. Not so. My friend the theologian, after hearing my narrative, told me that his problems with the encyclical were almost the same as mine. Having talked by phone with Byrne, my friend knew that Byrne expected some helpful decision to issue from our counseling session. To satisfy Byrne, and to help me, my friend suggested that I accept the invitation to teach at St. John's in Santa Fe. Neither of us expected that a semester in New Mexico would resolve my difficulties about the encyclical. But we did agree that a few months away from pastoral and episcopal duties might give me some welcome leisure and time to reflect on what options were open to me. It also gave me some solace to hear him say that he re-spected my unwillingness to state publicly my reservations about the encyclical. His comment eased the growing sense of hypocrisy I felt as a result of my internal dissent and external silence.

Archbishop Byrne was dismayed to learn that the theologian whom he had chosen as my counselor shared my reservations about the cen-tral thesis of *Humanae Vitae,* and even more upset at the counsel that I should accept the job in Santa Fe for the next semester. Reluctantly, he agreed to present my request for a leave of absence to "our superi-ors." His use of the plural puzzled me. We both knew that he had the complete authority to grant my request. The next day he went on vaca-tion and left me a note saying he would call me on his return but that I would not be able to reach him during the week.

First Binz and I had lost touch, and now Byrne and I were losing touch. By nature I am, I think, a sanguine person, confident that tomorrow will be better than today and that whatever happens tomorrow will be manageable. That native sense of security began to slip away from me during the Christmas season of 1968. For the first time in my life I knew genuine fear, a sense that something ominous was happening to me and that I could not prevent it.

While waiting for an answer on my request for a leave, I flew to Miami on November 30 to address the annual convention of the National Federation of Catholic Physicians' Guilds. The program chairman, Dr. Bernard O'Loughlin, a professor in the School of Medicine of the University of California at Los Angeles and an alumnus of the College of St. Thomas, had invited me to speak to the physicians about the college level education of medical students. I accepted his invitation only after he assured me that I would not be expected to talk about contraception.

My remarks that evening centered on the liberal arts as preparation for a career in medicine. After I had spoken, Archbishop Coleman Carroll, who at the recent meeting of the bishops in Washington had suggested to me that I should use my scheduled address in his diocese of Miami as an occasion to support *Humanae Vitae,* mounted the rostrum and told the doctors firmly that they should wholeheartedly and publicly endorse the encyclical. I knew from private comments heard before dinner that the audience was sharply divided on precisely this issue.

After dinner several doctors privately asked me to help them resolve the conflict on this point between their own conclusions and the clear-cut directives of Archbishop Carroll. I had four options: (1) no comment; (2) support the archbishop; (3) reveal my own difficulties on this point; or (4) use some mode of verbal fencing. I chose the last and merely rephrased their questions as best I could and left for my room as quickly as possible. These were dedicated Catholic doctors. They were not critics of the pope. They were uneasy to be at odds with the church and anxious to be shown some way out of their dilemma. Moreover, their opinions were, it seemed to me, both medically and theologically respectable. When I left them I felt, once more, that I had been dishonest in not stating clearly where I stood on the question at issue since they had been so open with me. Try as I might, I could not escape being drawn into new discussions of the encyclical with decent people who had a right to know my opinion but with whom I was reluctant to be open on this subject.

On December 5 the board of trustees of the Catholic University met on campus. One item on the agenda was the formation of a committee to select a new president for the university. Cardinal O'Boyle and Cardinal McIntyre stressed the importance of picking a president of unquestioned theological orthodoxy. I was aware that someone, without consulting me, had nominated me for the presidency. Fortunately, no nominees were mentioned that day. Hence I had no need to say that I did not wish to be a candidate.

That evening the trustees of the university gathered for dinner at the Madison Hotel. Cardinal Lawrence Shehan, archbishop of Baltimore, who had always been friendly to me, took me aside before dinner and suggested that I should spend a little time visiting personally with Cardinal McIntyre. In Shehan's words: "McIntyre is not as formidable as he appears. Go talk to him. Get to know him. Let him get to know you." I agreed to try.

That evening, at a reception prior to the dinner, McIntyre was sitting alone on a couch in a corner of the room. I approached him and asked if I might join him. "Certainly, young man." He always called me "young man" in a voice that reminded me of Lionel Barrymore. I sat down and we began to chat. Warming to my purpose and encouraged by the advice of Cardinal Shehan, I said that I hoped McIntyre and I might become better acquainted. He smiled agreeably without expressing galloping enthusiasm at this prospect. Then I made my fatal error. Referring to the NBC show and the subsequent vote by the bishops, I used the expression "I think, Your Eminence, that your letters to the bishops have injured my good name."

The old man turned red, jumped to his feet, and shouted, in a voice that could be heard all over the room, "How dare you? How dare you speak to me like that? Your good name is nonexistent." I was ready to die. I actually considered pulling him back down on the couch and clapping my hand over his mouth to shut him up. All conversation in the room stopped. All eyes were on us. McIntyre then turned and walked away, leaving me alone to explain as best I could to the assembled bishops what the outburst was all about. Cardinal Shehan, sensing what had happened, came over to me. I thanked him for his counsel and said, "So much for sweet reason with McIntyre."

Unaware of the issue which had provoked the shouting, several bishops quietly offered me words of consolation. I stayed for a lovely dinner and an evening of difficult small talk, punctuated by long pauses. It was the last time McIntyre and I ever spoke to each other.

On Christmas Eve in our rectory I received a call from Cardinal

Cody in Chicago. He was chairman of the search committee of the trustees of the Catholic University of America, charged with selecting a new president for the university. He told me that the slate of nominees for that post had been narrowed from thirty-one to four and that I was one of the four, the only bishop on the list. Would I allow him to propose my name to the trustees?

The Catholic University has a pontifical faculty of theology, officially accredited to the Holy See. It was unthinkable that my name could be approved in Rome for such an honorable and sensitive post. Without divulging my reasons to Cody, I expressed appreciation for his call and for the honor of being considered for the presidency of the university but asked that he remove my name from the list. He agreed to respect my wishes.

Having been a college president for a decade I had no burning desire to return to such a position. But it did disturb me to reflect that I had declined the nomination on the personal grounds that it could never be approved in Rome, not on the grounds that I had no desire to serve again as a college president.

Christmas came and went. Still no answer from Archbishop Byrne. Dr. Weigle was pressing me for an answer to his invitation. I explained that I expected but had not yet received permission from my superiors to leave the diocese.

About this time an enterprising reporter for the *St. Paul Pioneer Press* surprised me with a phone call and a question. Was it true that I was about to accept a teaching post at St. John's College in Santa Fe? He had already checked with Dr. Weigle, who confirmed that such a position had been offered to me. Without intending it, Weigle had blown my cover during a most delicate part of my negotiations with Archbishop Byrne.

I admitted to the reporter that the post had been offered but not yet accepted. When the news story appeared the next day, Archbishop Byrne concluded that I had tipped off the paper and was "going public" to put pressure on him. In an uncharacteristically curt letter he chided me for "pleading in the public forum...hardly the style or posture of bishops engaged in working together...[but] I suppose you liked it."

The fact is that I did not like it any more than he did. And I was hurt by his insinuation that I had planted the story and by his repetition of a quote he attributed to Bishop John Wright: "In Bishop Shannon's eyes the press can do no wrong."

Byrne, like Binz, could simply not comprehend how any bishop who had made a personal promise of loyalty to the pope could possibly question any formal teaching issued by any pope. Each time we met I assured Byrne of my unqualified belief in the gospel of Jesus Christ. And each time he came back to the point that the pope, as the vicar of Christ, cannot mislead the faithful on matters of doctrine or morals, and that my refusal of assent to a papal encyclical was an admission that I had lost my Christian faith. Leo Byrne was a very pious and deeply religious man. It seemed to him almost blasphemous for me to say that I could not assent to a papal position which, in my opinion, did not demonstrably rest on solid evidence from sacred scripture or philosophical necessity.

On three separate occasions, in the "parlor" of his residence, he and I retraced the same fruitless arguments about *Humanae Vitae*. These exchanges were never intemperate but they were exasperating for both of us.

Our final, brief meeting took place in mid-January in St. Joseph's Hospital, where Byrne was a patient. There he told me that my request had been granted. I could be absent from the diocese for four months, with official permission to teach at St. John's College in Santa Fe. I felt no sense of victory as I gave him my blessing that night and left the hospital.

I should have been happy. I was not. I was about to leave a parish, a diocese, a family, friends, and a ministry I dearly loved. I was not leaving because I coveted some position or reward outside my priestly ministry. I was going because I could no longer stand the ambiguity and ambivalence of my role as a lame-duck bishop unable to deliver the performance or the public witness expected of me by my religious superiors.

In our last conversation alone together Archbishop Binz had said to me, several weeks before I left the diocese, that I had become an embarrassment to him. Canonically, I was his auxiliary, his helper. I had tried, in every way that seemed feasible, not to let him down or to cast doubt on his earlier judgment in asking that I be named a bishop. But I, the helper, the auxiliary, had managed at last to become an embarrassment to the church and to my archbishop.

# CHAPTER SEVENTEEN

# SANTA FE

On Sunday, January 26, 1969, I offered the early Mass at St. Helena's, bade goodbye to my friend Father John McGrath, and set off by car alone on a journey which I then considered a four-month leave of absence but which has continued until the present. I did not know that I was making a permanent break. I did know that I was making a serious move.

My destination that night was Omaha — 840 Fairacres Road, my home away from home. My family there, Eileen Foxley, widow of my brother Bill, and her children, could not quite understand how or why a bishop would take a leave of absence. My replies to their polite queries were vague. They were too smart not to sense that I was evasive, but too decent to press me for an explanation. In candor I could not have given them a very satisfactory account of what I was about to do.

The next morning, with ominous weather reports of ice and rain in the West, I left Omaha and headed into the storm with a heavy heart and a great sense of sadness. The icy roads were so treacherous that I left the Interstate and followed gravel roads across Kansas. The foul weather took my attention off myself, at least for one day. The next day was cold and clear. And I was desolate as I pulled into Santa Fe my third night out.

I had implicitly asked Dick Weigle for a place on his faculty, and he had generously given it. I was "out West" where my psyche had always worked best. I was in a neutral zone where my views about contraception and papal encyclicals were no longer burning issues. And I was being welcomed royally by a goodly company of scholars at the lovely Santa Fe campus of St. John's. But I was sad, lonely, empty, and unhappy beyond words.

Santa Fe, cradled at the foothills of the Sangre de Cristo range of the Rockies, is a lovely place in any season. At seven thousand feet it has a more equable climate than almost any other city in the nation.

St. John's, with its classical, nonelective curriculum based on reading, over four years, the great books and scientific experiments which are the building blocks of Western civilization, was a refreshing new home and a healing atmosphere for me at a time I needed refreshment and healing.

I had been an early student of the "new program" at St. John's in Annapolis when Stringfellow Barr and Scott Buchanan, professors on leave from the University of Virginia, had persuaded the St. John's trustees to scrap their traditional collegiate departmental organization in 1937 in favor of a new plan for taking students through the classics of Western civilization in the sequence in which these basic elements of our culture were written. In the summers of 1941 and 1942 I had been a student in the "new program" at Annapolis and had contributed to their edition of classical texts my translation of Thomas Aquinas's treatise on teaching (*De Magistro*). While it was in print that little booklet brought me a handsome royalty check each year of about seventeen dollars.

The Santa Fe campus adjoins the national forest preserve and offers a sweeping view of the town, the Rio Grande Valley, and the Jemez Range to the west. If there is a platonic ideal for the site of a small liberal arts college it must resemble St. John's in Santa Fe.

My duties were not onerous. As an assistant to the president I helped with fund-raising, correspondence, administration, and recruitment for the summer session. As a substitute tutor I became reacquainted with the seminars, tutorials, and laboratory experiments which constitute the unique academic program at St. John's.

The bond between students and tutors there is close. Both groups welcomed me warmly. Their casual and comfortable dress, typical of the Southwest, contrasted with my black suit and Roman collar. But suit, collar, and all, I quickly felt at ease in their company.

The archbishop of Santa Fe at that time was James Peter Davis. He extended to me the "faculties" of the diocese (the right to preach, teach, and hear confessions) and went out of his way to make me feel welcome. I volunteered my services, as a priest or as a bishop, an offer he readily accepted. Like many western dioceses Santa Fe needed more priests than it had. As my availability became known I heard confessions and offered Mass in different parishes on weekends. On one occasion I conferred the sacrament of confirmation in a parish in Santa Fe. That great fraternity, the priests of the Catholic Church, were as cordial and generous to me in the West as they had been in Minnesota. The camaraderie of Catholic priests knows no geographical limits.

I did not at that time feel it necessary to take Archbishop Davis into my confidence about all the reasons which had led me to leave Minnesota. He did not inquire and seemed satisfied with my status in his diocese as a bishop on temporary leave from his own permanent assignment. He knew my fondness for the West and agreed that a sojourn in that salubrious climate now and again would be good for any Midwesterner who could get the time to make the trip.

Davis and I had been only nodding acquaintances at the bishops' meetings. After I settled in his diocese we became good friends. With his approval I prepared an altar in my apartment and offered Mass there each day that I was not asked to help in some parish.

Early in February I received a phone call from Archbishop Leo Byrne in St. Paul, telling me that the new apostolic delegate, Archbishop Luigi Raimondi, wanted to see me in Washington. I flew to Washington and went to the delegation the next morning. Raimondi and I talked alone, for more than two hours. He asked me to speak freely to him about my difficulties with *Humanae Vitae* and any other "problems of faith" which I might have. I told him I had no problems of faith and that my difficulties with the encyclical had been stated in detail in my letter of September 23, 1968, to Pope Paul, a copy of which had come to the delegate.

When I commented that my letter to the pope had never been answered or even acknowledged, Raimondi rose and went to a table nearby. On it was a letter which he then handed to me. It was a four-page typewritten letter addressed to me, signed by Pope Paul VI, and bearing the embossed crest of the papal coat of arms. I read it slowly as Raimondi waited.

The letter was kind, gentle, and solicitous about me, and in it the Holy Father promised to continue to pray for me. I was touched and grateful to have the letter, at long last. I had given up all hope of ever hearing from Pope Paul.

I thanked Raimondi and pocketed the letter. It was a clear, bright, chilly day. The delegate asked if I would like to take a walk with him to continue our discussion. I agreed. The Apostolic Delegation on Massachusetts Avenue is across the street from the Naval Observatory Grounds, now the official residence of the vice president of the United States. We crossed the street and began a series of slow circles of those well-manicured grounds.

As we walked Raimondi told me that if I had sought his counsel he would have urged me not to go to Santa Fe. But now that I had made the move west, he suggested that I stay there through the spring semester, return "for a few weeks" to the archdiocese of St. Paul, and then consider accepting a new assignment "in the service of the Holy Father."

I did not think to ask him what work he had in mind. I asked only "where" this work would be. He offered three possible sites: Rome, Jerusalem, or Switzerland. He asked me to think over this invitation and assured me that he would make the necessary arrangements once I decided where I would like to go. As we parted he asked whether I knew Father Theodore Hesburgh, C.S.C., president of the University of Notre Dame. I assured him that I did. He then asked whether I would be interested in asking Father Hesburgh to help me obtain an academic appointment at Tantur, the newly established center for ecumenical and interfaith studies in Jerusalem.

Father Hesburgh is a good friend of mine. But mention of his name by the delegate made me uneasy. If I were being offered a post "in the service of the Holy Father," why was there need to ask Father Hesburgh to pull strings for me? We parted on cordial terms and I agreed to consider his offer of a position for me in Rome, Jerusalem, or Switzerland.

On the plane back to Santa Fe I read and reread the letter from Pope Paul VI. It was dated February 28, 1969, four weeks after I took up residence in Santa Fe and more than five months after my letter to which it responded. Its tone was pastoral, paternal, and charitable. But its most important paragraph, apropos my concerns about *Humanae Vitae,* said, "We do not wish, therefore, to direct your thoughts so much to reasonings from natural evidence — since We feel able to understand that for you they may perhaps for the moment be lacking in sufficient force for conviction — as to sentiments of supernatural trust in the word of the Lord, who assures His continual assistance to the Church and to His Vicar on earth."

The pope put his finger precisely on my problem. Even accepting his premises from scripture and from tradition I still could not firmly assent to the proposition that every act of contraception is, for a married couple, always and necessarily mortally sinful.

It grieved me to seem to be withholding an assent which the pope assumed I could give, if only I had the right intentions and respect for him. As John Cogley had said in his expression of dissent to *Humanae Vitae,* Pope Paul VI was not just one more theologian. He was the pope and in Catholic tradition the legitimate successor to St. Peter, the bishop of Rome, and therefore the living representative of Jesus Christ among believing Catholics.

The letter could not have been more gracious. My letter had told the pope of my "weeks of anguish, days of prayer, and hours of fear" before writing to him. His letter confided to me that, prior to issuing his encyclical, he also had known "months of prayer and distress (because of the distress of those who were anxiously awaiting Our answer), of deep reflection and of wide and serious consultation."

I wrote the delegate to thank him for our visit and for the kind letter he had hand delivered to me from Pope Paul. In that letter I told him that I would not feel comfortable using my friendship with Father Hesburgh to arrange some kind of a nonpastoral position for me in Jerusalem, and asked for more time to ponder the other two options he had offered me: Rome or Switzerland.

In spite of the fond memories I had of Rome, I was not eager to be assigned there. As Cardinal Newman, after he became a Catholic, is alleged to have said, "I feel more comfortable in the Barque of Peter when I am farthest from its engine room." The prospect of an assignment in Switzerland became more attractive the more I thought of it.

Then I received an unexpected letter from Archbishop Binz. He had just been to Washington to see the delegate. He was writing to caution me that in his discussion with the delegate there was no mention of Switzerland as a possible site for my future labors. Hence the choices remaining open for me, according to Binz, were Rome or Jerusalem. I was not eager to accept either.

On March 17 the delegate wrote to me citing "a development of interest to Your Excellency" and invited me to visit him in Washington. I accepted and we met, alone, a second time at the Delegation. He asked whether I had decided about either of the options he had given me. I told him that I did not choose to accept either of them.

The "new development" he wished to explore with me was the possibility of working "in the service of the Holy Father in South America." I responded by saying that South America is a continent. What country did he have in mind? "Any country," came his reply. Surely they could not all have openings for someone like me. I knew at once that I was being rusticated, not reassigned. My instinct was to tell him right there that I would have no part of being shipped out of the country. But I agreed to consider his offer. He urged me to call him if necessary and assured me that my travel and living expenses, anywhere in South America, would be guaranteed. We had never before discussed living expenses. All our previous dialog had been about a foreign position "in the service of the Holy Father."

I continued to write my weekly column from Santa Fe for the *Catholic Bulletin* in Minnesota. I also continued to serve as the vice chairman of the press department of the bishops' conference.

The spring meeting of the bishops convened in Houston the second week of April. With Monsignor Francis Hurley, now the archbishop of Anchorage, I went to Houston two days before the conference to make preliminary arrangements for the conference and for the press briefings. With the tacit approval of Archbishop Dearden, then president of the conference, Hurley and I arranged the speakers' dais at the hotel so that it could accommodate none of the cardinals, all of whom had been accustomed to sit at the head table, where table microphones were within easy reach. It was to be my last session as a bishop. But I am told that our pattern has continued. The cardinals, who formerly broke into the dialog at will by using their individual table microphones, now sit in the body of the auditorium when the bishops assemble and walk to a microphone in the nearest aisle, just as the other bishops do, whenever they wish to speak.

The board of trustees of the Catholic University of America held a special meeting in Houston to set up a five-member study committee, under Cardinal John Krol, to continue the investigation of theologians on that faculty who had dissented from *Humanae Vitae*. I was asked to serve on the committee but begged off on grounds that my schedule in Santa Fe would prevent my traveling to Washington.

In May of that year Harold LeVander, the new Republican governor of Minnesota, asked me to accept a second term on the Minnesota Junior College Board, which I had chaired since March of 1967. I accepted reappointment and agreed to return to Minnesota for board meetings. The Minnesota network of junior colleges, now called community colleges, was expanding rapidly at that time, and I welcomed the opportunity to continue as chairman of the state board.

Before leaving Minnesota I had agreed to act as moderator for a debate between Father Gregory Baum, a Canadian priest-professor, and Dr. Charles Davis, a Catholic priest-professor who had resigned from the ministry and was then married and teaching in Canada. The debate, to be held in Si Melby Hall at Augsburg College in Minneapolis, was sponsored by a new and somewhat controversial lay group known as the Association of Catholics for Church Renewal (ACCR). I had worked with the founders of this group and considered them solid members of the Catholic community. After my move to Santa Fe they managed to irritate Archbishop Binz by publicly questioning a diocesan fund drive then in progress. Knowing nothing about their challenge to the drive, I assured them in early May that I would return to the Twin Cities on May 16 to moderate the debate as I had promised. This decision turned out to be a mistake on my part.

The "debate" between Baum and Davis was a very tame affair, but it attracted an enormous crowd. When I was introduced I received thunderous applause, which was duly reported in the local press. Without intending to take sides between the ACCR and the diocesan fund drive, I was perceived by some persons as taking a stand against the drive by my very presence on the platform. The day before the event I received a note from Archbishop Binz asking me not to take part in the program. Having reassured its sponsors that I would take part, I felt obligated to do so, and went on as scheduled that night.

The next day I went to see Binz. He was very displeased that I had moderated the debate and equally upset at the press coverage which reported "a standing ovation for Bishop Shannon." I apologized to him for going against his request. He considered my role in the debate an act of disobedience. I had to agree, even though I thought there were extenuating circumstances. It was an unpleasant session for both of us. Prior to my departure for Santa Fe he had instructed me to conduct all my business with Archbishop Byrne. I had done so and had not seen Binz in private for almost six months.

Binz asked what reply I had made to the apostolic delegate's invitation for me to accept a post outside the country. I told him that I had decided against it. He suggested that I reconsider and assured me that the archdiocese would be responsible for my living expenses for life. I told him that I had no stomach for becoming an expatriate for life.

He then cautioned me that if I did not voluntarily accept one of the delegate's invitations I might find myself being assigned by the Holy See to take up residence at a place of their choice. Binz reminded me of an American bishop we both knew who had recently been summarily and mysteriously "transferred" by the Vatican from his own diocese in the United States to take up residence in Rome and to live there without any assignment for the indefinite future. The unexplained departure and the subsequent replacement of this bishop had occurred very suddenly and quietly.

Binz mentioned the bishop by name and said, "You know what happened to him." I said I did not know what had happened but was very curious to find out. Binz quickly realized that he had almost shared with me some classified information about the bishop in question. Sensing that Binz was warning me that I might suddenly be "transferred," with or without my consent, I told him that this could never happen. I would resign from the ministry and seek other work if Rome should ever summarily try to send me into exile with a promise of "living expenses" but no assignment.

Binz could not imagine that a bishop would ever say "no" to a Vatican order. I told him I would do so, without a second thought, if the order in question were a transparent violation of my rights as a person and as a priest. He said he regretted citing the experience of the bishop who had been "rusticated" to Rome and asked me to forget the reference. I found that hard to do. Binz knew more than he was telling me about the "future" my superiors were planning for me. But when I refused to consider any foreign post, with a pension and no duties, at the age of forty-eight, he said that he would not press me but that I would be wise to reconsider.

We parted with mutual pain. I liked Binz. I think he liked me. But we had reached a point in our relationship where we could not understand each other. He was hurt by what he called my "disobedience" in moderating the Baum-Davis debate. In retrospect I am inclined to the opinion that he was right and I was wrong — on this issue. I should have told my friends at the ACCR that I could not keep my promises to them because my archbishop had asked me to withdraw.

Back in Santa Fe, Archbishop Davis invited me to dinner one evening and told me, in confidence, that a new diocese was about to be created in Phoenix and that it would be part of the metropolitan province of Santa Fe. Then the surprise. He had nominated me to Rome to head the new diocese.

By not having shared fully with Davis all the reasons why I was in New Mexico, I had unintentionally exposed him to serious embarrassment at the Vatican — not to mention the problems he would certainly face once Cardinal McIntyre learned that I was nominated to head a diocese in a territory which had, until then, been under McIntyre's jurisdiction.

I told Davis at once the whole story of my problems with *Humanae Vitae,* my letter to Pope Paul VI, my encounters with Cardinal McIntyre, and my letter of resignation as a bishop and as a pastor. He took all this surprising news in stride, thanked me for my candor, and assured me he would write to Rome at once to withdraw my name from the list of nominees.

As I drove home that night I was on the verge of despair. What future was there for me in the church? The prospect of being the bishop of the new diocese in Phoenix, with a fresh start in the Southwest, was most attractive. But all that was merely something that "might have been." It was no longer just a question of McIntyre's determination to prevent my advancement in the church. My file in Rome now had solid evidence that I could not give the assent to a papal encyclical which the pope expected every bishop to give readily and firmly. My own archbishop, Leo Binz, who was privy to my difficulties with the encyclical, could no longer in good conscience vouch for my orthodoxy.

The life of a priest living in a rectory or in a religious community has a quality of social security which is more psychic than economic. I, for one, had taken this steady sense of well-being for granted during my active ministry. Living alone in New Mexico I missed it. I hated to see the day end and to face the prospect of returning to a dark and empty house. Planning meals and shopping for food, not to mention preparing it, were skills I never thought I would need and had no taste to acquire.

Each morning I offered Mass alone, had breakfast, and walked to school. The sky is more blue and the air more clear in New Mexico than any other place I have ever lived. Walking to and from the campus each day were refreshing respites bracketing the time I spent in a sparsely furnished, all but empty, house where I regularly consumed unbalanced, occasionally burned, portions of food served in combinations which Julia Child would report to the Humane Society. I often had dinner with the students on campus, both because their food was better than mine and to delay as long as possible my return to my quaint, charming, empty adobe.

My work at the college as part-time tutor and part-time administrator was absorbing and varied. Tuning up my skills as a teacher, getting back in the swing of reading Greek, and helping with a range of administrative tasks gave me welcome contact with students, tutors, board members, the Santa Fe community, and the donors who make that unusual college possible.

Two-hour seminars were scheduled for all students two nights a week on Tuesday and Thursday. Friday nights were reserved for lectures, concerts, or movies. Downtown Santa Fe offered such crumby movies that the neighbors for miles around came to see good films and golden oldies at St. John's. One of these would occasionally attract Georgia O'Keeffe enough to make her leave her hilltop studio-home in Abiquiú to spend the evening with us.

There is a quality of intellectual excitement at St. John's which, though not unique to that campus, is unusually vigorous there. The basic premise of the Great Books curriculum is that a working knowledge of the major literary and scientific works on which Western civilization rests is essential for any person who hopes to maintain, improve, modify, or even replace that intellectual tradition.

The daily tutorials, in language, literature, mathematics, and science, are *intensive* one-hour sessions in which one tutor and a dozen students might spend the whole period analyzing the rhetorical elements of a single sentence in Plato or a single theorem in Euclid. In contrast, the twice weekly evening seminars, with two tutors and fifteen students, all around a huge table, are *extensive* and try to explicate a single complete book at each meeting and, if possible, relate it to the intellectual traditions which it supports or challenges.

The curriculum of the Great Books is not everyone's cup of tea. But it is mine. And I drank deeply during my brief tenure in that goodly company of learners, some of whom were masters, most of whom were novices. Usually I was one of the latter, as I tried to carry my end of the dialog with Job, Dante, Aquinas, Shakespeare, Milton, Locke, Newton, Jefferson, or Tolstoy.

I dreaded the weekends. They seemed to last forever. Knowing only a handful of persons off campus and not wanting to wear out my welcome with faculty friends, I would often take long drives alone on Saturday or Sunday afternoon. To Taos, to the Benedictine monastery Christ in the Desert, near Abiquiú, to Chama, or to Valle Grande (my favorite destination). Growing up in the family of a cattleman I had heard all about Valle Grande, a cattleman's dream ranch, years before I ever saw its spectacular beauty.

It is one of the widest expanses of well-watered grasslands in the West. What makes it unique is that it lies cradled in the top of a mountain range. Called, geologically, a caldera, this valley was formed eons ago by the collapse of a ring of volcanic mountains. Today its several streams, good grass, and protective shield of upland timber make it a uniquely handsome and well-endowed grazing meadow. I would often pack a lunch, drive over the Jemez Range above Los Alamos, park at some high point, and read, pray, prepare my classes, or simply watch the lovely scene below me.

Like Willa Cather, I always feel better when I am in the West. There is a noun in Latin, *suavitas,* which means sweetness, fitness, or rightness. Those lovely days alone in the clear sun above the meadows of Valle Grande always gave me just that sense of well-being, order, balance, fitness. I even said my prayers more reverently and with greater recollection in that quiet retreat than at lower elevations. *Suavitas.*

One day driving back from Valle Grande, it suddenly struck me that my lonely life in the West was also a life of freedom. I had missed the consolations of priestly ministry and the security of living in a supportive religious community so much that I was beginning to feel sorry for myself. I was looking so longingly to the past that I had failed to realize the value of the present and the promise of the future.

My appointment at St. John's was temporary. And my permission to be absent from Minnesota was near its end. But by then I was aware that the earlier pain of separation from home and ministry was lessening. I was making new friends. I was no longer apprehensive about my position on *Humanae Vitae*. In fact, on reflection, I realized that no one had even discussed that topic in my presence for over a month.

The trauma of my transition was passing. I liked my work. My new friends at the college accepted me as a professional and as a peer. I began to think that it might be possible for me to stay in New Mexico. Realistically, however, I could not expect an indefinite leave of absence from my home diocese. Nor had I been offered any permanent position at St. John's.

What kind of place was open for me back home? My ministry there as a bishop had been largely limited to conferring the sacrament of confirmation. New rules allowed the bishop of a diocese to delegate this power to any pastor. Hence my only previous episcopal function as an auxiliary bishop could be handled by any pastor in the diocese.

Was it likely that I would be named bishop of a diocese of my own? I had to admit that this prospect was exceedingly dim. Could Archbishop Binz recommend to Rome that I be entrusted with such a responsibility? How long would it take before the apostolic delegate would feel free to oppose Cardinal McIntyre's standing veto of my appointment to a diocese?

As a well known Yale alumnus and as the son of one of its most respected deans, Dr. Weigle was asked, early in 1969, whether he would endorse me as a nominee to receive the Wilbur Lucius Cross alumni medal at the Yale commencement that spring. I was not aware that I was a nominee until he told me of his correspondence with Yale and of his endorsement of my name for this honor. I assume that all graduates of Yale are proud of their alma mater. I am. And it pleased me to learn that Yale was also proud of me. This recognition came at a time when my psyche needed a boost.

The day he told me about the Yale medal Dick Weigle also told me that the St. John's Board of Visitors and Governors had authorized him to invite me to become vice president of the college and to handle his administrative duties when he was at the other campus (Annapolis).

The offer of the vice presidency told me, in effect, that my work at St. John's was acceptable and that the faculty and board were willing to turn my temporary position into a permanent one. That sign of acceptance from persons I respected as first-rate educators was important to me.

The invitation, however, posed a deeper question. Accepting it would be tantamount to cutting my ties with my home diocese.

While pondering this invitation I made a fund-raising trip to Denver for the college. One afternoon, returning to the Brown Palace Hotel, I found a team of newsmen and TV cameramen sitting on the floor in the hallway outside my room. As I approached they rose, introduced themselves, and asked if I would consent to a televised interview. Why me? Why then? They replied that a story the preceding day (May 28) in the *Minneapolis Star* alleged that I had submitted my resignation as a pastor and as a bishop before I had left Minnesota. Were these allegations true? Would I confirm or deny them?

The allegations, of course, were true. But my offers of resignation, submitted in November 1968, had never been officially accepted nor declined. Not being prepared to discuss these matters on television, I declined to be interviewed.

Once inside my room I learned that the hotel message desk had a flood of calls for me. One of these was from Archbishop Binz, calling me home to help him respond to the questions he was getting from the public and the press about my canonical status.

When I reached St. Paul I learned that our chancery had issued a statement denying that I had ever submitted any letters of resignation. Binz later defended this statement on the grounds that he had never shared my letters with his staff. Hence the chancellor was telling the truth when he said that he never saw any letter of resignation signed by me. I could not understand how Binz could let his chancellor, Monsignor Terrance Berntson, get caught in the cross-fire of the press when the truth would inevitably surface that I had indeed submitted my resignation in writing to Binz on November 23, 1968.

When asked by the press for my version of the story, I later admitted that the letters of resignation had been submitted by me to Archbishop Binz. Furthermore, in all of my dealings with the apostolic delegate it was my clear impression that his great concern for my future was definitely predicated on his knowledge of my letters of resignation.

While the issue of my resignation was still a hot topic in the press I flew to New Haven on June 9 to participate in Yale's commencement exercises and to receive the Wilbur Lucius Cross Medal from the Yale Graduate School Association. On a lovely sunny day several cherished friends surprised me by their presence in the Yale Yard: Monsignor John Sankovitz from Minnesota, Ann Asman and her family from New

Haven, Chris and Elaine Buckley from Cheshire, Connecticut, Betty Medsger, of the *Philadelphia Evening Bulletin,* and George Collins of the *Boston Globe,* reporters who regularly covered the bishops' meetings for their papers.

Other reporters were on hand to cover the Yale story but also to ask me about stories in the *New York Times* and the *Washington Post* on June 5 about my "alleged" resignation. I confirmed that I had asked to be relieved of my duties as a pastor and as an auxiliary bishop.

Not surprisingly, the apostolic delegate had also read the *Times* and the *Post* on June 5. He wrote me the same day and again on June 9 to say that the "offers" he had made to me for "service outside the country" had never been intended as exile but only as personal suggestions from one bishop to another. These statements about our two earlier visits were vastly different from the clear messages he and Archbishop Binz had given me about a "post in the service of the Holy See outside the United States."

In response to the news that I had offered my resignation as a pastor and a bishop and to the news that I had been offered posts outside the country a large group of my friends, priests, religious, and laity, using the slogan "S.O.S." (Save Our Shannon), held a prayer vigil at the Cathedral of St. Paul on June 13. Embarrassed at this spectacle, mounted by well-meaning friends, I wrote, wired, and phoned its sponsors asking them to desist. My plea did not stop them. Such demonstrations of support for me at that stage could, in my opinion, only hurt all interested parties.

Binz was upset by the wide press coverage given to the resignation story. At his request I returned to St. Paul to meet with him and Archbishop Byrne on June 20 and 21. It was to be my last visit with Binz. In the course of it, he told me for the first time that he would recommend my discontinuing my column, "The Pilgrim Church," published each week in our diocesan paper, the *Catholic Bulletin.* One of the recent columns about Cardinal McIntyre's high-handed administration in Los Angeles and one about priestly celibacy (reporting on five retreats I had given for priests) had, in his view, done more harm than good. I assured him that I would, in obedience, discontinue the column.

In a way I was relieved at the prospect of giving up the column. It had become a weekly chore for me, living in Santa Fe, to find a suitable current topic for discussion with readers in Minnesota. But it still hurt to have Binz tell me that, of late, the columns I considered mild were doing more harm than good for the church.

The touchiest topic in our final meeting was not my weekly column, but a letter I had written to Willmar Thorkelson at the *Minneapolis Star,* confirming the fact of my letter of resignation and also revealing the substance of the apostolic delegate's subsequent proposals for my future service to the church outside the United States.

When Thorkelson printed this story the delegate telephoned Binz and Byrne to say that he had never proposed to me any assignment in South America. I was in the room at Binz's residence the day the delegate made this call (June 21). I did not speak to him. But I was dumbfounded to learn that he denied ever talking to me about going to South America.

Archbishop Byrne asked if I would be willing to go with him to talk to the delegate. I was angry, but I was also anxious to confront the delegate with this discrepancy between what he had told me in private and what he had told Archbishop Byrne on the phone.

Before flying back to Santa Fe on June 21 I went home to see my mother. We talked alone for two hours, covering some of the same ground we had covered the previous December when I had told her my plans for going to Santa Fe "for a semester." I then told her that I had been offered the vice presidency at St. John's and that my experience that day with Binz and Byrne and the delegate had helped me make up my mind. I was going back to Santa Fe to accept the offer and to make my home there.

My mother and I were great friends. Because she was almost totally deaf, we had developed a bond of wordless understanding. It was seldom necessary for me to "explain" my decisions or my motives to her. It was enough for her that these were my decisions and my motives. That day she told me that she had feared, ever since I went to Santa Fe, that my "four months" there would inevitably be extended.

There were some tears as we parted. By then she had been confined to a wheelchair for almost a decade, ever since my father's death in 1961. It is awkward hugging someone in a wheelchair. We did the best we could. Death would claim her within a year. She and I had a private joke about the Old Testament tradition whereby only fathers, not mothers, conferred blessings on their children. Her final words to me were "Wherever you go, whatever you do, you do with my blessing."

On June 25 I met with Dr. Weigle in Santa Fe to discuss the administrative duties I would have as his vice president. His schedule, administering two separate campuses, required him to spend alternate months in Santa Fe and Annapolis, year around. While he was away I was to handle administrative affairs in Santa Fe. I was also to assist him in his never-ending pursuit of money for the college. Weigle was an excellent fund-raiser. He had checked on my record as a fund-raiser at St. Thomas and thought its success augured well for me as his assistant. I did not tell him that by the end of my decade as a college president, I had acquired a distaste for the interminable task of raising money for the college.

But I was impressed by Weigle's total dedication to the tradition of the liberal arts, his absolute confidence in the St. John's program, and his cordial assurance that he wanted me to be his helper. Each of us needs to know that we are needed and that our skills do produce something of value for others. This concept of service, of sharing my talent, training, and time with others, had been a central element in my vocation to the priesthood.

I knew (though I doubt that Dick Weigle was aware of it) that accepting this offer would violate the terms of my canonical leave of absence and implicitly terminate my ministry as a priest. I had not made my original commitment to the priesthood lightly. On my day of ordination as a priest in 1946 and as a bishop in 1965 I had solemnly promised to live out my years as an obedient priest and bishop in whatever assignment the church would give me.

All my training in the church and the example of all the priests I most admired told me that my duty was to decline the vice presidency, go back to Minnesota at the end of my leave, pick up the pieces of my life there as best I could, accept whatever assignment would be given me, and keep my thoughts about *Humanae Vitae* to myself.

I had a close friend, a few years my senior, at that time who knew that he would remain an auxiliary bishop for the rest of his life. I was never sure whether his chronic bouts of depression were the cause or the effect of his certain knowledge that the church would never ask him to assume greater responsibilities.

I had no fear that fits of depression might claim me, but I dreaded the prospect of becoming only a "confirming" bishop for the rest of my days. Since then some have called this attitude on my part pride. Some have called it disobedience. Some have called it a loss of faith.

In my opinion it was a loss of faith in the administrative process of the church and in my ability to deliver in the future the kind of service, obedience, and assent expected of me by my superiors. I feared that my forthcoming trip to meet the delegate in Washington would be a well-orchestrated effort to fashion some kind of press release which would absolve Raimondi of any intention of sending me into "exile" and which would also seal my fate as an auxiliary bishop permanently frozen in grade, with little future prospect of a ministry beyond that of bringing the sacrament of confirmation to parishes in the diocese.

On June 25, with some unexpressed but deep personal reservations, I told Dr. Weigle that I would accept the vice presidency, fund-raising and all. I then wrote to Archbishops Binz and Byrne to tell them of my decision. That letter, in its entirety, reads as follows:

June 25, 1969

The Most Reverend Leo Binz
Archbishop of St. Paul and Minneapolis
366 Summit Avenue
St. Paul, MN 55102

Dear Archbishop Binz:

I wish to thank you and Archbishop Leo C. Byrne for the several hours you gave last week to meeting with me on Monday, Wednesday, and Saturday in your home. Since those discussions, and greatly influenced by them, I have tried carefully and prayerfully to review my present and future position in the Church.

It is apparent to me now, as it has been apparent to you for some time, that I have become a sign of contradiction to the People of God. A bishop is supposed to be a sign and a source of unity in the Church. From our several extended discussions it would now seem that I have, without desiring it, become a source of disunity in the Church.

As I protested repeatedly with you last week I am today more firm in my faith in Jesus Christ, his resurrection, and his promises to his people than I was years ago as a young priest. Age, experience, a little suffering, and the help of wiser men have all helped to confirm my Christian Faith. But time and experience, especially within the past year, have eroded my confidence in many ecclesiastical persons and procedures within the Roman Catholic Church to such an extent that I have concluded that I am no longer able to serve the Church as a bishop and as a priest, in the manner which the Church expects us to do. Believe me I have tried to fulfill these honorable roles to the best of my ability.

Today I find myself the center of a great deal of public notoriety. I am embarrassed to have become a rallying point for many persons and movements in the Church which I cannot honestly espouse. My inability to give to Pope Paul VI's encyclical "Humanae Vitae" the internal and external assent it asks of all Catholics has been wrongly and widely interpreted as a sign of my rejection of the Church and of the pope. Neither of these assumptions is true.

However, at a time which calls for courage, confidence in Christ, belief in his promises, and high hopes for his Church, I have repeatedly found myself at odds with the timidity, secrecy, studied ambiguity, the curial style, and the heavy-handedness of many persons in authority in the Church. As you know, I have said often and will repeat now, I dearly love the Catholic Church. Its sacred teachings have shaped and formed me. Its Christian values are my daily guides, much and often as I fail to attain them. Hence I cannot deliberately do anything to hurt the Church. I pray daily for its renewal according to the mind of Christ, and I pray constantly that I may always be recognized by its founder and its judge as one of its members.

I have, however, concluded that it would be for the best interest of the people of God at this time for me to relinquish my duties as a bishop, as a pastor, and as a priest. You already have in writing, dated November 23, 1968, my formal resignation as a pastor and as an auxiliary bishop. I have no intention, now or ever, of seeking laicization. I simply hope to be able to live the rest of my days as a lay person in the Church. I realize that such a plan is unusual. At the present time it seems to me the only honorable solution to my present dilemma and yours.

The Board of Visitors and Governors of St. John's College, Santa Fe, has invited me to accept the position of vice president of this fine college. I have today agreed to accept this position. I am deeply grateful to St. John's, its president and its board, for this offer and for the confidence in me which it reflects.

It is not possible to explain in such a letter as this all the reasons which have led me to the difficult decisions stated above. Many of these are contained in detail in the several letters I have sent to you since last September and even more specifically in my extended verbal comments to you in our three long meetings last week.

I wish in closing to thank you sincerely for the many acts of kindness you have shown to me over several years. I promise you my earnest prayers that the Holy Spirit will guide you in your honorable and challenging role as a leader in these days of renewal within the Church. I ask also that you pray for me.

Respectfully yours in Christ,<br>
*James P. Shannon*

cc: Archbishop Leo C. Byrne
    226 Summit Avenue
    St. Paul, MN 55102

On June 28 I flew to Washington. Archbishop Byrne was waiting for me at the Delegation. The delegate asked if we would agree to have Father Thomas R. Gallagher, O.P., of the Delegation staff sit in on our meeting as a witness and a secretary. We offered no objection.

It quickly became clear that the purpose of the meeting was indeed to prepare a statement about me for the delegate to send to all the bishops of the country and to the press. Raimondi denied, as he had earlier on the telephone to Leo Byrne, that he had ever suggested that I accept a position in South America. I recalled for him specific elements in that conversation about my query of going to "any country" in South America, and about my saying that South America is a continent. He denied ever being party to such a discussion.

Then why had Raimondi written to me on March 17 to invite me to

Washington to discuss with him "a development of interest to Your Excellency"? The single purpose and sole focus of that visit in late March
had been to explore my readiness to take up residence "somewhere" in
South America. This was the "development of interest" which was the
occasion for the meeting.

I could not, and still do not, understand why our talk about South
America was any more sensitive than our earlier discussions about my
going to Jerusalem, Rome, or Switzerland. Raimondi did not deny that
he had proposed these places for me, but never, he said, in the sense of
an "exile."

The focus of our discussion was that his several suggestions to
me had been for "temporary" assignments, to last only as long as I
needed "rest and quiet" to consider the questions of conscience raised
for me by Pope Paul's encyclical. We concluded our meeting with an
agreement that the delegate would draft and send to all the bishops a
statement explaining his good intentions and my "misunderstandings"
or "misinterpretations" of his well-meant suggestions to me.

Once Archbishop Byrne and I were alone, I asked his reaction to
that part of our meeting which dealt with my allegation and the delegate's denial that during our last visit at the Delegation, in late March,
he had proposed that I accept a post "in the service of the Holy Father
in South America." Byrne waited several seconds before giving me his
careful reply: "Jim, the apostolic delegate is an honorable man."

Archbishop Byrne offered me a ride to the airport. I declined and
said that I would rather walk part way alone and then hail a cab. I did
not tell him that my career as his auxiliary bishop was over. He would
learn that when he read his mail the next day. We shook hands at the
door of the Delegation and said goodbye. I never saw Byrne again. He
died suddenly in 1974.

## CHAPTER EIGHTEEN

# A NEW LIFE

Canon law in the Catholic Church assumes that an adult male of sound mind can make a promise at ordination that he will give obedience to his bishop, live out his days in the service of the church, and live till death as a celibate. Typically, Catholic people have a deep and genuine respect for their priests, because most priests live up to these high standards which they voluntarily embrace in their youth.

The promise of obedience to one's bishop is usually not a great burden. Most bishops are fair and reasonable men. Seldom do they ask or expect the impossible from their priests. Keeping my promise of obedience under four different archbishops (Murray, Brady, Binz, and Byrne) had never been a problem for me.

Similarly the promise of celibacy which I made before ordination was a condition of that vocation which I willingly accepted. Recent public discussion of celibacy as a necessary condition for the priesthood has heard a growing number of priests either questioning or rejecting this threshold requirement for holy orders. My experience as a retreat master for priests, already cited, gave me some surprising new insights from priests who favor a change in this discipline.

Nonetheless, in my opinion, and based on my own experience, for most priests the promise to live a celibate life is a burden to which they steadily adjust as the fullness of their priestly vocation matures. The difficulty of staying celibate, as an active priest in the ministry, is, I believe, often exaggerated in our increasingly and excessively sex-conscious culture.

However, the record is equally clear that some good, generous, and honorable men, ordained to the sacred priesthood, reach a stage in their lives at which they find it impossible, for a variety of reasons, to deliver to the church and to the people of God the kind and the degree of priestly service which the church expects of them.

Obedience and celibacy are the best known, but not the only, and not always the principal, burdens of the priestly vocation. There is a line in T. S. Eliot's *Murder in the Cathedral* in which Thomas Becket, archbishop of Canterbury, describes the maturing process, "when we find no longer all things possible." That kind of noonday devil is probably better known to most priests at midcareer than any temptations to break their promises of obedience or celibacy.

It is a tragedy of record that priests can resolve this midlife trauma by deciding to bank the fires of their earlier zeal, take life a little easier, play a little more golf, take more and longer vacations, and counsel the housekeeper to set a better table in the rectory. Father Ernest Burner, the protagonist in J. F. Powers's short story *Prince of Darkness,* is probably the best-known member of this class of obedient, celibate, and relaxed gentlemen of the cloth.

Ernest Burner, with his consuming interest in good food, cold beer, days off, and long tee-shots, is not typical of the priests I know. But I had a growing fear that his lukewarm, self-serving ministry might shortly be a fair description of my lifestyle, if I should return to some assignment in my home diocese either after repudiating my known views on *Humanae Vitae* or with some tacit understanding that I would keep these opinions to myself.

Somewhere in my extended dialog with my superiors on what came to be known as my "problem" with Pope Paul's encyclical, I grew weary of the tedium of the ecclesiastical process and the administrative style of my superiors. When my friend Monsignor Terrence Murphy came to see me in Santa Fe, he asked whether I still wanted to be a bishop. The directness of the question surprised me. But I had to admit that I did not, given the conditions which I feared would accompany my return to the ministry. It shocked me to hear my own reply to his disarming question. The day he stayed with me we concelebrated Mass together in my little house. It was the last time I offered Mass. Somehow Father Murphy's direct query had forced me to recognize that I was trying to hold together two careers which I could no longer reconcile.

My decision to become vice president of St. John's College compromised my canonical status as a diocesan priest. I was, in effect, absent from my assigned duty without the permission of my bishop. Binz and Byrne both expressed strong disapproval, in the press, of my accepting the vice presidency. But they took no canonical steps to discipline or penalize me.

I was living in limbo. I still dressed as a priest. I attended Mass every Sunday and received the Eucharist, but I no longer performed any priestly functions. I knew that I was at a critical fork in the road. The options were clear: either resume my ministry and accept whatever status would be given me, or make a clean break with the past and try to fashion some completely new career for the future.

As my concepts of priesthood and ministry had matured over the years, I attached increasing importance to serving the needs of others as a central function of ministry. I believe firmly that the Holy Spirit speaks to each of us, and especially to priests, daily through the needs of other persons. I was also convinced, early on, that the Holy Spirit is licensed to broadcast on many more frequencies than are recognized in canon law.

Acting on these premises I had found it progressively easier in my years as a priest to find deep personal satisfaction and growth in serving the needs of others. I came to believe that the secret which lies at the heart of the life, suffering, death, and resurrection of Jesus Christ is that human growth, joy, happiness, and *suavitas* come into our lives only if, when, and to the extent that we take him at his word when he said: "Unless a wheat grain falls into the ground and dies, it remains only a single grain; but if it dies, it yields a rich harvest" (John 12:24).

More than two decades as a priest had given me ample opportunity to test this paradox. On the basis of my own experience I found it to be true. The persons I know who live it best are the best specimens of the human family I have ever met. Mother Teresa of Calcutta was probably the best-known practitioner of the Christian paradox in this century. But the rest of us who consider ourselves Christians are duty-bound to the same code of service as she. She merely did it better than the rest of us.

This mode of looking at the life of Christ and at my own life had, by 1969, given me a negative view of many ecclesiastical practices which the church expected me, as a bishop, to accept, practice, and endorse. *Humanae Vitae* had shaken my faith in the inerrancy of papal teaching on questions of morality. Dealing personally with two different apostolic delegates had weakened my original pride and confidence in the ecclesiastical process on levels higher than mine. And the inability of my two archbishops, both good men, to address or even to face Cardinal McIntyre when he was angry with me, had eroded the importance, in my mind, of continuing to function as a bishop in the church.

As I pondered my future in the church in 1969 more than one friend urged me to return to my own diocese, take any position assigned to me, and use that base and my status as a bishop to organize like-minded Catholics to speak out against the papal encyclical and, implicitly, against other regulations in the church which they and I considered ripe for reform. I had no stomach for this kind of a future. By instinct I am a peacemaker. All my life I have deliberately chosen to be a bridge builder. I could not change my style over the weekend and become a maverick bishop working against the system from the inside.

With the passing of time in Santa Fe and after the several meetings with my superiors in Minnesota it became clear that whatever future ministry was open to me would not be in my role as a bishop. But, like other priests about to leave the ministry, I had no clear idea of any alternative career that would offer me the "ministry of service" which I considered my only possible future course.

In considering this dilemma I did not sense the worry about money which other priests in this quandary had described to me. Although my financial reserves were extremely modest, I was confident of my academic credentials, of my administrative skills, and of myself. I knew, more by instinct than reason, that making a living in the secular world would not likely be a problem for me.

My real concern was whether, without the psychological support and the camaraderie of the priesthood, I could live alone and be reasonably happy. As a priest I had become accustomed to being and working alone most of the time. One reason that celibacy is a tolerable state is that it allows its practitioners more than the ordinary amount of time to indulge their interests in music, teaching, reading, prayer, writing, study, travel, athletics, or whatever. I had always found this regimen satisfying and fulfilling. I like to be alone. Some of the time.

After three months in Santa Fe I discovered the limits of my desire to be alone. Peace and quiet are nice. But being alone in all my off-duty hours was a condition I quickly learned I could not endure permanently.

At first the thought of marriage scared me. I feared that I was a confirmed bachelor who would find adjustment to marriage impossible. But I was also apprehensive that, cut off from the support of the priesthood, I could not face the prospect of living alone for life. As I pondered the possibility of marriage I feared that my family, cherished friends, and what Archbishop Byrne called "my following" would be scandalized and injured, some beyond repair.

Knowing all this I first began to consider the prospect of marriage in the late spring of 1969. I had met Ruth Wilkinson in Washington, D.C., in 1964, when she was the personal secretary for Senator Kenneth B. Keating, and I was the chairman of the Association of American Colleges. Keating and Ruth were both natives of Rochester, New York. She was a lifelong and very active member of the Christian Church (Disciples of Christ). At the time we met, she worshiped at the

National Christian Church in Washington, but retained her permanent membership in the Christian Church in Rochester. Her hometown congregation was then debating whether to retain or sell their old church in the inner city and move to the suburbs. When she asked my counsel about the moral obligation of a Christian congregation to stay in place when its neighborhood starts to "change," I gave her some things to read on the subject of racism, including a piece by me on this topic. Later she wrote me to express her agreements and problems with what I had written. I responded as tactfully as I could, not wanting to be drawn into any more ecclesiastical rhubarbs than the ones I already had. She persisted and I replied with courtesy, if not enthusiasm. She is a very strong-minded woman who does not find it difficult in any spirited discussion to say, "I repeat the question."

After Senator Keating lost his bid for reelection to Robert Kennedy in 1966, Ruth returned to Rochester to be with her family and her father who was then dying of cancer. I heard from her at the time of his death and on occasion after that.

When I moved to Santa Fe early in 1969 our correspondence resumed. During the spring vacation that year I visited her in Rochester and shared with her the full story of my status in the church and my dilemma about the future. After that we corresponded more frequently and I invited her to visit Santa Fe. She liked the town and the college, but not the wide open spaces of the West. What I considered friendly expanses of clear air and blue sky she considered lonely, empty, and desolate. She is really a city person.

During that visit we first talked, most cautiously, about marriage. We were both apprehensive that such a union would be under impossible strains from the beginning. She had been married and divorced before we met. Her former husband had died in 1964. She was anxious not to make that mistake again. I was far from confident of my ability to be a good marriage partner.

We admitted to each other that our lives were lonely. But we were old enough to know that successful marriage calls for more common ground than this negative bond. She was candid about her preference for living in a city. I was equally candid in saying that I felt I could not possibly leave New Mexico. I already knew that she was just as devoted to her Protestant tradition as I was to my Catholic origins. She also told me that she had attended a short course on Catholic doctrine and practice, but still felt that she could not in good conscience end her affiliation with the Disciples of Christ. I quickly assured her that I did not expect her to become a Catholic. On balance that visit brought into the open some fundamental differences we both considered serious. When she left New Mexico, I considered the visit a failure.

We did agree that marriage at our age, with our disparate backgrounds, was an extremely high risk venture. For different reasons each of us considered the word "love" a classified term to be used most cautiously. We were reluctant to admit that we were in love if we could not reach the further conclusion that we were prepared to marry and live with the consequences of this decision.

From our first meeting I admired Ruth's style. She is a strong person. She was a liberated woman long before that term acquired its current vogue. Her youthful formation in the Christian Church also gave her a deep sense of stewardship, the conviction that all we have is from God and that all God's gifts to us are to be shared with other persons. My formal theological training was more extensive than hers, but I soon learned that she suffers, vicariously, with other persons much more intensely than I do.

For more than a decade she had been a legal secretary for New York State Senator Thomas Laverne. As his administrative assistant during the legislative sessions in Albany she acquired her abiding interest in the political process, and as his legal secretary in Rochester she gained her knowledge of the law and her considerable administrative skills.

In World War II she had been in the WAVES. Only half in jest, she modestly admitted that, had she stayed in the Navy, she might be an admiral today. Kidding aside, I agreed. When she told me that some of her friends called her "Auntie Mame," I knew at once why they did. It fits her. She has a zany streak that I find fascinating.

We talked seriously about religious belief, life, death, and prayer. Once we got away from ecclesiastical regulations, hers and mine, we found that we had much in common. She shared my view that God speaks to each of us continually through the evident sufferings of other persons. Her concern for the poor and the disenfranchised is vintage Christian doctrine.

Sharing the stories of our lives I also learned that she had more psychic scar tissue than I had. When I spoke of being lonely for six months in Santa Fe she smiled as though I did not know what loneliness is. She knew. She had lived it. It had only visited me — briefly.

We wanted to believe that we could beat the odds and fashion a solid, loving, supportive marriage. We knew the odds were against us. But I did not have the courage to make either of the two crucial decisions facing me: to leave my priestly ministry and to ask her to marry me.

The offer of the vice presidency at St. John's gave me the occasion, the economic security, and the courage to make both of these decisions. After my final visit with the apostolic delegate in Washington in late June, I wrote a detailed long-hand letter to my mother, telling her of my decision to ask Ruth to marry me. The day mother received it she had my sister Mary place a long distance call to me. Mother could not hear on the telephone. She could only speak into it. Once Mary had me on the line mother came on and said, "I have read your letter a dozen times. I do understand. You have my blessing. God be with you and Ruth. Please bring her to see me as soon as you can." I could not thank her. She could not hear me.

Over the July 4 holiday I flew to Rochester, proposed to Ruth, was accepted, and got a marriage license. We were relieved to have that decision behind us and buoyed at the prospect of helping each other build new lives together.

A month later on August 2 we were married in the Christian Church in Endicott, New York, with the Reverend Hugh Kelly as minister. Ruth's son, Peter Van Wieren, and his wife, Elaine, were our attendants. Ruth's mother, three sisters, and two brothers-in-law were also with us for the ceremony and for a family dinner later that day.

We left New York the same day by car for Santa Fe, by way of Minnesota, to visit my mother and family. Driving west this time, with Ruth beside me, was vastly easier than my earlier solo trip in winter from Minnesota to New Mexico.

## CHAPTER NINETEEN

# LOS RANCHOS
# AND LAW SCHOOL

Our first day in Santa Fe was a Sunday. We went to morning Mass at the cathedral and were astonished to find ourselves named in the homily. The first news of our marriage was in the paper that day. The priest celebrating Mass used the story about us as a text for his sermon. He compared us to the hippies who roamed the Santa Fe Plaza with "no aim or purpose in life but to please themselves." We were off to a bad start in our new home town. That encounter was a salutary early warning for both of us not to take for granted the warmth of earlier friendships.

We soon learned to wait for others to make the first overture of friendliness. Code words and body language became signals telling us that some old flames of friendship no longer burned brightly. Fortunately, in Santa Fe there were very few such cool encounters. Our landlady, Henrietta Harris, gave a champagne brunch for us at her home that first morning after Mass, and our neighbor Farona Konopak hosted a fancy dinner the next night for our close neighbors on Camino del Monte Sol.

Our house, brand new in April, still lacked a woman's touch. Ruth said it looked like a monastery. At first I took that as a compliment. She thrives on challenges. Within a month she transformed the place. She is by nature an organizer, with some of the traits of a benevolent despot.

Santa Fe is lovely in any season. But in August, on many afternoons at about 4 P.M. a soft rain shower lasting about ten minutes rinses the dust from the piñon trees. After the rain, when the sun hits the wet pine boughs, evaporation gives the warm air a fresh pine fragrance. As our home took shape and as our days fell into a regular routine, the West began to state its charm for Ruth. I was already a true believer.

Summer and fall passed quickly. As vice president of the college I was expected to represent Dr. Weigle at social events when he was in Annapolis. Ruth and I were soon at ease in the dual "town and gown" roles we were asked to fill.

Often as we awoke in the morning that summer she would say, "I can't tell you how great it is to wake up in our own home and not have to go to work." It pleased me to see her so happy. We were off to a fresh start in a new life together.

Within a month of our wedding a small stream of letters began to reach me from priests around the country. Many asked if they could come to see me. Most of them were weighing the decision to remain in the priestly ministry or to resign. I answered each letter and granted every interview requested, but never urged any of my new pen-pals to leave the priesthood. Many of them did later choose to resign. But in each instance the burden of my counsel was that they should continue in the priesthood, if possible. As these men passed through our home, Ruth often remarked that they were some of the finest persons she had ever met. I modestly admitted that she was absolutely correct.

The daily mail also brought me from time to time two other kinds of letters: requests from laymen asking me to ordain them to the priesthood or requests from priests asking me to ordain them to the episcopacy. Canonically, I am still a priest and still a bishop. Foolish or not, these writers knew enough about holy orders to understand that I still had the power, if not the canonical authority, to ordain men validly to the priesthood and to the episcopacy. They did not know that I was unwilling to exercise this power contrary to the canonical discipline of the church. Without knowing me, they had assumed that, because I could not assent to *Humanae Vitae,* I had become some kind of episcopal maverick, ready to join any group challenging the traditions or the discipline of the church. The Catholic Church is my spiritual home. I owe it an enormous debt of gratitude and respect. I could never use the priestly or episcopal powers which it had given me to injure it.

Santa Fe is one of the few state capitals in the nation without major airport facilities. The natives want it that way. They have turned down federal funds offered to widen and strengthen the runways on their landing strip. The big jets can land in Albuquerque, sixty miles to the south, and Santa Fe can keep its identity as a small town where writers, artists, and craftspeople quietly turn out work they are proud to sign.

Artists abound in Santa Fe, but the biggest industry in town is politics and the state bureaucracy. The lively brand of politics produced by the interplay of Indian, Spanish, and Anglo cultures, with all their cultural nuances, makes life in New Mexico, but especially in the capital city, a fascinating laboratory for anyone interested in the political process. Ruth was in her element. It was a long way from Albany and

Washington. And it wasn't just the old familiar two-party system. But it was never dull. She loved it and was soon involved as a volunteer in the gubernatorial campaign of Bruce King. She organized a "coffee" at our house for the neighbors to meet Bruce. We took our fair share of the credit when he became the new governor.

The war in Vietnam was then at its peak. CALCAV had an active chapter in Santa Fe. We signed up and helped plan a candlelight vigil at the capitol and a march for peace around the plaza and to the cathedral. Archbishop Davis marched and sang with us. National sentiment was by then swinging slowly against the war, but Davis was still the only archbishop willing to hit the streets to protest U.S. involvement in it.

Occasional fund-raising trips for the college took me to New York, Washington, Texas, or California, but most of my work for the college was on campus. The tutorial I led in Greek met four mornings a week. I also helped out as a substitute seminar leader whenever another tutor was ill or out of town.

One rule at St. John's is that students are asked *not* to take part in seminar discussions if they have not read the book under discussion. Hence when a tutor notices a student not participating in the dialog, it is reasonable to assume that the student is unprepared. But if the same student is silent two nights in a row, the tutor will find an occasion to have coffee and chat to find out if there is some problem deeper than merely being unprepared for a single class. The tutors keep a slack rein and try not to monitor students too closely. But once "a flag is on the field" that a student is having trouble, the St. John's system swings into action quickly to find out what's wrong and what can be done about it. Not all colleges have such dependable rapport between the masters and the novices.

There is a saying at St. John's that there are no administrators on campus, only tutors, some of whom do a little part-time work as administrators. I was one of these hybrids. Jack Rule and Bill Darkey, the dean of students and the dean of studies, were my fellow tutors who also did (quite) a little part-time administrative work. Rule had been a professor of mathematics at Massachusetts Institute of Technology before coming to Santa Fe, and Darkey was one of the early graduates of the "new program" at St. John's in Annapolis. We were a complementary team. They became my closest friends and trusted counselors.

Through Jack Rule I was also invited to join Santa Fe's oldest permanent, floating, male chauvinist monthly dinner club. "Quien Sabe?" is a fascinating crowd of eighteen writers, artists, educators, lawyers, doctors, and businessmen who meet on the first Friday night of each month for deep talk, shop talk, good food, and a few cheering glasses.

Another friend whose bond with Ruth and me grew stronger after our marriage was Bishop Charles Buswell of Pueblo, Colorado. On Halloween night of 1969 he was driving through Santa Fe and stopped for dinner at our home. Our meal was repeatedly interrupted by local small-fry calling for "tricks or treats." He helped us dish out the treats at the door. When he left, Ruth apologized that his dinner, with all the door calls, had probably been cold. He wrote her the next day to say that there is an old spiritual maxim which he learned at Louvain: "Cold dinners with hob-goblins are always better than warm dinners with no hob-goblins."

Another new friend in our early days in Santa Fe was Bruce Rolstad, pastor of the Christian Church (Disciples of Christ) in Santa Fe. Bruce and his wife, Jacque, were active members of CALCAV (as I was). We marched and prayed with them for peace.

There is a strong military and federal tradition in New Mexico. Payrolls at Kirtland Air Force Base, White Sands Proving Grounds, Cannon Air Force Base, Los Alamos Research Laboratory, Sandia Laboratory, and the Bureau of Indian Affairs pump federal dollars steadily into the New Mexico economy. Furthermore, a career in the military, as a draftee or a volunteer, has always been in our society an honorable avenue of social mobility and a prelude to future education for the members of low-income families. Hence local units of the American Legion and the VFW, not to mention many church elders, took a dim view of academic or ecclesiastical "peaceniks" marching and praying for the war to end.

In the fall of 1969 I was named director of the St. John's Graduate Institute, the master's degree summer program, also based on the Great Books. Planning the curriculum and recruiting the faculty and students for the summer session of 1970 were my principal tasks that winter and spring. Occasional trips to Annapolis introduced me anew to the "other" campus and the rest of the St. John's faculty.

The corporate structure of St. John's was unique. It was then a single corporation, with one president and one board, operating two campuses. From time to time faculty members in Santa Fe or Annapolis would ask whether the time had come to split the schools and create two separate corporations. Faculty opinion in favor of such a split became strong early in 1970. A joint meeting of the two faculties with the board of governors brought the discussion to a head. President Weigle and the board favored the status quo. But as a compromise position the board decided to create a new administrative post of provost on each campus. The person in this position was to be the chief operating officer for each campus, reporting to President Weigle.

The faculty in Santa Fe voted to offer this post to me. I was honored by the invitation, but uncertain about accepting it. Dick Weigle urged me to accept. It was clearly an advancement for me in an academic community I respected.

Ruth and I took some time to ponder our response. I asked Weigle whether the new position would involve me in more extensive fund-raising. He said it would. Weigle relished the role of fund-raiser. I do not. I was neither eager nor ready to leave St. John's or Santa Fe. But on balance, the fund-raising duties tipped the scales for us against accepting the post. Weigle asked me to reconsider but assured me that I would still be welcome to stay on as a tutor, even if I chose not to be the provost. The duties previously assigned to me as vice president were to be assigned to the new provost.

I did not think it fair to turn down the position of provost and then stay on to look over the shoulder of whoever would fill that new role. With Ruth's agreement, but without knowing our next step, I offered my resignation as vice president of the college, effective at the end of the summer session in August of 1970.

I had no other job offer and no clear idea what I wanted to do. Ruth had been a volunteer that year at St. Vincent's Hospital, but held no other job. My resignation at St. John's was the occasion for her to tell me that her new role as housewife had begun to lose its original charm. She is a high-drive person. She missed the excitement and the engagement of her political careers in Albany and Washington. It was time for each of us to look for a new position.

In that first year we learned that we were both attracted to the study of law. One of her employers, an attorney in Rochester, had urged her at one time to become a lawyer. My interest in the law had been quickened by the Supreme Court decision in 1954 in Brown vs. Board of Education. This landmark case, declaring segregated public schools unconstitutional, came down at a time of great social unrest, country-wide. As a witness at Selma and as a critic of Vietnam, I had been as active in the civil and human rights movements of the '60s as my other assignments would allow.

In the role of social activist I had grown increasingly uncomfortable with many of my liberal associates who were more eloquent in describing the ills of society than in formulating workable solutions for our civic and moral dilemmas. These dedicated citizens were regularly motivated by good will but often lacked the knowledge or skill to devise constructive programs to alleviate the civic maladies they would eliminate.

The decisive action of our Supreme Court in Brown vs. Board of Education impressed me with the continuing vigor of the Anglo-American legal system for righting wrongs and charting equitable social courses. With Ruth's encouragement I took the Law School Aptitude Test and applied for admission to law school at the University of New Mexico. We agreed that if I were accepted we would move closer to Albuquerque and she would find a job to support us while I went to school. She welcomed the prospect of a little more excitement than tending a house which she usually had shipshape by 9:00 A.M. daily, and I was intrigued at the possibility of studying law.

In my interview with Thomas Christopher, dean of the law school, I learned that his admissions committee had some doubts about admitting me. In his words: "The track record in law school for forty-nine-year-old freshmen is not good." He asked about my plans for the future. I admitted that I wanted an education in the law more than a future law practice. That admission did not help my case. But after our visit I was admitted. Classes were to start in late August.

Early in 1970 my friend Bower Hawthorne, editor of the *Minneapolis Tribune,* had invited me to begin writing in the Sunday *Tribune* the "Pilgrim Church" column I had done weekly for the *Catholic Bulletin* until Archbishop Binz asked me to stop in 1969. The *Tribune* did not then have a separate religion page. It preferred to use its opinion-editorial pages as a forum for the discussion of the religious, moral, or ethical aspects of current political and social questions. I accepted the offer and began the column in March of that year. It appeared regularly for the next twenty years, but without the title "Pilgrim Church." I had great latitude in choosing subject matter for it. On occasion it treated ecclesiastical topics, but usually addressed questions of wider concern.

On July 1 word came that my mother had died in her sleep the previous night. She was in her ninety-fifth year. A few weeks earlier I had been to Minnesota to see her. She told me then that she was ready for death. I knew that was our last meeting. She did too. It was a difficult parting. She was a valiant woman, who gave courage, strength, and good cheer to everyone who knew her. She had survived two husbands and three sons. In times of sorrow she was fond of saying, "Remember, children, the fire that melts the butter hardens the iron."

Her funeral Mass at St. Augustine's Church, our home parish, drew "the full of the house," as my Irish father would have put it. Archbishop Leo Binz and scores of my fellow priests came to pay their final respects to her.

At the end of the summer session Ruth and I left St. John's and Santa Fe. We bought a comfortable adobe house, part of it allegedly a hundred years old, on two acres "with ditch rights" in the village of Los Ranchos near the Rio Grande, just north of Albuquerque. Ruth whipped the place into shape, made new curtains, sent me off to law school, and got herself a job as a secretary. Family funds were low, but we splurged and bought a 1962 Volkswagen "bug" for me to drive to school.

Without realizing exactly when it had happened I had failed to catch on when Ruth stopped saying how glad she was not to be going to work each day. Once she got back in the regimen of working outside our home, however, I realized how much she had missed it.

I had a lot of catching up to do in understanding the feminine psyche. I was not a quick study in this new venture and often misread the signals I should have caught. Ruth missed her family more than she had ever told me. In our first year together I was extremely busy. I would regularly get up at 5:00 A.M. to prepare classes or to complete unfinished office work. We socialized a lot on college affairs, but had very little leisure alone together. It slowly dawned on me that I had asked a lot more of Ruth than I knew the day I asked her to marry me. While I was scrambling to fashion a new professional career for myself at St. John's, I had assumed that Ruth found her days equally busy and fulfilling. I was mistaken. The move to Los Ranchos came at a good time for each of us.

That move also brought Nancy and Howard Stump into our lives. They were our nearest neighbors in the village and quickly became our dearest friends. The week we arrived they gave a party to introduce us to the neighbors. They fed our dogs and took in our mail when we were away, brought us fresh bread on "bake day," made a path to our door, shared windfalls of chili, apples, and zucchini with us, and made us feel like "family" from day one.

Law school professors like to think that they engage their students in "Socratic dialogs." God forgive them. Socrates must be spinning in his grave. A Socratic dialog is a rhetorical art form between a master and a novice which leads steadily, by subtle increments, to some satisfying shock of recognition at the end of the exercise.

In contrast, old style law school pedagogy is essentially a tricky quiz game, loaded to demonstrate the industry or virtuosity of the professor and the slothfulness or stupidity of the students. In its worst form it once made women students cry and male students curse. Since women's liberation, I am told, it makes men cry and women curse. In fairness, I must say here that all but two of my law school professors were first-rate students of the law and excellent teachers. Those two, however, were from the old school. One day, in my first semester, listening to an endless harangue by one of these tedious quizmasters, I raised my hand in exasperation and asked whether we could not get on with learning the law instead of listening to his withering attack on a hapless student who had not read the cases assigned for that day. That professor never spoke to me during the next three years. Just as well.

Programs in clinical law, designed to introduce the student to the elements of civil and criminal practice outside the classroom, were just then coming into vogue. In my first semester I worked two afternoons a week in the county jail and the court house in the "release on recognizance" program sponsored by the district court. All the judges, save two, were in favor of the program and helped us learn the law from the inside. One of the two judges who enjoyed making life miserable for law students once explained to me that in the real world there are mean judges and we should get ready to deal with them. I suppose that argument has some merit. But not much.

In my second and third years I was a teaching assistant, drawing a small salary, supervising the drafting of the pleadings framed by fellow students in their clinical law courses. Ruth did double duty in those days, working by day in the personnel department at the Hilton Hotels in Albuquerque and Santa Fe, and helping me by night to learn my way in the world of pleadings, motions, and legal affidavits she knew far better than I.

There were then eight district judges in Bernalillo County. In the middle of my second year Daniel McPherson, the presiding judge, called me into his chambers to say that his associates had voted to offer me the job of court administrator. It was a full-time position. To take it I would have had to quit law school. I thanked him and declined. Law school was fascinating, full-time work for me.

I also found time that first year to run for office — a seat on the Los Ranchos village council. I lost by the widest margin in recorded history and put to rest forever any political ambition lurking in my psyche.

On Sundays we worshiped at Aquinas Chapel on the university campus where Dominican priests, some of whom I had known in Minnesota, ministered to the Catholic community. In those days following Vatican II many traditional Catholics had difficulty in accepting the less formal liturgies then becoming popular. One Sunday the celebrant at Mass, Father George Welch, told us all that we were too uptight. He urged us to loosen up and sense the joy of the liturgy. Then he played a banjo recording of "When My Baby Smiles at Me" as the offertory hymn. He had the whole congregation in smiles. I could only say, "Thank God Cardinal McIntyre can't hear this." He would have blown a gasket.

In the summer of 1971 I clerked in the office of the attorney general of New Mexico. The round trip to Santa Fe, every day, was 110 miles. Coming home against the sun made for some long days. But in the clear air of morning the drive to Santa Fe was a treat. On a clear day in New Mexico you can often see a dozen "contrails" high in the sky, the wake of transcontinental jets. Coming up over La Bajada from the Rio Grande Valley and then dropping down into the Santa Fe basin is a far more interesting drive to the office than most commuters ever see.

Early in 1971 I had agreed to deliver the keynote address "Neighbors in the Global Village" at the Twelfth Annual Biblical Institute at Barat College, Lake Forest, Illinois. When Cardinal John Cody of Chicago learned that I was scheduled to speak in his diocese, he ordered the program cancelled unless I was removed from the list of speakers. He told the sponsors of the conference that inviting me to address a biblical studies symposium on a Catholic campus was "an insult to the American hierarchy." When I heard this I offered to remove myself from the program. The sponsors refused to cancel my address and moved the entire meeting to the campus of George Williams College in Downers Grove, Illinois, just outside Cody's jurisdiction.

Another break in our routine occurred in the summer of 1971 when Phil Donahue telephoned me one day at the A.G.'s office. I had never heard of him. In those days, before he became a national television celebrity, Donahue was doing a local TV show in Dayton, Ohio. It was a low-budget production, with no stipends for the guests, but he could provide round-trip air fare tickets for Ruth and me to Dayton. Would I be a guest on his show? I think we accepted just to get the plane trip. We had very little money for such frivolous junkets. I think Donahue, a Catholic, was disappointed in my responses to his questions about Vatican II and church reform. He thought I would be more radical. I asked him to pass that opinion on to Cardinal Cody if they should ever chance to meet.

In the summer of 1972 I clerked, again in Santa Fe, but this time for the law firm of Sutin, Thayer and Browne. I began to get the feel of a busy law practice. But that daily round-trip of 110 miles had lost its charm, even for me, by the end of that second summer.

During Christmas vacation that year, my final year in law school, I was invited to lunch at the Petroleum Club in Albuquerque by the managing partners of Sutin, Thayer and Browne. They had kind words about my work as a clerk that previous summer and invited me to join the firm. I was flattered. That firm had produced Irwin Moise, chief justice of the New Mexico Supreme Court, Lewis Sutin, associate justice of the New Mexico Court of Appeals, Franklin Jones and Norman Thayer, each in turn New Mexico commissioners of revenue, and Paul Bardacke, later to be New Mexico's attorney general.

In law school I had acquired a considerable interest in water law, a field of practice which was, and still is, expanding steadily in what are called the arid regions of the West. I asked the partners whether the firm had any interest in water law. Early on, they said, it did have a considerable water law practice before Irwin Moise, a specialist in that field, left to join the Supreme Court, but after he went on the bench that specialty had declined. If I wanted to pick up where he left off, they assured me, I was welcome to try. Fair enough. I signed on.

When our class graduated in May I was asked to deliver the commencement address. I passed the bar exam in August and went to work on September 1. The day I reported for duty I was the junior member but the oldest of twenty-one attorneys in our two offices. My first client was the law school. Dean Fred Hart asked the firm to release me twice a week to teach the law school class in legal ethics. I was a little nervous, entering the same classroom as a professor that I so recently had left as a student. But the firm liked to have its attorneys invited to teach. And I was secretly eager to try it. With no experience in legal practice I was, to say the least, rash in accepting that appointment. The class went reasonably well. At least I did not try to palm off my performance as a "Socratic dialog."

The practice of our law firm was mostly corporate matters. My assignments ranged across administrative law, water law, municipal government, Indian affairs, and school administration. I was not one of the trial lawyers but worked on one occasion with Norman Thayer, head of the trial section. A friend of mine, Doctor Patrick McNamara, had been denied tenure by the University of New Mexico, after fulfilling all the stated requirements for that recognition. I asked Thayer if we could help Pat have this decision reversed. Thayer said that professors almost never win against universities on tenure questions. The odds are too great.

Before I told Pat we would not represent him I asked Thayer to read the file which McNamara had prepared. Norman took it home that night, read it, and called me the same evening: "Tell your friend we'll represent him. What they did to him is an outrage."

We took it and we won it. The instruction I got, watching Thayer in action on each level of the academic appeal process, was the kind of instruction every new lawyer needs but seldom gets after passing the bar. The name of that game is meticulous preparation. McNamara was later named chairman of the department of sociology at the University of New Mexico.

A considerable part of my practice centered on the new community Cochiti Lake, built by developers on a ninety-nine-year lease granted by the Indians of the Cochiti Pueblo on reservation lands overlooking a man-made lake on the Rio Grande. The senior lawyer on this project was Stephen Charnas. The whole concept of a residential development on lands leased from an Indian tribe raised legal questions for which the statutes and reported cases had no precedents. Who has primary police authority in the town? The sheriff or the B.I.A.? Can Indian range cattle nibble shrubs and graze on the manicured front lawns of lessees? Can guests in a commercial hotel on a reservation buy alcoholic beverages? Is the Rio Grande, behind the dam, a navigable stream subject to federal supervision? Does the U.S. Department of the Interior or the State Bureau of Game and Fisheries control fishing rights on Cochiti Lake? What authority or legal sanctions does the homeowners association have in a town populated by non-Indians in the middle of an Indian reservation?

Charnas and I never learned Tewa, the Pueblo language. We did, however, learn a lot about the delicate arts of contract negotiation, arbitration, building amity between Indians and Anglos, and jawboning endlessly on legal issues never mentioned in Felix Cohen's classic *Manual of Federal Indian Law*.

Learning the law starts *after* a lawyer is admitted to practice. That process consists of watching skillful practitioners "move the pieces on the board." New lawyers in the Sutin firm in my day were fortunate to have Chief Justice Irwin Moise and Franklin Jones, founders of the firm, as frequent visitors always ready to listen to the elements of a new case, to suggest legal theories to address it, and to warn novices like me where the quicksand lay.

There is a lot of "grunt work" in the practice of law. Keeping time

sheets, searching the reported cases, drafting and redrafting memo-
randa of law are as tedious as the daily routine in many other profes-
sions. But the product of these boring routines can be a craftsmanlike
document or an equitable settlement which more than compensates for
the hours spent in reaching the result. The variety of our practice, the
competence and the competitiveness of my associates, the good name
of the firm, a certain "grace under pressure," and a streak of zaniness in
that office made life there interesting and challenging.

I was just beginning to get the hang of it when an old friend called,
in July of 1974, from Minneapolis. Atherton Bean was on the search
committee for the Minneapolis Foundation, looking for a new executive director. Would I come to Minnesota for a visit, to discuss
this position? Ruth was delighted. I was ambivalent. Minneapolis, she
reasoned, was thirteen hundred miles closer to her family than Albuquerque. I knew that. But I had nameless fears about returning to my
old hometown.

What would it be like? Would we be welcome? Should I leave a good
firm and a secure future? Would my presence "back there" embarrass
the Catholic community?

I had a week's vacation coming. We drove to Minneapolis to recon-
noiter the situation. Atherton Bean and Judson Bemis, members of the
search committee, had anticipated my concern about returning to the
archdiocese where I had served as a priest and as a bishop. Before Bean
called to discuss the job with me, he and Bemis had gone to see Archbishop Leo Byrne. They did not offer the archbishop any veto power
but told him they were thinking of asking me to come back to Minnesota and that they were not anxious to create a situation which might
later embarrass him or the diocese, the foundation, or me. Byrne told
them that he and I had serious differences but that he would not dis-
courage them from offering me the position. Since then it has been a
matter of genuine regret for me that I was never able to thank him for
his courtesy to Bean and Bemis. He died suddenly in his sleep a few
weeks after their visit with him.

The Minneapolis Foundation is what the Internal Revenue Service calls a "public charity." In a dynamic community known for its
philanthropic and corporate generosity to worthy public causes, this
foundation exercised a catalytic role far greater than its modest endowment (at that time) would warrant. Russell Ewald, who had directed
the foundation for four years, spent three days with me explaining how
it operated and describing the job of the executive director.

The service role of the foundation appealed to me as it had to him.

Ewald is an ordained priest of the Episcopal Church. The work of the foundation is, in my terms, a "ministry of service."

Ruth was charmed at the prospect of living in Minnesota. She is at heart a city girl who never really bought the whole package "Out West." We accepted the position, rented a house in Wayzata, and headed back to Albuquerque for a month of packing and farewells.

CHAPTER TWENTY

# HOME AGAIN

Board members of the Minneapolis Foundation who did not know me had called around to check on my credentials. One such call went to Roger Kennedy, a good friend, then vice president of the Ford Foundation in New York City. After the call Kennedy promptly called me. He asked whether I had any fears of "old ghosts back home." Of course I did. Only a fool could believe that returning to the scene of his priestly ministry would not evoke happy memories of earlier times.

On balance though, it was a risk I was willing to take. The friendship of one cherished brother priest in Minneapolis, Harvey Egan, went a long way to allay such fears. He invited dozens of my friends to a buffet dinner and open house at St. Joan of Arc rectory every Monday evening for three weeks in a row — to meet Ruth, to see me again, and to break bread. These cordial reunions were occasions of grace for both of us. They showed her my priestly fraternity in its best light and gave each of us welcome occasions to meet old friends or to make new ones.

One shadow hanging over our return to Minnesota was my clear memory of the Minneapolis Foundation as a dormant, not to say lifeless, trust fund. Although it is the second oldest community foundation in the nation, started in 1915, it had shown few signs of life during my decade as a college president (and grant-seeker).

This shadow faded quickly once I learned how much Russ Ewald (with the professional assistance of Richard Nordby of the First Bank System) had accomplished in his four years as its director. As an Episcopal priest and community activist Ewald was well known and widely admired. His diplomacy in persuading several elderly board members, many of whom were early donors to the foundation, to resign (and still be friends) was a big first step in rebuilding the structure and the program of the foundation; and his personal "preferential option for the poor" made me eager to try my skills as his successor.

A month before I took over, the board had authorized Russ to hire a new program officer. He wisely opted to leave the selection of this person to me but recommended that I consider Tom Beech to fill it. A little "due diligence" on my part proved that Beech, then director of the Apache corporation's community affairs office in Minneapolis, had precisely the kind of experience and passion for community service that I wanted. I hired him the day I met him — and got a lifetime friend in the bargain. With Tom as my associate, Russ Ewald as our mentor, and an energetic board of directors, I was off to a great start in a new career. Ruth was charmed to be a partner in this challenging venture.

As a young priest Russ Ewald had served as chaplain for the Hennepin County jail, a role that gave him new insights into the lives of persons who needed help to start over. As a foundation director he persuaded his board to create a discretionary fund capable of quick response to meet emergency needs, like bail bonds, rent money, transportation costs, funeral expenses, or medical emergencies. In four years Ewald had given the foundation a human face, a warm heart, and an open hand.

In 1969 Congress had passed a tax reform act, aimed at bringing nonprofit philanthropic agencies under new federal controls. My board informed me that my credentials as a lawyer had tipped the scales of their judgment in my favor for my new post. The new tax act had many and vocal critics. But alert boards of directors were eager to comply with its demands, even as they sought ways to lobby for its future emendation.

In my efforts to learn the ropes of being a foundation executive I profited greatly by my rediscovery of the works of Robert Greenleaf, especially his now classic essay "The Servant as Leader." I had first met Greenleaf in 1953 when I was a graduate student at Yale and he and Peter Drucker were coleaders of a seminar sponsored by the American Management Association at the old Astor Hotel on Times Square in New York City.

Having forgotten, or neglected, Greenleaf's work for more than two decades, I found his writings directly responsive to my new needs as a foundation director in 1974. As a personnel officer at A.T.&T. Greenleaf had been a talent scout within the human resource department of that enormous company. His assignment was to locate, motivate, and mentor promising young employees already on A.T.&T.'s payroll who had the talent, with a little help along the way, to become the future leaders of the company. His bosses soon realized that Greenleaf had the "eye" to spot talent early on among his charges. As his fame and their success grew, he formulated his list of traits which separated the real winners from the "also rans" in the corporate world.

His list included the obvious virtues of integrity, industry, vision, energy, and several less obvious virtues like a collegial style of decision making, an active concern for team-building and cooperation (vs. the more common style of corporate competitiveness at every level), a continuing search for win-win situations which assured all team members of ownership in the outcome of joint efforts, and a fondness for leadership by personal example (vs. leadership by mandate, fear, threats, or manipulation).

Although Greenleaf's hypotheses about leadership are equally valid in for-profit or nonprofit agencies, it was clear by the time I came on the scene in philanthropy that his ideas were particularly well suited for service in the nonprofit or voluntary sector. Volunteers abound in the nonprofit sector; and volunteers seem to have an abiding affinity for a leadership style based on what I have already described as the "authority of service," as distinguished from the authority of appointment or election.

It was easy for me to find overtones of the gospel of Jesus Christ in the writings of Greenleaf, even though he stoutly contended that his theses were the empirical results of induction and experience in the real world, not deductions or corollaries from the life of Christ.

In truth, Greenleaf had a personal bias that, sooner or later, all churches tend to become narcissistic, spending more energy defending their own bureaucratic systems than in serving the human needs of their members. He refused to believe that his concept of the servant as leader is vintage Judaeo-Christian doctrine. In contrast, I have felt from day one that the altruistic spirit of his central thesis is clearly a corollary of Judaeo-Christian theology.

In the last year of Greenleaf's life I had the welcome opportunity of spending an afternoon alone with him in the lovely Quaker retirement center at Kennett Square, Pennsylvania. In that visit I had the temerity to tell him my thesis about his thesis. He smiled and said, "Maybe." Whether his theory or my theory about his work is correct, it has always been clear to me that my early formation in the Judaeo-Christian doctrine and his experiential insights about what character traits identify good managers and leaders are complementary at every level and that their compatibility is demonstrated daily in the careers and the work-products of thousands of practitioners who have no difficulty in melding two lines of thought which he (at least at one time) considered unrelated.

Another new friend and mentor came into my life in 1975. Eugene Struckhoff, an attorney from New Hampshire, had literally "written the book" on community foundations just as I entered this field of work. His two-volume opus on how to manage community foundations is still the basic text in this fast-growing arena of philanthropy. "Struck" went out of his way to help me learn the elements of this craft and to introduce me to his network of friends across the nation. In my career in philanthropy Struck personified for me the open spirit of generosity and friendship which I would discover are key personality traits among folks who seek careers of service in the voluntary sector.

Acting on Struck's sage advice, I also wrote a letter to each member of the foundation board (thirty-five in all), requesting a personal interview: to introduce myself, and to give each of them a private opportunity to share with me any counsel they had for me or our staff.

As Struck had predicted, in these private sessions board members spoke much more candidly about the strengths and weaknesses of the foundation than they would have in any open board meeting. In these sessions I took no notes but paid close attention and quickly drafted a memorandum for my files immediately after each such meeting. In time this file proved valuable to me in building bonds of rapport and trust between and among the board, our staff, and myself.

The art of managing a metropolitan community foundation depends primarily on the ancillary arts of scanning the local horizon regularly and of listening carefully for signs of local need or opportunity. One reason that the Minneapolis Foundation board is so large is that it gives high priority to these twin arts of seeing and hearing what is happening (or about to happen) in a very dynamic urban setting.

Minneapolis and its surrounding metropolitan area have more than their fair share of volunteer agencies dedicated to helping the disenfranchised, the talented, the underprivileged, and the visionaries. Linking arms with these agencies, or persons, to help them help themselves was satisfying and exciting work for me. On occasion it could also be emotionally draining, when the urgent needs or obvious merits of worthy programs exceeded our limited grant-making capacity. On balance, though, I knew at once that this was the right job for me.

Although the grant-making dimension of my new job was its most attractive feature, I soon learned that an equally important part of it was fund-raising. The federal Tax Reform Act of 1969 mandated that all community foundations take a proactive role in raising new money for their foundations. It was no longer permissible for us to wait passively for legacies promised to us in the wills of benevolent community members. Even though, as I have said more than once in this narrative, fund-raising is not one of my favorite activities, I accepted this requirement as a necessary part of my new job and resolved to do it as zealously as I could.

The philanthropic process which pledges private means to meet public needs is neither widely known nor well understood by the American public. Yet from the beginning of this nation private philanthropy has been essential to the growth of education, religion, social service, and health care, and to the nonprofit agencies which comprise the extensive third sector (nongovernmental and nonbusiness) of our national economy and society.

Visitors and residents in the Twin Cities often comment on the attractive "quality of life" which prevails there. No one has ever defined this nebulous term. Whatever its definition, it signifies a community endowed with a variety of support systems designed to answer a wide spectrum of family and personal needs for education, worship, the arts, job security, entertainment, recreation, equal opportunity, and health care. In a modest but significant way the Minneapolis Foundation is a catalytic agent which places small grants in strategic locations to enhance the general quality of life and to promote the common good of its region.

It quickly became clear to me that serving as its executive director was, for me, a ministry of service. Healthy communities tend to be places where a significant number of residents accept responsibility for advancing the common good of society. In a private vocabulary used at our foundation office we called persons of this type "weight bearers." For some reason that is not entirely clear, Minnesota has more than its fair share of weight bearers. Whatever the reason, the fact is clear: community well-being is a value highly prized and well served in this state. One result of this happy condition is that foundations in this region never seem to want for good ideas promoting worthy causes.

Community foundations are specifically mandated to work within their designated geographic areas and to be alert within such areas, to address new problems or opportunities in the nonprofit sector. They are also expected to be convenors of interested parties capable of creating new service programs and of charting new public policies to guide these programs. I found this role of convenor for community dialogues an especially attractive part of my new work.

From its founding in 1915 until 1974 the Minneapolis Foundation had acquired, mostly through legacies, an endowment of $10 million. At the board's request I made a detailed study of how this sum had been acquired. It surprised the board and me to find that the typical contribution to the fund had been a legacy of about $25,000. A significant number of these gifts came from former Minneapolitans who had spent their retirement years in California or Florida. Not having put down roots in their retirement areas, they chose, in making their wills, to share their estates with the city in which they had lived, been educated, married, and earned their livelihood.

Prior to this study, members of our board and I had erroneously assumed that our endowment had come to us over almost six decades in large gifts. Not so. In fact, until 1977 the foundation had never received a gift of $1 million. In that year we received three such gifts. No thanks to my fund-raising skills, the Tax Reform Act of 1969, by creating a new, hybrid legal entity called the "Founder-Adviser Fund" with increased tax deductibility for donors, had made such gifts to community foundations most attractive to new donors.

Subsequent federal statutes, enacted since 1969, have made community foundations the "darling" of the Internal Revenue Code and vastly more attractive as recipients for tax-deductible contributions. At this writing the Minneapolis Foundation has an endowment of $300 million, an increase of 2900 percent over the past twenty-three years!

In 1975 a small group of Minnesota foundation executives began meeting occasionally to discuss the wisdom of creating a Minnesota Council on Foundations. For some years there had been a paper organization with this name, but it was only that, a letterhead used on occasion to alert the governor or the legislature that some act pending at the state house was seen as a threat to organized philanthropy.

The federal Tax Reform Act of 1969, however, had alerted the nonprofit sector, both grant-makers and grant-seekers, that a new day had dawned for philanthropy. It was no longer enough for us to act as "firefighters" to oppose threatening new laws. The time had come for interested parties to be in dialog regularly, not just during crises, about the kind of new legislation, at the federal and state levels, that would be needed to help the growing nonprofit sector actualize more of its potential as a regular and active partner with governments (at all levels) and business in promoting good public policy for tax-exempt entities.

By this time regional associations of grant-makers (later to be known as RAGs) had sprung up in a handful of the more progressive states to create a forum in which the new dialog with government would be shaped proactively by the voices of the citizenry. One such RAG, in Michigan, was already up and running and gaining considerable visibility for its enlightened and creative programs.

In 1975 foundation executives in Minnesota voted to incorporate the Minnesota Council on Foundations (MCOF), asked me to serve as its first volunteer board chair, and invited Judith Healey to be its chief executive. Judy and I promptly flew off to Michigan to learn all we could about the new art of building a regional association of grant-makers.

Thanks to Judy's energy and administrative skills over a span of four years, and those of her successor, Jacqueline Reis, in that post for the past nineteen years, the Minnesota Council on Foundations today is recognized nationally for its strong programs, energy, and creative vision. I served as its chair person for its first six years.

In the spring of 1978 I confided to Ruth that I had a growing desire to find or make some time in my schedule to write a narrative of my "odyssey" as a priest, teacher, bishop, lawyer, foundation executive, and as a married man. I wanted this narrative to be written by me, in the first person, not by some critic or some friend. With Ruth's encouragement I set up a regimen of rising at 5:00 A.M. to add an hour of writing time to my daily schedule. The press of other duties at the foundation and in the larger community soon made it clear that I was burning my candle at both ends. I needed to find larger hunks of time than just one hour daily at daybreak. That schedule had worked fine for some of my friends, but I soon found that it made me run out of gas at about 3:00 P.M. daily.

In the back of my mind was the thought that my father had died of a heart attack at age seventy-six. If his life span was to be any measure of mine, I had to get some leisure or create some quality time to do the research, the writing, and the rewriting that this narrative would take, while I was still in good health.

I discussed my dilemma with Thomas Crosby, Sr., who was then chairman of the board of the Minneapolis Foundation. As always, he was a good listener and a wise counselor. He suggested that we consider a six-month sabbatical for me. In my view, the task I had in mind would require much more time than that. Further dialog with Ruth and Tom Beech finally led us to decide that I would resign from the foundation and budget at least a year of writing time for my narrative, with the hope of finding some kind of new employment at the end of that span. In retrospect it now seems to me a highly improvident plan, but at every step of it, Ruth was strongly supportive, and at this distance I still think it was the right thing for us to do.

The solid performance of Tom Beech as associate director of the foundation over a span of almost four years encouraged me to recommend him as my successor. The foundation's board of directors shared my admiration for Tom and readily named him executive director to succeed me. In June 1978 Tom took over as CEO of the foundation and I embarked on the task of writing this book. Ruth's cordial endorsement of this move gave me the courage to make it, even though we had very modest savings and no other visible means of support. Fortunately (or providentially) a new friend came into our lives at this time.

John M. Musser, of St. Paul, president of his endowed family foundation (the General Service Foundation), invited me to lunch one day and asked if I would be able to help him, on a part-time basis, as program officer for his foundation. Ruth and I readily accepted the invitation, and for the next year we worked, part-time, as a team to review and evaluate all incoming proposals for the foundation and to prepare the agenda for the board meetings of the foundation.

In the process we became fast friends with John and Betty Musser and their extended family, a bond that added enormously to our education in the field of philanthropy. At every meeting of the General Service Foundation board we heard experts of worldwide reputation, recruited by John and Betty to enlighten us on the elements of responsible domestic and international grant-making. This was my first exposure to the larger world of global philanthropy.

In his business career John Musser had been a senior executive of the Weyerhaeuser Company, an avid world-traveler, and a dedicated environmentalist. Given the range of his extraordinary interest in world affairs, the ecosystem, and sound public policy, my hours spent reviewing grant proposals with him were like being enrolled in graduate courses in the university of the world.

Our part-time work with the General Service Foundation extended from June 1978 through December 1979. During this span my energy focused principally on writing a first draft of this book.

By the end of 1979 I felt that I had put down on paper the essence of what I wanted to say about my life's journey. But for reasons I could not quite explain I had reservations about going public with the manuscript at that time. In retrospect I think that this reluctance stemmed partly from my hope that this book would neither be nor be seen as one more volume in that genre which came to be called "exit books" written by angry priests as they left their sacred ministry. I have never been angry at the Catholic Church, even though I was on more than one occasion deeply disappointed by the style, the standards, and the conduct of some of its highest-ranking ecclesiastics.

My hesitancy about going public with the manuscript in 1980 was seconded by kindly but clear letters of rejection from two different publishers to whom I sent it. Secretly relieved that I would still have more time to edit and tighten the text, I filed two copies of it in separate secure places and readily turned my attention to finding some kind of gainful employment. Once more, the job sought me.

An unsolicited phone call from Paul Parker, a senior vice president at General Mills, Inc., asked if I would be interested in applying for a position coming open there as executive director of the General Mills Foundation. I was more than interested; I was eager to explore such an attractive opportunity.

General Mills, an international corporation organized by James Ford Bell in 1929, is the successor-in-interest to the original Washburn Crosby Milling Company founded in Minneapolis in 1866 by Cadwallader Washburn, a legendary entrepreneur from Maine. Students of Minnesota history may recall that although the Washburn Crosby Company was then primarily a flour milling company, it applied for and received one of the first federal licenses to operate a radio station in Minnesota. To this day, the call letters of that station (WCCO — i.e., Washburn Crosby Co.) are well known, under different ownership, across the Midwest.

In my four years at the Minneapolis Foundation I had come to know and admire the General Mills Foundation as a model corporate grant-maker in Minnesota and in the other states where General Mills had manufacturing plants or subsidiaries. After short interviews with Robert Kinney (CEO and chairman), Bruce Atwater (president), and Paul Parker, I was invited to join the company as associate director of the foundation on January 1, 1980, and to become its executive director and a vice president of General Mills on August 1, when my friend Bill Humphrey would retire from these two positions.

Paul Parker was to be my boss at General Mills for the next six years. We hit it off from the beginning. I liked his breezy style. In our first session together he cautioned me, "I'll be candid with you. There are some highly placed executives in this company who are making book that you will be a failure in this job." When I asked what prompted such a gloomy prediction, he replied: "You come from two separate 'soft' backgrounds, the church and academia." Having heard these hoary chestnuts often over the years, I said, "Let's just wait and see whether the local gamblers win their bets." Paul agreed.

Paul's official title was senior vice president, but in fact it could have been "company ombudsman." Ardently loyal to General Mills, he was known for his readiness to help newcomers like me to learn the folklore and adjust to the culture of the company.

In our first business session he told me that all employees, including corporate officers, were expected to take an active role as volunteers in civic community affairs. I was free to decide where and how to pledge my time as a volunteer, but at year's end, part of my bonus would depend on my documented record of community service outside the company.

On a lighter note that day he also told me that his principal interests, outside the company and his family, were the Republican Party, Sherlock Holmes, and the Chicago Cubs (whom he fondly calls "The Little Bears"). Emulating his candor I told him that I was a lifelong Democrat and a fan of the Atlanta Braves, but suggested that we might build on our mutual interest in Sherlock Holmes.

Bearing in mind his cautionary tale about the executives who were betting that I would not succeed in my new role as a corporate executive, and recalling how much I had learned at the Minneapolis Foundation by interviewing each of my board members individually, I sent a memorandum to every officer of the company (forty-four in all at that time at our headquarters location). In it I introduced myself as a newcomer and asked each of them for a half hour of their office time to help us become better acquainted.

In these private sessions, I asked a series of questions about their place of origin, educational background, history with the company, family, extracurricular interests, and for any advice they might have for me in my new job. My file on these interviews became in time a useful and valuable reference resource for me.

Each of these encounters, save one, was positive, cordial, and encouraging. In that one, scheduled at the end of a working day, my host busily signed his outgoing mail during our visit, took all incoming calls, and told me at the end of it that, in his view, the purpose of the company was to make money, not give it away, and that my job and our giving program were both big mistakes. I cut the session short and thanked him for his candor. The incident is important here only because of its sharp contrast with the other forty-three interviews, which showed a universal consensus and considerable pride, company-wide, in our corporate giving program.

Having endorsed my nomination as a new employee at General Mills, Paul Parker was clearly eager to help me in my new post. Specifically, he took care to instruct me about the differences between official rules and the folklore of the company. When I expressed concern that one senior executive did not share my definition for community service, Paul put me at ease: "Don't worry. His idea of doing community service is that he drives his daughters to dancing lessons once a week."

I found the style of open and informal communication ("No three-page memos, please") and the collegial style of decision making at General Mills attractive and refreshing. Every office door in the executive wing, from the chairman on down, was open to me, on short notice or without notice.

There is an axiom in corporate managerial folklore, posed in the form of two questions, about the ideal relationship between a chief executive and a board of directors: does the board say to the executive, "Stop until we say go"?; or does the board say, "Go until we say stop"? If the board favors the first of these alternatives, it will guarantee a do-nothing operation. I learned quickly that General Mills favors clear-cut and detailed job descriptions up front, followed by equally clear orders to "Go until we say stop."

In my nine years at General Mills I had ample opportunity to compare the company with its peers, nationwide. Then and now I rate it as a superlatively strong company in any category on which a publicly held corporation can be judged. My time there was challenging, rewarding, and deeply satisfying. I was, in effect, the CEO of a separate (nonprofit) corporation. I reported to a board, made up of the seven senior officers of the company. I was older than the eldest member of this group by almost a decade. More than once I told them that they trusted my judgment too much and should spend more time evaluating my performance. They replied that they would get around to this chore later on.

In my first year at General Mills the company's philanthropic budget was set at 2 percent of corporate pretax profits. Our grants budget that year amounted to $4.5 million. When I retired in 1988, 3 percent of pretax profits ($9 million) were pledged to grant-making and community support in the twenty cities where we had a significant corporate presence. (At this writing, the General Mills annual grants budget totals $16 million.) In each of our plant-site cities (including Toronto, Canada, Guatemala City, Guatemala, and Managua, Nicaragua) a committee of local employees counseled me and my staff on grants and community efforts appropriate in these locations.

One managerial trait that made my job different, if not unique, was that my corporate board of directors counseled me early on and often that our grant-making budget was not an adjunct to the company's marketing or advertising budgets. My job was not to sell more Wheaties, Cheerios, or Betty Crocker cake mixes. It was to scan the horizon regularly in all the cities where General Mills had a "significant presence" and to find creative ways in which our corporate resources (only one of which was money) could help underwrite programs to make these areas healthier and more humane communities. Very few of my corporate peers in the field of grant-making worked under such an enlightened mandate. Then, and to an even greater degree today, the typical grant-making arm of a publicly held company wants its grants "to produce more bang for the buck." I was blessed in having no such mandate from my board.

At that time the General Mills Foundation was a member of five national watchdog agencies: (1) the National Council on Foundations and (2) the Independent Sector, both in Washington, D.C., and (3) the Foundation Center, (4) the Contributions Council of the Conference Board, and (5) the National Charities Information Bureau, in New York City. In time I came to serve on the boards of all five of these agencies. More than once, on my return from their annual meetings, I wrote a memorandum to my chairman (Bruce Atwater) at General Mills, expressing my appreciation for the caliber of our wide-angle community affairs program and its enlightened view of the role of corporate grant-making within the larger fields of corporate management and leadership.

Working and traveling for General Mills widened my horizons. At the Minneapolis Foundation I had learned the vital importance of site visits to meet with grant-seekers on their own turf and to see their programs in action. This was the microcosm of grassroots philanthropy. At General Mills my travels put me in touch with the macrocosm of community leaders across the nation and with representatives of other nations then joining the network of global grant-seekers and grant-makers. While one can say that organized philanthropy got its start in the United States, its reach and its works now circle the global village.

Over the years I have come to realize that schoolwork (in college or seminary or law school) covers only the ABC's of learning in any field. The best stuff comes later, by experience in observing and listening closely to persons who exemplify the best standards of their calling. Thanks to General Mills I met and worked with world-class exemplars of servant-leadership, like Elmer L. Andersen, Judson Bemis, Carol Berde, Susan Berresford, Robert Bellah, Landrum Bolling, Tom Buckman, Alice Buhl, Thomas M. Crosby, Sr., Humphrey Doermann, John Edie, Pablo Eisenberg, Sarah Engelhardt, Russell Ewald, John W. Gardner, Robert K. Greenleaf, A. A. Heckman, Virginia Hodgkinson, Dorothy Johnson, James A. Joseph, Henry S. Kingman, Jr., Burt Knauft, Lynn Luckow, Char Mollison, John Nason, Brian O'Connell, Martin Paley, Lois Palmquist, Robert Payton, Bob Smucker, Eugene Struckhoff, Lauren Weck, Clifford Whitehill, Leonard Wilkening, and

Paul Ylvisaker. From each of these masters I learned more about the separate pieces of what keeps the voluntary sector of our society healthy and thriving. And in the process I came to know and share some of the passion and conviction of this cadre of dedicated and generous persons who exemplify in their own lives the values on which a humane society is predicated.

# CHAPTER TWENTY-ONE

# RECESSIONAL

After retiring from General Mills in 1988, I was invited by the Council on Foundations in Washington to serve as one of three senior consultants who are, in essence, circuit riding troubleshooters, on call when needed by any of the fifteen hundred philanthropic foundations which make up this council. My first assignment was to identify and recruit a select group of writers from twenty-five corporate foundations to produce a manual to be entitled *The Corporate Contributions Handbook*. It was completed and published by Jossey-Bass in 1991. From then through 1994, work for the Council kept me on the road or in the air much of the time. Although occasionally these trips cast me in the role of referee between a foundation's board of directors and its chief executive officer, I enjoyed meeting and working with an expanding national network of foundation executives, many of whom were newcomers to the field. Near the end of 1994 it became clear to me — and to Ruth — that I should taper off on travel, spend more time at home, and try, belatedly, to get at least a passing grade in "Retirement 101," whatever that means.

In my personal vocabulary I translate "retirement" to mean freedom: freedom from schedules and deadlines set for me by my supervisors or my employer. Today my calendar is often just as full as it was in the days of my nine-to-five career. But now it is filled with meetings, writing, counseling, and occasional travel that I have chosen, not with tasks and deadlines set for me by others to whom I report. Ruth says that I am "allegedly retired."

On occasion in recent years at public functions I have been introduced by well-meaning masters of ceremonies as an "ex-priest." In each such instance, without making an issue of the matter, I have courteously told the audience and the M.C. that I am not an ex-priest.

On February 27, 1921, at St. Augustine Catholic Church in my hometown I received the sacrament of baptism and became a member of the Christian community. On June 8, 1946, in the Cathedral of St. Paul, I received the sacrament of holy orders and became a Catholic priest. On March 31, 1965, in the same cathedral I received "the fullness of holy orders" and was ordained a bishop in the Catholic Church. The sacraments of baptism and holy orders mark a permanent, irreversible, ontological change in persons who receive them. I am still a Christian. I am still a Catholic. I am still a priest. I am still a bishop. I continue to be proud of each of these honorable identities. Persons who do not know me might be tempted to assume that, because I have been unable to give internal or external assent to Pope Paul's encyclical *Humanae Vitae,* I am no longer an active member of the Catholic community. Quite the contrary, I continue to be proud of my Catholic identity and to try to live each day according to the saving doctrine of the church. If I had my life to live over again I would readily opt to do so in a Catholic family and in Catholic schools. The balance which Catholic theology strives to maintain between the twin values of faith and reason continues to impress me as an admirable standard which every religion would do well to espouse and practice.

Granted, my marriage in 1969 ended my priestly ministry. In a press interview at that time Archbishop Byrne stated that I was automatically excommunicated from the church by my marriage. Under the 1918 Code of Canon Law he was correct. However, the new Code of Canon Law, promulgated in 1983, following Vatican II, abolished this penalty, and this abolition applied, retroactively, to my situation. The new code orders that I be "suspended" from my apostolic role as a priest (such as offering Mass or administering the sacraments); but it does not separate me from the Catholic community.

It has never been difficult for me to believe in the providence of God. What others see as luck, fate, chance, or coincidence has often seemed to me a "beneficent provision" of opportunity, energy, or a second chance from some power beyond my ken. The best things that have happened in my life were events I could never have foreseen, planned, or executed. The greatest of these was the appearance of Ruth in my world just at the time that my life was coming apart.

Several subsequent "beneficent events" fall into the same category. When I realized that I could no longer function in my role as a priest and bishop in the manner expected of me by my superiors in the church, I knew instinctively that whatever new career I would choose had to be some kind of work in the service of others. But I had no clear perception of where or what that would be. I actually turned down the first invitation that came to me to work in philanthropy. I have since told Atherton Bean, who extended that invitation and who persisted in renewing it, that I clearly see him as an agent of God in my life.

The field of philanthropy was tailor-made for me. It has offered me a rich ministry of service that I could neither have envisioned nor planned. It has helped me actualize far more of my own human potential than any other kind of work I can imagine. It has enabled me to work with world-class leaders, mentors, and teachers I could never have dreamed of meeting; and it has given me the kind of psychic satisfaction that I knew intimately as a priest and bishop but that I once feared I would never know again.

Another (providential) opportunity that I almost failed to grasp was an invitation in 1983 to serve on the board of the Institute for Ecumenical and Cultural Research, proffered by its executive director, Robert Bilheimer. Uneasy about my "negative baggage" (my term), I declined. Exactly one year later Bilheimer repeated the offer, this time citing the unanimous consensus of his board (which included Abbot Jerome Theisen, O.S.B.). Having long admired this international center and its impressive programs, founded by Father Kilian McDonnell, O.S.B., and his confreres at St. John's Abbey, Collegeville, Minnesota, in 1967, I accepted. Fortunately, over time my fears have proved to be groundless. Meeting the scholars (from six continents) who have been in residence at this institute and sharing dialogue with them, especially in our summer consultations, about the present position and the future prospects of the Christian community in local and world affairs has been, for me, an occasion of great grace.

Participants in the summer gatherings are asked to speak consistently in the first person about their own journey of faith, and not to see themselves as spokespersons for their respective denominations. This guideline, and the correlative one assuring speakers of anonymity during and after the conversations, make the consultations of the institute and their subsequent work-products models of low-keyed, candid, amicable, if sometimes hard-hitting, dialogue about how persons who call themselves Christians in the modern world ought to go about the business of this sacred calling.

It has been a humbling experience for me to learn from mainline Protestant, Anglican, Orthodox, Evangelical, Pentecostal, Holiness, and fellow Catholic participants how much more I still have to learn about the imitation of Jesus Christ in the modern world. I have been touched and heartened repeatedly by the faith, hope, and charity which these dedicated Christians have demonstrated and willingly shared with me on my journey of faith in a society that is continuously tempted to retreat into ever smaller enclaves of denominational or individual separatism.

In St. Paul's letter to the young Christian community at Ephesus he tells them (and us) that followers of Jesus Christ share the privilege of confessing "one lord, one faith, one baptism." If this bond is indeed a common ground on which all Christians agree, how do we reconcile this bed-rock consensus with all the cultural and historical variations, not to say antipathies, of our several Christian denominations? It is, in part, the mission of the Ecumenical Institute to phrase and rephrase this central paradox in our joint efforts to become recognizable followers of Jesus Christ in a multicultural society replete with challenges and roadblocks to this admirable goal.

One of the obstacles we encountered early on at the institute in our efforts to bring more Christian denominations into ecumenical dialogue was the erroneous perception, among some of these would-be participants, that somehow our objective is to "homogenize" several denominations into some kind of new and different Christian potpourri, or that we want to convert them to a denomination different from their own. Abundant experience over three decades now confirms that both of these fears are groundless. Quite the contrary, our record shows a regular pattern of strong new bonds of mutual respect and cooperation, across denominational lines, for participants who often find that they have more in common with fellow Christians of other denominations than they have with some of the members of their own church. These participants also report developing over time a much stronger appreciation for their own denomination than they had before coming to the institute. Somehow hearing others speak, candidly but lovingly, about the human weaknesses of their own church lead ers or about shortcomings of the polity or programs of their own church inclines their listeners to be equally candid and equally forgiving of similar shortcomings in their denominations. Forgiveness begets forgiveness. The healing process works both ways. All this is in sharp contrast to the ancient and now discredited adage: "Outside *my* church there is no salvation."

In the category of other providential events during the twentieth century I would, without hesitation, cite the Second Vatican Council, convened by Pope John XXIII in 1962, as the single most graphic illustration of divine intervention in human affairs in this century. It is, by a wide margin, the most remarkable religious event in my lifetime.

The influence of this worldwide, four-year assembly cannot be measured. It can only be estimated. Its ripple effects, in all churches and in civil society, are continuing and will continue: in the fields of worship, liturgy, sacred scripture, catechetics, ecumenism, seminary training, homiletics, collegiality, parish life, interfaith relations, church polity, the role of women in the church, lay leadership, and numerous variations on all of these themes.

In spite of recent, welcome, and overdue changes in these several fields of religious life, thanks to Vatican II, it troubles me to hear occasionally that many adults in the Catholic Church, three decades after Vatican II, have, at best, only a vague notion of what that Council was all about and what it promulgated as official Catholic teaching in its sixteen published documents.

Possibly we could have anticipated that these far-ranging and carefully annotated statements of belief and practice would become the occasion for polarization within the church, as indeed they have. Certainly we could have done a better job, since the Council, of explicating these documents, their origins, their purpose, and their enormous promise for the future of the church. But even admitting such pedagogical shortcomings, it is clear that the essential teachings of Vatican II have taken root, are growing vigorously, and have been warmly received by the people of God within the worldwide Catholic communion and in the larger Christian world.

At the same time it is sobering to realize that current dialogue between Catholics at both ends of the spectrum of opinion often lacks civility and on occasion is even venomous. Shortly before his death in 1996, Cardinal Joseph Bernardin expressed the personal hope that both of these groups might alter their tactics, lower their voices, and search more charitably for wider common ground. Within a week three of his fellow American cardinals stated publicly that Bernardin's proposal would not fly. One of them came close to resurrecting the hoary chestnut of days gone by: in theological debate, error has no rights. In June 1996 Archbishop John Quinn, the retired archbishop of San Francisco, in a masterful address at Oxford University, called on all segments of the Catholic community to recall the gospel spirit of Vatican II, with its emphasis on a collegial style of open dialogue, civility, courtesy, and charity.

How did we come to this juncture in our intramural Catholic relations? In viewing the scene today I can hardly believe that our church is the same one that concluded Vatican II in December 1965 on a high note of almost euphoric optimism about change, love, joy, peace, justice, and growth.

On our return from Vatican II Archbishop Leo Binz asked whether I would be willing to take on the task in our archdiocese of explicating for our priests and people the essence of Vatican II. I was charmed to be asked and leaped at the chance. As I have said earlier in this narrative, Binz was a social liberal and an ecclesiastical conservative. A true Roman, he found it extremely difficult to accept some of the changes and especially the rate of change recommended by the decrees of Vatican II, even though he acknowledged privately to me that he had voted in favor of "most of these changes." His sense of *Romanità* demanded that he give unquestioning endorsement to any papal decree, but psychologically he found it difficult, and possibly frightening, to order the implementation in his home diocese of the new *modus operandi* officially called for by Pope Paul VI at the conclusion of Vatican II.

It pleased me to have my archbishop show such trust in me as to ask my help in doing what he felt had to be done but which he found personally difficult to do. I understood his dilemma, and he seemed to sense my eagerness to accept his invitation.

The enthusiasm I carried home from Vatican II was enormous. I was forty-four, in good health, had a pilot's license and access to a rental Cessna 180, a clear mandate from my archbishop, and an ardent desire to tell our priests and people all I could about what I had learned from three months of the most intense and inspiring educational experience of my life. I was also absolutely confident that our joint mission was a true apostolate, assuredly inspired by the Holy Spirit.

In retrospect I now worry on occasion that my eagerness to pursue this assignment from early January 1966 through all of 1967 and the first three quarters of 1968 must have negatively affected my final semester at the College of St. Thomas and my entire tenure at St. Helena's parish. None of my associates at the college or the parish ever chided me about neglecting them, but in looking back on that era I chide myself for unwittingly favoring my ad hoc assignment (on Vatican II) at the expense of my principal duties as a college president and as a pastor.

As we approach the end of the twentieth century it is most encouraging to hear Pope John Paul II say in a recent apostolic letter: "The best preparation for the new millennium...can only be expressed in a renewed commitment to apply, as faithfully as possible, the teaching of Vatican II to the life of every individual and of the whole church." Meaning no lack of appreciation to the participants in Vatican II, I think it is fair to say that their remarkable work-product is but the prelude to our more difficult long-term task of turning the grand design they set out in theory into a specific action plan for the church in the new century.

One reason for writing this book was my desire to express appreciation to friends who have made my odyssey richer by their kindness and to express regret to those I have injured or disappointed by actions of mine which they could neither understand nor endorse. I hope that it will be at least moderately successful in addressing one or both of these goals.

Ruth and I knew early on that marriage was a huge risk for us and that making a success of it would test our best efforts. Our pastor, who has counseled thousands of couples over almost five decades of priestly ministry, tells us and our fellow parishioners that he has yet to see a "perfect marriage." While we agree with his seasoned and reasoned opinion, we would still defend the proposition that our marriage is a happy, stable, solid union of two committed Christians who ask God each day to help them use to good advantage the blessings he has given them so abundantly: our health, our loving and extended families, our host of good friends, frequent opportunities to serve others, and, above all, the gift of the saving gospel of Jesus Christ.

At this writing we have just celebrated the twenty-eighth anniversary of our marriage, well aware that we have been granted length of years even beyond the biblical ideal of "three score and ten."

As a lifelong and dedicated member of the Disciples of Christ Christian Church, Ruth was engaged in ecumenical dialogue long before I was even aware of this dimension of the Christian mandate. Sixty years ago her mother was active in interdenominational dialogue and ministry as a deacon in the Christian Church. Ruth's family life, not to say their weekly schedule, centered on their bond with the church and the gospel.

True to this tradition she has recently completed eight years of volunteer service, working from ten to five, five days a week as a fundraiser at Interfaith Outreach and Community Partners, a coalition of twenty local congregations, seventeen Protestant and three Catholic, ministering to the religious, human, social, medical, and legal needs of poor families in our county.

Earlier in this narrative I have said that she suffers vicariously with the poor and the disenfranchised with a degree of personal involvement that is vintage Christian activism. Her reason for stepping down from her career as a volunteer now, I think, is her desire to set a good example (of disengagement) for me and to help us both learn something about the elements of "Retirement 101." She tells me that she knows I can spell the word "leisure," but that I probably know little of its meaning, much less its rewards.

Of late we find ourselves being reminded that much will be expected from those to whom much has been given. Much has been given to